THE SEVENTH SENSE

THE SEVENTH SENSE

A Study of
Francis Hutcheson's Aesthetics
And Its Influence in Eighteenth-Century Britain

by
PETER KIVY

BURT FRANKLIN & CO., Inc.

For Lindley

© 1976 Burt Franklin & Co., Inc.
New York

Library of Congress Cataloging in Publication Data

Kivy, Peter.
The seventh sense.

Bibliography: p.
Includes index.
1. Hutcheson, Francis, 1694-1746. 2. Aesthetics,
British. I. Title.
B1504.A33K58   111.8'5   75-28447
ISBN 0-89102-044-6

This book has been printed on
Warren 66 Antique Offset,
chosen for its high
degree of permanency, good quality,
and acid-free characteristics.

Frontispiece:
Francis Hutcheson.
From an engraving by F. Bertolozzi.

CONTENTS

PREFACE

I have tried to do two things in this book: first, to make an analytic study of Francis Hutcheson's *Inquiry Concerning Beauty, Order, Harmony, Design* in some detail and completeness; second, to trace the development in Britain of its leading idea, the sense of beauty, to its decline at the close of the eighteenth century. Part I occupies itself with the former task and can be read as a self-contained unit. Part II, along with relevant portions of Part I, can be read as a history of the sense of beauty in the British Enlightenment. And Parts I and II together are what the subtitle of this book describes: *A Study of Francis Hutcheson's Aesthetics, and Its Influence in Eighteenth-Century Britain.*

I see my work as a study in eighteenth-century *aesthetics*, and I have, therefore, not scrupled to use the noun "aesthetics" and the adjective "aesthetic" wherever they have seemed to me to be appropriate. But in spite of the fact that the terms, in *something* like the way we now use them, were coined in the first half of the eighteenth century, and that philosophers since Plato have been concerned with metaphysical and epistemological issues raised by the concept of the beautiful, and what *we* now call the fine arts, objections have been raised to the use of these terms in describing the work of the eighteenth-century critics and philosophers.

There are two answers to these objections: a short answer and a long one.

I do not know exactly what the long answer is. It would require a detailed study of Enlightenment reflections on art and beauty with the specific end in view of determining what was being done and whether what was being done differed significantly enough from what we do in the name of "aesthetics" to be denied that name. The present study, along with many other works of eighteenth-century scholarship, may contribute to the eventual long answer. But the long answer cannot be given here.

The short answer is that surely what was done in the eighteenth century in the way of philosophy of art, of taste, of criticism, and of beauty is more like what we call "aesthetics" than it is like anything else. It is different, too, of course. But who would expect it to be in every respect the same? A theory can be different from a contemporary aesthetic theory and still be an *aesthetic* theory. There was, to be sure, no word in eighteenth-century Britain that exactly captured our word "aesthetics"; for although the word was coined, it was not currency in the British Isles until after the period with which we are concerned. But Newton, after all, did what the seventeenth and eighteenth centuries called "natural philosophy." Should we boggle at calling it "physics"? Such linguistic scruples would be too fussy — and misleading in the bargain.

It is with pleasure that I acknowledge, now, some old debts, and some newly incurred ones. To my former teachers, Arthur Danto, Albert Hofstadter, Richard F. Kuhns, Jr., and James J. Walsh, this book owes much substance and much of the philosophical spirit it may have. To George Dickie and Elmer Sprague it now owes further improvements in its philosophical and historical content. It owes its mistakes to its author.

New York City   P.K.
June, 1974

PART I

HUTCHESON'S FIRST "INQUIRY"

"I have here followed the common opinion of men's having but five senses, though, perhaps there may be justly counted more . . . . "

John Locke

I

JUST BEFORE HUTCHESON

(1) The name of Francis Hutcheson is associated in ethics and aesthetics with the doctrine of "internal senses." The Third Earl of Shaftesbury, Anthony Ashley Cooper, is generally credited with having established the notions of the moral sense and sense of beauty in Britain. But the doctrine in its characteristic form, that is, the doctrine which represented moral and aesthetic judgments as perceptual or emotive rather than rational, was the work, mainly, of Hutcheson.

Hutcheson was convinced by the analogy between sense perception and critical judgment. The ability to perceive, Locke had claimed, is innate, immediate, not under the control of the will: so also, Hutcheson insisted, is the ability to recognize the beautiful (and other aesthetic qualities). There was, of course, nothing particularly novel in this; such observations were rife in the seventeenth century. Hutcheson's originality lay in his re-expression of these insights in Lockean terms.

In this chapter I attempt to introduce *some* seventeenth-century concepts which presaged, in one way or another, the aesthetic sense doctrine as Hutcheson later formulated it. And as the aesthetic sense doctrine is so largely a British product, for the most part I confine myself to its British forerunners. To do anything more would require catching Leviathan with a fishhook.

(2) In seventeenth-century British philosophy there were already full-fledged theories of inner senses and faculties, both

1

moral and aesthetic; and there can be very little doubt that they were familiar to Shaftesbury, who was looked upon by those he influenced as at least co-founder of the aesthetic sense school. Shaftesbury's philosophical debt is owed most heavily to the Cambridge Platonists.[1] They, in their turn, are indebted, in a negative way, to Hobbes; for "it was largely in conscious opposition to Hobbism that they defined their position."[2] But the Cambridge Platonists are indebted also to a pre-Hobbesian thinker, Lord Herbert of Cherbury, often called the father of Deism, who, as early as 1624, in the *De Veritate,* had set forth a position in clear anticipation of the Cambridge group, as well as the later aesthetic sense school.[3]

Lord Herbert's foreshadowing of the sense of beauty is revealed in his doctrine of "Natural Instincts" and the "Common Notions" to which they give rise — a doctrine which may derive its general features from Stoic philosophy.[4] For Lord Herbert, the criterion of truth is common agreement; such agreement is guaranteed by common subjective faculties and divinely established harmony between these faculties and their objects. "Whatever is believed by universal consent must be true and must have been brought into conformity in virtue of some internal faculty." The internal faculties or natural instincts are bestowed upon men by "divine Providence, some measure of which is imprinted upon our mind."[5]

Natural instinct seems to denote both an active and a passive faculty. It is passive in that the presence of an object is required to occasion its activity: "when it is stimulated by objects, whether things or words or symbols, we must believe that a Common Notion will result." The Common Notions pertain to the totality of human knowledge, including nature, religion, morality, and the beautiful:

> [N]atural instincts are expressions of those faculties which are found in every normal man, through which the Common Notions touching the internal conformity of things, such as the cause, means, and purpose of things, the good, bad, beautiful, pleasing, etc., especially those Notions which tend towards the preservation of the individual, of species, of kinds, and of the universe, are brought into conformity independently of discursive thought.[6]

Surely there is a superfluity of innate principles here. "At first sight," as W. R. Sorley remarked, "this seems like the faculty-psychology run mad."[7] Yet Sorley added, and I think with some justice, that the very number of the "faculties" Lord Herbert is committed to militates against their being thought of as entirely distinct principles. "They are so numerous that it would be almost impossible for Herbert to assign them that degree of independence which was frequently ascribed to the 'faculties of the mind' by psychologists of a recent generation."

The immediacy of the Natural Instincts is continually emphasized by Lord Herbert. "Common Notions are brought into conformity immediately, provided the meaning of the facts or words is grasped; while discursive reason works slowly by means of species and its Questions, moving for ever to and fro, without recourse to apprehension." This immediacy, opposed to the deliberate operation of the "discursive reason," is, according to Lord Herbert, particularly exemplified by the perception of beauty:

> Natural Instinct anticipates reason in perceiving the beauty of proportions of a house built according to architectural principles; for reason reaches its conclusions by a laborious consideration of the proportions, first severally and then as a whole, and even in the process itself is constrained to rely on Common Notions. And the same point can be noticed in judging beautiful features, or graceful forms, or harmony in music. For it is not necessary to call any plain man who takes immediate pleasure in such things a mathematician or a musician.[8]

Lord Herbert's conception of an aesthetic instinct — with its emphasis upon the anticipation of reason by a faculty of immediate perception — is very close indeed to the early aesthetic sense school, although there is as yet no attempt to classify judgments of the beautiful as sensate.

(3) Among the Cambridge group, external evidence points to three men as obvious influences on Shaftesbury: Benjamin Whichcote, whose *Sermons* Shaftesbury brought out in 1698, Henry More, and Ralph Cudworth, both of whom are referred

to in Shaftesbury's writings. In the realm of moral theory, More is particularly important for our purposes. Shaftesbury was basically a moral aesthetician: in the Platonic tradition, he saw no distinction between the philosophy of the good and the philosophy of the beautiful. "Beauty . . . and good," he wrote, ". . . are *one and the same*."⁹ Thus, any anticipation of the moral sense can, in relation to Shaftesbury, be considered at the same time an anticipation of the sense of beauty. And we have in More's *Enchiridion Ethicum* (1666) a clear anticipation of the former, which must have been well known to Shaftesbury.

More argues that "there is something which is simply and absolutely good, which in all human Actions is to be sought for."¹⁰ This simple quality of goodness (if we may be permitted to use the phrase of a different Moore) is recognized by reason; but it is "savored," so to speak, by a moral "sense": "the relish and delectation thereof, is to be taken in by the *Boniform Faculty*." Thus, although the discovery of goodness, ultimately, is a rational discovery, the pleasure that we take in its contemplation arises from a distinct moral faculty: a *sense of Virtue*.¹¹ More gives us, then, "a specifically ethical sense, perceiving and desiring absolute good, and in no way co-extensive with the will, the intellect, or both."¹²

More's *sense of Virtue* is not, properly speaking, a faculty of judgment; that is still the province of reason. It perceives "absolute good" only in the limited sense of *tasting*, not *discovering*. But it is a *sense;* it is a moral faculty which feels. So although More has not made the crucial distinction between "perceiving the true" (knowledge) and "sensing the good" (feeling) which Kant attributed to Hutcheson and his school,¹³ he has, nevertheless, made a great stride in that direction by positing a sensate moral faculty. He is half way, and more, toward Hutcheson's moral sense.

(4) While the seventeenth-century British philosophers approached the sense of beauty, a second stream of thought was converging on it from another quarter. I make reference to the concept of "taste" as a faculty of judgment, which was bequeathed to the Enlightment by the French critics.

The history of the term "taste" in its aesthetic and critical use has never been exhaustively treated[14]; nor can such a task be undertaken here. It must suffice for our purposes to examine some characteristic "aesthetic" uses of the term in seventeenth-century criticism which may have been of direct influence in the development of the aesthetic sense.

The introduction of "taste" as a full-blown mental faculty seems to have been accomplished by the Spanish moralist Baltasar Gracián in the mid-seventeenth century. Of particular influence was his *Orácula manual y arte de prudencia* (1647), which was translated into Dutch, English, French, German, and Italian during the seventeenth century. Good taste is not treated here purely as an aesthetic or critical concept, but rather as a faculty of liking and disliking in relation to a wide variety of objects — the wider the better, in fact: "The extent of a man's capacity is to be known by the loftiness of his taste. Great ability requires many objects to satisfy it . . . . "[15] Such "loftiness of taste" seems to be an acquired, rather than an inborn, disposition — emphasis, in any case, being placed upon its development. "There is room for cultivation here, just as in the case of mind . . . ," Gracián writes.

As a critical and aesthetic concept, "taste" developed most fully during the seventeenth century in the writings of the French. It came to be associated more and more with feeling (*sentiment*) and instinct; it was a subtle, nonrational faculty of perception, that which it perceived an equally subtle quality, often characterized by the timeworn phrase *je ne sais quoi*. Gracián's influence seems to have reached France as early as 1656, at which time Saint-Evremond (of particular interest here because of his long residence in London) was already writing of "taste" (*gout*) as a disposition to be pleased by the "refined" (*delicat*) in various objects.[16] Shortly thereafter the Chevalier de Méré was writing extensively of taste and the *je ne sais quoi*. [17] Important, too, are Dominique Bouhours' *La Manière de bien penser dans les ouvrages d'esprit* (1687) and the earlier dialogues, *Entretiens d'Ariste de d'Eugène* (1671), one of which is concerned explicitly with *"Le Je ne sais Quoi."*

For Bouhours the *je ne sais quoi* is not solely a critical

concept: rather, it still bears the wider connotations of Gracián's "taste"; he writes,

> [I]t is a grace which brightens beauty and other natural perfections, which corrects ugliness and other natural defects, . . . it is a charm and an air which informs every action and every word, which has its part in the way one walks and laughs, in the tone of the voice, and even in the slightest gesture of the socially acceptable person.[18]

But there is little doubt that Bouhours thought of it as a quality peculiarly relevant to beauty in general, and art in particular.

> The *je ne sais quoi* belongs to art as well as nature. For, without mentioning the different manners of painters, what charms us in those excellent paintings, in those statues so nearly alive that they lack only the gift of speech, . . . what charms us, I say, in such paintings and statues is an inexplicable quality.[19]

The "inexplicable" *je ne sais quoi* is perceived by a nonrational faculty: a "tendency and instinct of the heart, . . . the most exquisite feeling of the soul for whatever makes an impression on it, a marvelous liking and what might be called a kinship of the heart . . . ."[20] This "instinct" bears two characteristics later to be associated by Hutcheson with the sense of beauty: immediacy and freedom from control of the will, both of which were considered by Hutcheson and many others as infallible marks of sense perception. Bouhours states:

> [T]hese mysterious qualities which produce the effect of beauty or ugliness, so to speak, cause in us mysterious feelings of inclination or aversion which are beyond reason and which the will cannot control. They are impulses which forestall reflection and freedom. We can stop them in their course but we cannot prevent their arising. These feelings of liking or disliking take shape in an instant and when we are least aware of them. We love or hate at once without awareness in the mind, and, if I dare say so, without knowledge in the heart.[21]

But if Bouhours' "instinct" is nonrational, it is by no means in conflict with reason. Reason and instinct tell the same tale, although in a different way; they are in perfect rapport. Thus,

Bouhours later defined taste as "a harmony, an accord of the spirit and the reason." [22] If the Enlightenment saw a separation between reason and such faculties as taste and the sense of beauty, that separation did not imply an estrangement; and one should therefore exercise restraint in the application of a term like "romantic" to the nonrational in Enlightenment philosophy of art.

(5) The term "taste" in the language of British criticism goes back at least as far as Sidney's *Apologie for Poetrie* (*c.* 1583) — thus to its very beginnings. With regard to certain cases of dislike ("mislike") in poetry, Sidney argues, "the faulte is in their iudgements quit out of taste, and not in the sweet foode of sweetly vttered knowledge." [23] The passage is puzzling. On the one hand, it seems almost to equate "taste" with judgment, not merely with liking or disliking. Or, on the other hand, it may mean that one can dislike a poem and still judge it to be good. In this case the phrase, "their iudgements quit out of taste," would imply that one is judging correctly but not experiencing the feeling proper to the judgment; that is, "misliking," liking what one knows to be bad or not liking what one knows to be good. Such an interpretation would allow for a sharp distinction between judgment, the faculty of understanding, and taste, the faculty which merely likes or dislikes. It would not imply that Sidney thought of the critical judgment as a species of sense perception rather than reason.

The concept of taste does not seem to have taken firm hold in Britain during the seventeenth century although the term remained in use. To some, "taste" was the taste about which there was no disputing; it implied relativism in criticism. This may be inherent, for example, in Robert Howard's preface to *The Great Favorite* (1668):

> [I]n the Differences of *Tragedy* and *Comedy*, and of *Farce* itself, there can be no Determination but by taste; nor in the Manner of their Composure; and whoever would endeavour to like or dislike by the Rules of others, he will be as unsuccessful, as if he should try to be persuaded into a Power of believing: not what he must but what others direct him to believe. [24]

The implication here seems to be that we do not merely like or dislike independently of reason ("the Rules"), but that we make aesthetic or critical distinctions on the basis of liking and disliking. This, at least, is what Dryden (Howard's brother-in-law) made of the passage, severely criticizing it for its apparent identification of liking or disliking something with its goodness or badness. "The liking or disliking of the people," Dryden writes in the preface to the *Indian Emperor* (1668),

> gives the play the denomination good or bad, but does not really make or constitute it such. To please the people ought to be the poet's aim, because plays are made for their delight; but it does not follow that they are always pleased with good plays, or that plays which please them are always good. [25]

The notion of taste which the French promulgated and to which the British fell heir in the eighteenth century had unquestionably helped push critical judgment away from the reason and toward sense perception. "Thus taste," Ernst Cassirer writes, "is no longer classified with the logical processes of inference and conclusion but placed on a par with the immediacy of the pure acts of perception — with seeing and hearing, tasting and smelling." [26] And taste was essentially a faculty of those who look at, or listen to, or otherwise contemplate, aesthetic objects, not those who create them; it emphasized aesthetic perception rather than the creative process — an emphasis that was to characterize future speculation in eighteenth-century Britain, in marked contrast to seventeenth-century thought.

Why did the notion of taste, with its stress upon perception, take such firm root in British soil? The answer perhaps lies with the growing *audience* that was provided in Britain by the rising middle class. If the "consumer" in the arts is himself well schooled and likely to be a "creator" as well, there will be a rapport between himself and the professional (or we should say, rather, the accomplished) artist. There is no real gap between them, and therefore no real need for two separate aesthetic psychologies. Creator and perceiver are one. However, with the growth of an audience that consists not of dilettantes and dabblers, but, rather, laymen who wish to purchase entertainment (tired businessmen, in fact), there must inevitably arise a gulf between artist and audience, between creator and perceiver. Eighteenth-century London presented, to an extent never before known, a vast audience involved in the process of aesthetic perception but far removed from the process of creation. A new aesthetic phenomenon was born, and with it a new aesthetic study.

There is a certain irony in the fact that John Locke "who was of all the great seventeenth-century philosophers the most supercilious toward poetry" inspired this "entire new esthetic movement." [27] There is actually a double irony here; for although Locke "inspired" the new British aesthetics, its real founder was the Third Earl of Shaftesbury: a Neoplatonist, a philosophical reactionary, and an outspoken critic of Locke's empiricism (in spite of his being Locke's pupil and friend). So we are faced at the beginning of the eighteenth century with this peculiar state of affairs: a new aesthetic philosophy, inspired by an "unaesthetic" philosopher, founded by a conservative very much more interested in reviving an old doctrine than in promulgating a new one.

As perplexing as this situation appears on the surface it is nonetheless, from Shaftesbury's point of view at least, eminently reasonable. Empiricism alone, Shaftesbury felt, could never be delivered of a viable aesthetic theory; Locke's position had essentially "devalued" the universe. " 'Twas Mr. Locke," Shaftesbury wrote in a letter to his young protégé Michael Ainsworth, "that struck at all fundamentals, threw all order and virtue out of the world and made the very ideas of these . . . *unnatural* and without foundation in our minds." [28] For Shaftesbury, the empirical view was barren of values, aesthetic and moral. What it required was fertilization from another source; and this fertilization Shaftesbury himself could provide. For if Locke's universe was a bloodless dance of particles, Shaftesbury's, on the contrary, was a veritable orgy of virtues, beauties, and designs. It was a marriage of the new way of ideas and the most venerable of ancient philosophies, Platonism, that had issue in the new British aesthetics.

(6) That this is the best of all possible worlds Shaftesbury believed wholeheartedly and for reasons not by any means original. All evil is apparent evil only. If one sees the total picture, one understands that the apparent evil serves some distant good. All the parts serve the whole; see the relation and purpose of the parts and you see the good of the whole. "Only connect . . . " is a motto that, in the metaphysics of morals, Shaftesbury would have endorsed without question. "Only connect . . . " and you will perceive *"That whatsoever the Order of the World produces, is in the main both just and good."* [29] This is the faith that permeates Shaftesbury's writings — the faith of "perfect *Theism*," as he terms his position.

The good of the universe is constituted by the orderly arrangement of its parts; and although the idea is old, it is clothed by Shaftesbury in a modern vision: the Newtonian system of the world. Around the sun

> all the PLANETS, with this *our Earth,* single or with Attendants, continually move; seeking to receive the Blessing of his Light and lively warmth! towards him they seem to tend with prone descent, as to their Center; but happily controul'd still by another Impulse, they keep their heavenly Order; and in just Numbers, and exactest Measure, go the eternal Rounds. [30]

There is excellence in this structure: God saw that it was good. And the contemplation of it is pleasant to us. As Fontenelle told the elegant ladies of France (in describing the rival Cartesian cosmology), *"the Physical Ideas are in themselves very diverting; and as they convince and satisfy reason, so at the same time they present to the Imagination a Spectacle, which looks as if it were made on purpose to please it."* [31] In short, the universe is not only good, but beautiful as well. It is a harmonious whole and as such is beautiful in the contemplation.

For Shaftesbury the central concept of morality and aesthetics alike is harmony; it is in the *harmony* of parts — be they parts of the cosmos, a landscape, a musical composition, a man's character — that virtue and beauty lie. And all such beauty flows ultimately from God:

For Divinity it-self . . . is surely beauteous, and, of all Beautys the
brightest; tho not a beauteous body, but that from whence the
Beauty of Bodys is deriv'd: Not a beauteous Plain, but that from
whence the Plain looks Beautiful. The River's Beauty, the Sea's,
the Heaven's, and the Heavenly Constellations, all from hence as
from a Source Eternal and Incorruptible. As Beings partake of
this, they are fair, and flourishing, and happy: As they are lost to
this, they are deform'd, perish'd and lost. [32]

A vision worthy of Plotinus: and like Plotinus, Shaftesbury sees
a hierarchy of beauties whereby we rise from the physical to the
moral realm.

There are *"Three Degrees or Orders of Beauty,"* the beauty
of all resting in the harmonious relation of parts. At the lowest
level are physical objects, both natural and manmade: *"the dead*
Forms . . . which bear, a Fashion, and are form'd, whether by
Man, or Nature; but have no forming Power, no Action, no
Intelligence."[33] Among these are to be numbered objects of art;
painting, sculpture, music, and the like.

At the second level are *"the Forms which form;* that is,
which have Intelligence, Action, and Operation."[34] Thus, for
Shaftesbury, the beauty of inanimate objects derives from a
higher beauty, from the beauty of the intelligence that forms
them. And we are now in the moral realm; the beautiful and the
good are one. With respect to intelligence, virtue lies in the
beauty of mind, the beauty of mind in the harmony of parts,
and their harmonious relation to the universe as a whole. In so
far as man imbues external objects with harmony, he is an
artist; and in so far as he makes himself — his inner self — harmonious, he is also an artist: the maker of his own beauty and
virtue, "the *Architect of his own Life and Fortune.*"[35] So the
highest *moral,* as well as aesthetic, compliment that can be paid
to a man is that he has *good taste.*

Finally we reach the *"last* Order of *Supreme* and *Sovereign*
Beauty," the godhead from which all beauty flows. In that
beauty of the "second order" derives from God, and beauty of
the "first order" from the second, all can be subsumed under
the highest principle. "Thus Architecture, Musick, and all which
is of human Invention, resolves itself into this *last Order.*"[36] But

it is in the higher order that the Platonist will dwell. "What beauty could one still wish to see after having arrived at vision of Him who gives perfection to all beings . . . ?" asked Plotinus. [37] Shaftesbury, perhaps the most eloquent Platonist of modern times, echoes these sentiments.

> For whate'er is void of Mind, is *Void* and *Darkness* to the *Mind's* EYE. This languishes and grows dim, whene'er detained on foreign Subjects; but thrives and attains its natural Vigour, when employ'd in Contemplation of what is like it-self. 'Tis this *improving* MIND, slightly surveying other Objects, and passing over Bodys, and the common Forms, (where only a Shadow of Beauty rests) ambitiously presses onward to its *Source*, and views *the Original* of Form and Order in that which is intelligent. [38]

It is to the "Mind's EYE," then, to the sense of beauty, that harmony, at least of the higher kind, appears. But what of physical beauty? Is there a sense appropriate to it? Shaftesbury's position with regard to the sense of beauty is a complex one; it may perhaps be inconsistent, and it is certainly a position that evolved and deepened in the course of his intellectual development.

(7) Shaftesbury inaugurated his literary career with the preface to his edition of Whichcote's *Sermons* (1698). Shortly thereafter his *Inquiry Concerning Virtue or Merit* (1699) appeared in a pirated edition: "an imperfect thing," he later wrote, "brought into the world . . . contrary to the author's design, in his absence beyond the sea [Shaftesbury was in Holland at the time], and in a disguised, disordered style." [39] Between the appearance of the *Inquiry* and Shaftesbury's next published work, *A Letter Concerning Enthusiasm* (1708), lies a considerable gap [40]; but after the *Letter,* the remainder of Shaftesbury's writings to be published in his lifetime followed in short order. Thus, the publication history of Shaftesbury's works suggests that the *Inquiry Concerning Virtue or Merit* be considered as an early work, somewhat apart from the later writings; and we shall so treat it in the ensuing examination of the sense of beauty in Shaftesbury's philosophy.

Shaftesbury's first allusion to the aesthetic and moral sense proper occurs early in the *Inquiry*. It is a historically important passage and deserves quotation at some length.

> The Case is the same in the *mental* or *moral* subjects, as in the ordinary Bodys, or common Subjects of *Sense*. The Shapes, Motions, Colours, and Proportions of these latter being presented to our Eye; there necessarily results a Beauty or Deformity, according to the different Measure, Arrangement and Disposition of their several Parts. So in *Behaviour*, and *Actions*, when presented to our Understanding, there must be found, of necessity, an apparent Difference, according to the Regularity or Irregularity of the Subjects.
>
> THE MIND, which is Spectator or Auditor of *other Minds*, cannot be without its *Eye* and *Ear*; so as to discern Proportion, distinguish Sound, and scan each Sentiment or Thought which comes before it. It can let nothing escape its Censure. It feels the Soft and Harsh, the Agreeable and Disagreeable, in the Affections; and finds a *Foul* and *Fair*, a *Harmonious* and a *Dissonant*, as really and truly here, as in any musical Numbers, or in the outward Forms or Representations of sensible Things. Nor can it with-hold its *Admiration* and *Extasy*, its *Aversion* and *Scorn*, any more in what relates to one than to the other of these Subjects. So that to deny the common and natural Sense of a SUBLIME and BEAUTIFUL in Things, will appear an Affectation merely, to any-one who considers duly of this Affair. [41]

There are a number of points of interest here. To begin with, one wonders about the distinction between subjective and objective qualities, which was to become such a bone of contention in the aesthetic speculations of Hutcheson, his followers, and his critics. "Beauty or deformity," Shaftesbury tells us, is the result of "Shapes, Motions, Colours, and the Proportions of these latter being presented to our Eye." Is the *result* a subjective quality (like the taste of the apple), or an "emergent" tertiary quality? Is beauty the subjective result, while the "Shapes, Motions, Colours, and Proportions of these" are *out there*? Or is beauty an objective quality, composed of, or emerging from, objective qualities? I presume Shaftesbury meant the latter, although he is not explicit. But if one reads Shaftesbury with the subjective - objective distinction already formed, along the lines of Locke, as Hutcheson undoubtedly did, then the former interpretation is likely to jump out of the page. In this case it would seem that Shaftesbury's silence was as influential as anything he ever wrote.

The parallel between value judgment and sense perception had already, as we have seen, become something of a common-place, characteristic of various movements in seventeenth-century philosophy and criticism. Both moral and aesthetic judgment, for Shaftesbury, exhibit the immediacy of sense per-ception; and we also find the notion of moral and aesthetic judgment as beyond the control of the will — a further implica-tion of the sense perception analogy. When the object appropri-ate to any sense is presented to it under the proper perceptual conditions, the perception "necessarily results." So also with the "sense" of (moral) beauty. But what must be emphasized here is that, for Shaftesbury, all of this is analogy only. Shaftes-bury never concludes that because value judgment is similar to sense perception in certain respects, it *is* sense perception. That step awaited Hutcheson. (Whether the inference is indeed justi-fiable, we will discuss when we come to Hutcheson's presenta-tion of it.)

The exact nature of Shaftesbury's "common and natural Sense of a SUBLIME and BEAUTIFUL in Things" is difficult to make out. It has been the opinion of many, from Shaftesbury's time to our own, that no coherent view emerges; and I am inclined, in the last analysis, to agree. But, nonetheless, some explication is possible before one surrenders to Shaftesbury's inherent indeterminateness.

At times Shaftesbury seems to equate sense with feeling: "SENSE or *good Affection*," he writes on one occasion.[42] But the term is never used in the *Inquiry*, so far as I can see, with the connotation of an autonomous faculty, atomic and unana-lyzable. There is, rather, something here of that "common sense" which implies no hidden or occult faculties but merely those rational powers that all men can be supposed to possess. When Shaftesbury refers to a sense of right and wrong, or beauty and deformity, he is not necessarily appealing to some extra faculty, but rather to a sensibility — a talent for perceiv-

ing — that all men may be assumed to have diffused through
their normal faculties of reason and perception, at least to some
degree. Thus there seems to be a real affinity between Shaftesbury's use of "sense" and the notion of "good sense" or "common sense" which Thomas Rymer imported from France. And
for Rymer, the apostle of *reason* in seventeenth-century British
criticism, the term "sense" never implied sense perception or
feeling. Nor was any special faculty intended, but merely a level
of understanding which might be supposed of the cultivated
mind. In critical judgment, he insisted, "there is not required
much learning, or that a man must be some *Aristotle*, and *Doctor of Subtilties*, to form a right judgment in this particular:
common sense suffices . . . ."[43]

The most prominent feature of Shaftesbury's early theorizing
with regard to the aesthetic and moral sense, however, is the
lack of a feature: there is no theory of critical judgment at all.
Nowhere in the *Inquiry* does Shaftesbury refer to a faculty of
artistic judgment or a faculty of judgment whose object is natural beauty, nor is there any significant discussion of critical
theory. In fact, as we have seen, the analogy on which this early
theory is based ascribes the perception of visual beauty not to
an aesthetic sense but to the sense of sight, the perception of
beauty in sound not to an aesthetic sense but to the sense of
hearing. There is no question but that the mind plays a part
both in the judgment of visual beauty and auditory beauty, as
well as in moral beauty. In the passage quoted above, we must
interpret Shaftesbury in this way:

> It [the mind] feels the Soft and Harsh, the Agreeable and Dis-
> agreeable, in the Affections; and [the mind] finds a *Foul* and *Fair*,
> a *Harmonious* and a *Dissonant*, as really and truly here, as in any
> musical Numbers, or in the outward Forms or Representations of
> sensible Things. Nor can it [the mind again] with-hold its *Admira-
> tion* and *Extasy*, its *Aversion* and *Scorn*, any more in what relates
> to the one [moral beauty] than to the other [visual and aural
> beauty] of these subjects.

So there is a meaning of "perceive" in which the eye perceives
visual beauty, the ear perceives aural beauty, and the moral

sense perceives moral beauty. There is another meaning of "perceive," however (or perhaps "judge" would be better here), in which the *mind* perceives (or judges) visual, aural, and moral beauty. Jerome Stolnitz, in a recent article on Shaftesbury's aesthetic theory, offers this interpretation with regard to the perception of physical beauty: "The object enters awareness through the sense-organs, but its beauty is only discerned subsequent to physical ·sensation . . . . " [44] And, interestingly enough, Henry More — a thorough rationalist in aesthetics, as well as a direct influence on Shaftesbury — stated his own position in very much the same way some fifty years before. Beauty, he maintained, "is convey'd indeed by the outward Senses into the Soul, but a more Intellectual Faculty is that which relishes it; as a *Geometrical Scheme* is let in by the *Eyes*, but the Demonstration is discover'd by Reason." [45] However we interpret Shaftesbury on this point, the fact remains that there is, at least in the *Inquiry*, no faculty of aesthetic judgment apart from what is designated by the ubiquitous term *mind* itself, which has the beauty of art objects or natural beauty as its data.

(8) Shaftesbury continued, in his later writings, to expound the position which he had first stated in the *Inquiry Concerning Virtue or Merit*. In *The Moralists* (1709), he still clung to the analogy between the perception of external beauty by the senses of sight and hearing, and the perception of moral beauty by the moral sense. [46] Shaftesbury never seems to have deviated from this basic position; but other currents began to flow, and the problems of critical judgment, ignored in the early *Inquiry*, began, more and more, to occupy his thoughts.

Evidence of Shaftesbury's increasing interest in critical problems is to be found in the *Soliloquy: or, Advice to an Author*, first published in 1710. Here Shaftesbury seems to be timidly extending his theory of the moral sense to literary criticism. For the same analogy that had, in the *Inquiry* and *The Moralists*, served as an illustration of the moral sense, is now alluded to in reference to a literary sense: "a CRITIC'S *Eye*," as Shaftesbury calls it. [47] But there is no real independence of the moral sense: it is the ability to recognize moral beauty, wherein, for Shaftes-

bury, the excellence of the author lies. The fittest subjects for
the author are the beautiful actions and sentiments of men; and
a beautiful action or sentiment, as we have seen, is just another
name for a moral one. So Shaftesbury concludes,

> [T]here can be no kind of Writing which relates to Men and
> Manners, where it is not necessary for the Author to understand
> *Poetical* and *Moral* TRUTH, *the Beauty* of Sentiments, *the Sub-*
> *lime* of Characters; and carry in his Eye, the Model or Exemplar of
> that *natural Grace*, which gives to every Action its attractive
> Charm. If he has naturally no Eye, or Ear, for these *interior Num-*
> *bers*; 'tis not likely he shou'd be able to judge better of that
> *exterior Proportion* and *Symmetry* of Composition which consti-
> tutes a *legitimate Piece*.[48]

If there is a "critical sense" in the *Soliloquy*, it is identical with
the moral sense; it is the moral sense applied to literary occupations.

This rather tentative formulation of a critical "sense" was
followed by more extensive theorizing in the *Miscellaneous Re-*
flections (1714), one of the last works that Shaftesbury lived to
see prepared for publication (he died in 1713). Here the concept of taste gains currency; through this work, more than any
other perhaps, it becomes firmly established in British aesthetics.

What Shaftesbury meant by the term "taste" is as hard to
determine as his previous intentions with regard to the moral
sense; and it appears, in fact, that in the realm of moral beauty,
"taste" became, for Shaftesbury, another name for the sense of
beauty. The man of taste in art and manners is a "gentleman";
the man of taste in the moral realm is a true philosopher and a
moral being. "To *philosophize*, in a just Signification, is but to
carry *Good-breeding* a step higher," Shaftesbury writes. "For
the Accomplishment of Breeding is, To learn whatever is *decent*
in Company, or *beautiful* in Arts; and the Sum of Philosophy is,
To learn what is *just* in Society, and *beautiful* in Nature, and
the Order of the World." The gentleman and the philosopher
have but a single goal: "Both *Characters* aim at what is excellent, aspire to *a just Taste*, and carry in view the Model of what

is *beautiful* and becoming."[49] Thus it would appear but a step
from lace ruffles and a pinch of snuff to the moral law within — a convenient arrangement for a peer of England.

In his later writings, then, Shaftesbury seems to consider
taste and moral sense as interchangeable. One is tempted to
argue, therefore, that "taste" when used as a critical term in the
arts carries with it the characteristics which were ascribed, in
the early writings, to the moral sense. And if this is the case,
then Shaftesbury's position with regard to critical and aesthetic
judgment has altered somewhat; for, as we have seen, there was
in the early *Inquiry Concerning Virtue or Merit* no faculty of
aesthetic judgment per se. However, Shaftesbury nowhere refers
to taste in art as a "sense" or "faculty." And even if we were
correct in assuming that he thought of it in the same terms as
the moral sense, we are not much closer to a full-fledged aesthetic faculty; for the moral sense, as we have previously argued, is
far less an autonomous faculty than a generalized ability to
perceive, involving no extra talent or internal sense. Hence, it is
a mistake to maintain, as a recent student of Shaftesbury has,
that Shaftesbury himself advanced "the notion that there is a
faculty of aesthetic judgment, *a special sense which can be identified with taste . . . .* "[50]

(9) Shaftesbury is a transitional figure in the history of
aesthetics: though he was the nominal founder of a new tradition, he had one foot planted firmly in the past, not only the
past as represented by the Italian Renaissance, but that of classical antiquity as well. So we find that his treatment of the
problem of taste is at once characteristic of the Enlightenment
quest for a *subjective* critical standard and, to a greater extent,
of the Renaissance tradition of objectivity and reason in art. It
is only by taking into account Shaftesbury's divided allegiance
that we can fathom the rather moderate and, from the Enlightenment point of view, indecisive stand that he finally takes.

Shaftesbury often compared the moral sense to an instinct;
and it was in criticizing Locke's denial of innate ideas that the
term "instinct" often occurred. With regard to "the Notions
and Principles of *Fair, Just,* and *Honest,*" Shaftesbury wrote in

The Moralists, "if you dislike the word *Innate*, let us change it, if you will, for INSTINCT; and call *Instinct*, that which *Nature* teaches, exclusive of *Art, Culture* or *Discipline*."[51] Shaftesbury agreed with Locke that one is not born with a catalogue of precepts and principles imprinted on the *tabula*[52]; but this, he maintained, is no argument against innate principles. (It is doubtful that Locke thought it was either.) He wrote to Michael Ainsworth,

> The question is not about the *time* the ideas entered . . . but whether the constitution of man be such that, being adult and grown up, at such or such a time, sooner or later (no matter when), the idea and sense of order, administration, and a God, will not infallibly, inevitably, necessarily spring up in him.[53]

Following this line of thought, we would naturally conclude that aesthetic standards are to be found in man's innate structure; through his innate aesthetic and moral instincts, the precepts of beauty and morality "infallibly, inevitably, necessarily spring up in him." With regard to the aesthetic, in Kant's words, "We are suitors for agreement from everyone else, because we are fortified with a ground common to all."[54]

An important question, however, remains unanswered. If men possess innate moral and aesthetic instincts in common, why do they, nevertheless, differ in their judgments of right and wrong, beautiful and ugly? Shaftesbury's answer, an answer not uncommon in the eighteenth century, is that such instincts are liable to deflection and perversion; and they must, therefore, be guided. Thus, Shaftesbury was grossly overstating his position when he spoke of value judgments as conforming "exclusive of *Art, Culture* or *Discipline*." This is particularly true of taste in art, as Shaftesbury made quite clear in the *Miscellaneous Reflections*, where he wrote:

> Now TASTE or *Judgment*, 'tis suppos'd, can hardly come ready form'd with us into the World. Whatever Principles or Materials of this kind we may possibly bring with us; whatever Facultys, Senses, or anticipating Sensations, and Imaginations, may be of Nature's Growth, and arise properly, of themselves, without our Art, Promotion, or Assistance; the general *Idea* which is form'd of

all this Management, and the clear *Notion* we attain of what is
preferable and principal in all these Subjects of Choice and Estima-
tion, will not, I imagine, by any Person, be taken for *in-nate*. Use,
Practice and Culture must precede *Understanding* and *Wit* of such
an advanc'd Size and growth as this. A legitimate and just TASTE
can neither be begotten, made, conceiv'd, or produc'd, without
the antecedent *Labour* and *Pains* of CRITICISM.[55]

Taste, then, does not just happen; it must be made to happen.

But we are now faced anew with the problem of aesthetic
standards. For if taste must be formed in order to become a
reliable organ of critical judgment, the question must arise: According to what standard is it to be formed? What is the standard by which the critic judges taste to be good or bad? If the
standard is his own taste, then what is the standard on which *his*
taste was formed? And the answer that Shaftesbury ultimately
falls back on is the answer of tradition: reason is the judge,
harmony the law.

For HARMONY is Harmony *by Nature*, let Men judge ever so
ridiculously of Musick. So is *Symmetry* and *Proportion* founded
still *in Nature*, let Mens Fancy prove ever so *Gothick* in their
Architecture, Sculpture, or whatever other designing Art.[56]

The ignorant may *feel*, but the artist and connoisseur know:
"The Philosopher and virtuoso alone [are] capable to prove,
demonstrate. But the idiot, the vulgar man can feel, recognize."[57] And if the vulgar recognize the beautiful, it is only by
luck or because their taste has been correctly formed by the
man of reason. Taste makes a big noise in Shaftesbury's later
writings; but reason is the still small voice.

What function, then, does taste perform? One suspects that
in the last analysis it is the function of Henry More's *Boniform
Faculty*: a faculty of delectation but not of judgment. In art we
may savor with our taste, "feeling only by the Effect, whilst
ignorant of the cause"[58]; but, ultimately, it is reason that teaches us what is beautiful. Taste is but right opinion: reason is
knowledge. If we judge the beautiful by a "sense," it is a sense
that reason has formed; and reason is the epistemologically pri-

or principle. "Art it-self is severe: the *Rules* rigid. And if I expect *the Knowledge* shou'd come to me by accident, or in play, I shall be grossly deluded . . . . "[59]

For Shaftesbury, critical and aesthetic judgment still function through knowledge, not perception. Shaftesbury was a man of the past; he looked into the abyss and quickly withdrew to safe ground — rational ground. But that look was of vital import to the Enlightenment; and Hutcheson rushed in where Shaftesbury feared to tread.[60]

II

THE SENSE OF "SENSE"

(1) The first phase in the history of the aesthetic sense in Enlightenment thought closes with Francis Hutcheson's *Inquiry Concerning Beauty, Order, Harmony, Design*, the first of the two treatises which comprise his *Inquiry into the Original of Our Ideas of Beauty and Virtue* (1725). It is certainly the first systematic philosophical treatment in English of what we would now call "aesthetics."

Hutcheson makes an end point and a synthesis of an era in aesthetics and criticism: an era in which the sense of beauty — the seventh sense — played a progressive role, turning speculation away from the art object toward the perception of that object, away from the rational judgment toward the perceptual, away from the "old" aesthetics of the Renaissance toward the "new" outlook of the Enlightenment. From Hutcheson's time, the sense of beauty came to be seen, for the most part, as a conservative influence; and it would have lived out a quiet old age in Scotland had it not received a temporary new life in Kant's *Critique of Judgment*.

Hutcheson's aesthetic theory surely owes something to Shaftesbury (with whom his contemporaries often associated him). Of far greater importance is the influence of Locke. Hutcheson himself pays ample tribute to the author of the *Characteristicks*. The title page of the first edition of the *Inquiry into Beauty and Virtue* reads, in part: "IN WHICH The Principles of the late Earl of Shaftesbury are explan'd and defended against the author of the *Fable of the Bees* [i.e., Mande-ville] . . . . " In the preface Shaftesbury is again referred to: "THIS moral Sense of *Beauty in* Actions *and* Affections *may appear strange at first view: Some of our* Moralists *themselves are offended at it in my* LORD SHAFTESBURY . . . . "[1] And Hutcheson further apotheosizes Shaftesbury in the following terms: "TO *recommend the* LORD SHAFTESBURY'S *Writings to the World is a very needless attempt. They will be esteem'd while any* Reflection *remains among Men.*"[2] But it is Shaftes-bury the moralist whom Hutcheson is most often eulogizing: seldom is it the aesthetician. And it becomes apparent from the very outset of the preface that Locke is the guiding spirit of Hutcheson's aesthetic theory. His aesthetics, unlike Shaftes-bury's, is permeated with the psychological and epistemological language of the *Essay Concerning Human Understanding.* The first *Inquiry* speaks the language of Locke even in its criticism of him: its "field of study itself is defined in Lockean terms. The method of inquiry is therefore also Locke's — the new way of ideas, conceived as a psychological programme."[3] Thus, Hutcheson's work in aesthetics is the first fruit of a union of empiricism and English Platonism which the philosophy of Locke and his pupil made possible. Shaftesbury gave Hutcheson his subject: aesthetics as a respectable and even central concern of the philosopher. Locke gave him the method of pursuing it.

(2) Hutcheson believed that he was embarking, in his aesthe-tic and moral treatises, on a voyage whose course had not be-fore been charted, namely, *"inquiring into the various Pleasures which* human Nature *is capable of receiving."*

> *We shall generally find in our modern philosophic Writings, no-thing further on this Head, than some bare Division of them into* Sensible *and* Rational, *and some trite commonplace Arguments to prove the* latter *to be more valuable than the* former. *Our sensible Pleasures are slightly pass'd over, and explain'd only by some in-stances in* Tastes, Smells, Sounds, *or such like, which Men of any tolerable Reflection generally look upon as very trifling Satisfac-tions. Our* rational Pleasures *have had much the same kind of treatment* .[4]

There cannot be much doubt that Locke's *Essay* is the principal representative in Hutcheson's mind of the "modern philosophic Writings"; and Hutcheson's characterization of it is substantially correct. "Delight or uneasiness, one or other of them," writes Locke, "join themselves to almost all our ideas both of sensation and reflection: and there is scarce an affection of our senses from without, any retired thought of our mind within, which is not able to produce in us pleasure or pain."[5] But he nowhere pursues the topic with any great thoroughness. That was the task Hutcheson made his own: to do for "delight" and "uneasiness," "pleasure," and "pain," what Locke had left undone, which Hutcheson (I think rightly) believed was almost everything.

Hutcheson, as we have seen, divides pleasures into two kinds: *sensible* and *rational*. The sensible pleasures are those that are felt directly by the external senses: thus, the pleasant sound of a musical instrument's timbre, the disagreeable taste of a bitter herb, the pain of looking directly at the sun, the pleasant warmth of a fireside. And these pleasures or pains, satisfactions or dissatisfactions, are, Hutcheson urges (as did Locke) unaffected by the wishes and desires of the perceiver: which is considered one indelible mark of sense perception. Hutcheson writes:

> IN *reflecting upon our* external Senses, *we plainly see, that our Perceptions of pleasure or Pain do not depend directly upon our Will. Objects do not please us, according as we incline they should: The Presence of some Objects necessarily pleases us, and the Presence of others as necessarily displeases us* .... *By the very* Frame *of our* Nature *the one is made the Occasion of Delight, and the other of Dissatisfaction.*[6]

But, Hutcheson continues, the pleasures we are capable of receiving are not confined to the immediate pleasures of sense perception: *"for there are many other sorts of Objects, which please, or displease us as necessarily as material objects do when they operate upon our Organs of sense."*[7] And among these are the objects which we would now call "aesthetic." They are distinguished from the former in that the pleasures we receive directly from external sense perception are pleasures taken in simple qualities: a sound, a color, a smell, a taste, a touch. Whereas the pleasures that we call "aesthetic" are pleasures received in the contemplation of complex qualities: collections of simple qualities exhibiting some form or arrangement.

> *Thus we shall find our selves pleas'd with a regular* Form, *a piece of* Architecture, *or* Painting, *a composition of* Notes, *a* Theorem ... *and we are conscious that this Pleasure necessarily arises from the Contemplation of the Idea, which is then present to our Minds, with all its Circumstances, altho some of these Ideas have nothing of what we call sensible perception in them; and in those which have, the Pleasure arises from some* Uniformity, Order, Arrangement, Imitation; *and not from the simple Ideas of* Color, *or* Sound, *or mode of* Extension *separately considered.* [8]

Hutcheson concludes: "THESE *Determinations to be pleas'd with any Forms or Ideas which occur to our Observation, the* Author *choses to call* SENSES; *distinguishing them from the Powers which commonly go by that Name, by calling our Power of perceiving the* Beauty *of* Regularity, Order, Harmony, *an* INTERNAL SENSE . . . ." [9]

It is important to note, in distinguishing between external and internal senses, that in the final version of the passage just quoted (the fourth edition) Hutcheson replaces the phrase *"any Forms or Ideas which occur to our Observation"* with *"certain complex Forms."* [10] The internal senses, for Hutcheson, receive pleasure from "ideas"; but so, too, do the external senses, on the Lockean model of "representative" perception, to which Hutcheson adhered. The distinction between an external and an internal sense is not that the former receives pleasure from an "external" object and the latter from an "internal" one; for both are here on the same footing. It is that the latter receives pleasure from complex ideas, the former from simple ones (and thus a uniform patch of color, or a single note cannot, for Hutcheson, give *aesthetic* pleasure). The alteration which Hutcheson made in the fourth edition of the *Inquiry Concerning Beauty* makes this clear: the internal senses do not receive pleasure from *any* forms or ideas, but only from certain *complex* forms or ideas.

(3) The first mark of sense perception for Hutcheson, as we have just seen, is its nonvolitional character. The second mark is *innateness*. Our sense of beauty is a *sense* of beauty because the pleasure it perceives, it perceives whether we will or not; but it is a sense, too, because, like the external senses, we possess it *"By the very* Frame *of our* Nature . . . . " *"There is,"* Hutcheson urges, *"some Sense of* Beauty *natural to men."* [11]

But the notion of an innate sense immediately raised for followers of Locke the specter of *innate ideas* which Locke was at such pains to exorcise. And so Hutcheson is adamant in his insistence "That an *internal Sense* no more presupposes an *innate Idea*, or Principle of Knowledge, than the external." [12] What, then, does it mean for the sense of beauty to be innate? And what does it mean for it *not* to be an innate idea?

When a Cartesian claimed that certain ideas or principles are innate, there is certainly one thing he did *not* mean: he did not mean to say that infants or children have (are conscious of) these ideas or principles. Yet when Locke criticized the doctrine, this is exactly the form which it took. Thus, he argued, we can "show these propositions not to be innate, if children alone were ignorant of them." [13] Now there is one thing, although it is not the only thing, which Locke perhaps meant to show with such arguments: that the phrase "innate idea" is a misleading one if it does not signify "idea in consciousness since birth." [14] Locke must have been perfectly well aware that when Descartes said the idea of God is innate, he did not mean that infants are conscious of this idea, but that, under the proper conditions, such an idea will inevitably arise. We have an innate capacity of framing such an idea. But why then call the *idea* innate? This leads us away from the very thing which, for Locke, was the most crucial to a sound theory of knowledge: the *process* which, not necessarily in fact, but in rational reconstruction, brings the idea to consciousness. It is more than mere carping to insist that a thing be called by its right name, even if one is not mistaken about the nature of the thing. To call the idea of God innate is to fix attention on the idea as we have it. To call the capacity of framing the idea of God innate is to fix attention on how, under what conditions, the capacity can be exercised. And it is in fixing on the latter, Locke believed, that the empiricist's claim can be supported. [15]

For Hutcheson to claim that the sense of beauty is not an innate idea, then, is to allow for the obvious and trivial fact that we are not born making aesthetic distinctions: "*It is probably some little time before Children do reflect, or at least let us know that they do reflect upon Proportion and Similitude . . . .* " [16] But it is to call attention also to the manner in which our innate capacity to make aesthetic distinctions is realized. This is a topic which will occupy us more properly when we come to discuss the standard of taste and the universality of the sense of beauty. However, we must at this point establish the sense in which the sense of beauty is an *innate* capacity; and it will be best to begin by determining how many innate aesthetic senses Hutcheson is willing to countenance. This, however, will require a slight historical detour.

(4) One of the most important and most frequently remarked upon aspects of eighteenth-century British aesthetic theory is the emergence of aesthetic (as opposed to rhetorical) categories — categories of aesthetic *experience*. The dichotomy between the beautiful and the sublime, which Samuel H. Monk made the subject of his now classic study, is, of course, the most prominent division. Late in the century the picturesque emerged as another full-blown aesthetic category, making such a noise in the world that Jane Austen was moved to some lovely satire in reaction. Other critical terms such as "novelty" and "ridicule" also reared their heads, but never quite achieved individual identity to the extent that the sublime and picturesque had.

In examining the proliferation of inner senses, which the emergence of aesthetic categories inevitably brought about, we must return to the opening years of the eighteenth century and, specifically, to the work which really inaugurated the new way of ideas in aesthetics, Addison's *Pleasures of the Imagination*. Addison was one of the first Enlightenment authors to write of taste as an autonomous faculty. He was also one of the first to attempt a clear distinction between such aesthetic categories as the beautiful and the sublime on a subjective level. What the relation between taste as a faculty and the categorization of aesthetic experience undertaken in the *Pleasures of the Imagination* is, Addison never reveals. But that he was, in part, responsible for their merging, there can be no doubt.

Addison defines the "pleasures of the imagination" in this way:

> I mean only such pleasures as arise originally from sight, and . . . I divide these pleasures into two kinds: my design being, first of all, to discourse of those primary pleasures of the imagination which entirely proceed from such objects as are before our eyes; and, in the next place, to speak of those secondary pleasures of imagination which flow from the ideas of visible objects, when the objects are not actually before the eye, but are called up into our memories, or formed into agreeable visions of things that are either absent or fictitious. [17]

The "primary pleasures" take in the realm of natural beauty. The "secondary pleasures" include, for the most part, imitative beauty and, therefore, the beauty of the fine arts (except music, which owes its power to imitation proper in only a small degree). But the secondary pleasures include also the pleasures of *imagining*. Thus, if I view some natural beauty, I experience a primary pleasure of the imagination; and if that beauty is called to mind by a work of art which imitates it, or merely by an act of imagination in some moment of reverie, I experience a secondary pleasure.

The primary pleasures of the imagination are divided by Addison into three categories which "all proceed from the sight of what is great, uncommon, or beautiful." [18] These are, in the more familiar terminology of the later Enlightenment, the ideas of *sublimity, novelty,* and *beauty,* respectively. (Sublimity, of course, as well as the tripartite division of categories, Addison and his age appropriated from the celebrated pseudo-Longinian treatise *On the Sublime.*[19]) A psychological explanation accompanies each of the first two categories to account for its pleasing character. The object of great magnitude pleases through the mind's innate disdain to be bounded. "The mind of man naturally hates to fancy itself under a sort of confinement, when the

sight is pent up in a narrow compass . . . ." [10] The pleasure of
uncommon, novel objects is owed, essentially, to the relief of
mental tedium: "We are indeed so often conversant with one set
of objects, and tired out with so many repeated shows of the
same thing, that whatever is new or uncommon contributes a
little to vary human life, and to divert our minds for a while
with the strangeness of its appearance." Such explanations, or
variations of them, survived in Britain throughout the century.

With regard to the pleasure of beauty, Addison gives us no
explanation, but, rather, a description of its effect, which
immediately suggests the French school of taste, as well as
Hutcheson's aesthetic sense.

> But there is nothing that makes its way more directly to the soul
> than beauty, which immediately diffuses a secret satisfaction and
> complacency through the imagination, and gives a finishing to any
> thing that is great or uncommon. [Thus, for Addison, the aesthetic
> categories are not exclusive of each other; for the "great" or "un-
> common" can at the same time be "beautiful."] The very first
> discovery of it strikes the mind with an inward joy, and spreads a
> cheerfulness and delight through all its faculties. There is not per-
> haps any real beauty or deformity more in one piece of matter
> than another, because we might have been so made, that whatso-
> ever now appears loathsome to us might have shown itself agree-
> able; but we find, by experience, that there are several modifica-
> tions of matter which the mind, without any previous considera-
> tion, pronounces at first sight beautiful or deformed. [21]

The pleasure of beauty is a "secret satisfaction" — essentially a
je ne sais quoi. Its effect is immediate, without "previous consideration"; thus it operates in the manner of Hutcheson's internal senses in this regard. And like Hutcheson (as we shall see),
Addison maintains that for the beautiful, in a certain sense, to
be is to be perceived, although beauty is correlated by a benevolent Deity to "several modifications of matter" for our utility
and amusement, as are the pleasures of novelty and sublimity.

Addison concludes that the primary pleasures of the imagination are ultimate mysteries "because we know neither the nature of an idea, nor the substance of a human soul, which might
help us to discover the conformity or disagreeableness of the

one to the other . . . . " What remains for the aesthetician is a job of catalouging and, at last, the way of final causes, which, Addison writes, "though they are not altogether so satisfactory, are generally more useful than the other [i.e., "necessary and efficient causes"], as they give us greater occasion of admiring the goodness and wisdom of the first Contriver." [22] We need not bother ourselves with the Spectator's theology except perhaps to observe that Hutcheson seems to have incorporated some of it into his own aesthetic theory.

But we should take time to notice how striking the influence of Locke is on Addison here. Simple ideas, for Locke, are the irreducible elements, the brute facts, of experience. Complex ideas can be explained in terms of their simple constituents; we cannot go beyond simple ideas. Definition means the breaking down of complex into simple. Once ultimate simplicity is reached, definition must end: "The names of simple ideas are not capable of any definition; the names of all complex ideas are." [23] Thus we cannot know "the nature of an idea" (we must understand Addison to mean simple idea here) because our explanation could but consist in some kind of reduction to more simple constituents which, *ex hypothesi*, is impossible since the most simple constituents are what we are attempting to explain. The "substance of a human soul," too, is inexplicable, Locke believes: we are "in the dark concerning these matters," ignorant "of the nature of that thinking thing that is in us, and which we look on as ourselves." [24] Addison has, clearly, learned the language of Locke and his *Essay*.

With regard to the secondary pleasures of the imagination, the pleasure in imitation (its most populous species) is, of course, a major aesthetic category in the Enlightenment, embracing, as it does, almost the whole corpus of eighteenth-century art. It is a completely autonomous category since its effect relies neither upon the sublimity nor novelty nor beauty of its objects, although it can involve them all. Imitation is, as we have seen, perceived by the intellect, according to Addison, since this perception involves a comparison of an object (or remembered image of an object) with its imitation. The pleasure which such perception arouses "may be more properly called the pleasure of the understanding than of the fancy [or imagination] ," writes Addison, "because we are not so much delighted with the image that is contained in the description [Addison is discussing poetic imitation here], as with the aptness of the description to excite the image." [25] But whether a pleasure of the intellect or imagination, imitation emerges as an aesthetic category of major importance.

Addison never referred to the pleasures of the imagination as "senses" although they certainly bear characteristics which Hutcheson attributed to his sense of beauty. Both Addison and Hutcheson couched their aesthetic principles in Lockean terms; and both recognized essentially the same aesthetic categories, Hutcheson, in fact, admittedly following Addison in this regard. Thus, Addison himself was but a step away from the proliferation of aesthetic senses, as was Hutcheson at the time of the first *Inquiry*; and Hutcheson eventually took that step.

(5) In 1725, the year which saw publication of the *Inquiry Concerning Beauty*, Hutcheson also published a series of papers in the *Dublin Journal,* the first three of which were later collected under the title *Reflections Upon Laughter.* He there wrote: "The implanting then of a sense of the ridiculous, in our nature, was giving us an avenue to pleasure and an easy remedy for discontent and sorrow." [26] This "sense of the ridiculous" is obviously cast in the same mold as Hutcheson's other inner senses, being an "avenue of pleasure" implanted "in our nature." And if a sense of humor can be considered an *aesthetic* sense, we can begin our list with it. [27]

In the *Inquiry Concerning Beauty* Hutcheson seems to recognize five basic aesthetic categories: *original beauty, relative (imitative) beauty, harmony (beauty of sound), novelty,* and *grandeur (sublimity)*. At this time Hutcheson never speaks of more than one aesthetic sense (called, alternately, the *sense of beauty* and the *sense of harmony*), and it would appear that he thinks of all his aesthetic principles as subsumed under this single sense. It is fairly certain this is true of the first three; whether it is true of *novelty* and *grandeur* as well is more difficult to say, for Hutcheson refers to them only in an offhand manner, as if

they were second thoughts, and refers his readers to Addison
for further explication. [28]

In his next published work, the *Essay on the Nature and
Conduct of the Passions and Affections* (1728), Hutcheson's
epistemology has virtually exploded into "senses" of every description, although it is still not certain that he acknowledges
more than one aesthetic sense. Hutcheson states:

> If we may call *every Determination of our Minds to receive Ideas
> independently on our Will and to have Perceptions of Pleasure and
> Pain*, A SENSE, we shall find many other *Senses* beside those
> commonly explained. Tho it is not easy to assign accurate Divi-
> sions on such Subjects, yet we may reduce them to the following
> Classes . . . . In the 1st Class are the *External Senses*, universally
> known. In the 2d, the *Pleasant Perceptions* arising from *regular,
> harmonious, uniform* Objects; as also from *Grandeur* and *Novelty*.
> These we may call, after Mr. ADDISON, the Pleasures of the Imagina-
> tion; or we may call the Power of receiving them, an *Internal Sense*.
> Whoever dislikes this Name may substitute another. 3. The next
> Class of Perceptions we may call a *Publick Sense, viz* 'our Deter-
> mination to be pleased with the *Happiness* of others, and to be
> uneasy at their *Misery*' . . . . 4. The fourth Class we may call the
> *Moral Sense*, by which 'we perceive *Virtue*, or *Vice* in our selves,
> or others' . . . . 5. The fifth Class is a *Sense of Honour*, 'which
> makes the *Approbation*, or *Gratitude* of others, for any good ac-
> tions we have done, the necessary occasion of Pleasure' . . . . [29]

I have quoted here at some length to indicate the freedom with
which Hutcheson was now applying the term "sense" in his
value theory, both moral and aesthetic.

The list of aesthetic categories is approximately the same as
that in the *Inquiry*, and the kinship with Addison's pleasures of
the imagination is made quite explicit. It is particularly worthy
of note that Hutcheson considered "pleasure of the imagination" as equivalent to "sense" — a clear indication of Addison's
role in the proliferation of aesthetic senses and, in general, the
development of the internal sense doctrine in aesthetics. But
whether Hutcheson at this time thought of each aesthetic category as having a sense appropriate to it, or thought of them all
as arising from a single sense, is not clear. The crucial passage is
this: "we may call the Power of receiving them an *Internal*

Sense." Does Hutcheson mean that one *"Internal Sense"* perceives all of "them," or that each of "them" is perceived by a
different *"Internal Sense"*? Perhaps at this juncture we are
merely splitting grammatical hairs. For if Hutcheson is not now
committed to the proliferation of aesthetic senses in letter, he is
already committed in spirit.

But Hutcheson's advance along the multiplication table of
aesthetic senses does not seem to have been a steady one: for in
the *Short Introduction to Moral Philosophy* (1747), a halt has
been called. We now have eight aesthetic categories and (unequivocally) but one "sense" appropriate to them.

> The external senses of Sight and Hearing we have in common with
> the Brutes: but there's superadded to the Human Eye and Ear a
> wonderful and ingenious Relish or Sense, by which we receive
> subtiler pleasures; in material forms *gracefulness, beauty and pro-
> portion*; in sounds *concord* and *harmony*; and are highly delighted
> with observing exact *imitation* in the works of the more ingenious
> arts, Painting, Statuary and Sculpture, and in motion and Action;
> all which afford us far more manly pleasures than the external
> senses . . . . And the very *grandeur* and *novelty* of objects excite
> some grateful perceptions not unlike the former, which are natu-
> rally connected with and subservient to our desires of know-
> ledge. [30]

Hutcheson's last work, the posthumously published *System
of Moral Philosophy* (1755), finally reveals the proliferation of
aesthetic senses that had been lurking near the surface since
1728. The categories are still basically those of the earlier
works: *beauty, imitation, harmony, design* (fitness of means to
ends), *grandeur,* and *novelty.* But now Hutcheson is willing to
call each category a sense;

> To the senses of seeing and hearing, are superadded in most men,
> tho' in very different degrees, certain powers of perception of a
> finer kind than what we have reason to imagine are in most lower
> animals, who yet perceive the several colours and figures, and hear
> the several sounds. These we may call the senses of beauty and
> harmony, or, with Mr. Addison, the *imagination.* Whatever name
> we give them, 'tis manifest that, the several following qualities

[i.e., beauty, imitation, harmony, design, grandeur, novelty] in
objects, are sources of pleasures constituted by nature; or, men
have natural powers or determinations to perceive pleasure from
them. [31]

Hutcheson has at last made explicit what was obvious from the
start: if one is to remain entirely within the Lockean camp,
every simple aesthetic perception which merits the name of a
distinctive aesthetic category must imply a corresponding
"sense," or "power," "determination to be pleased," or something of the kind. One must be satisfied with a single aesthetic
category, or not balk at the multiplication of internal senses —
or, break away from the strict tutelage of Locke. To accept the
first alternative would have been to turn one's back on the most
interesting aesthetic and critical development of Hutcheson's
age; to accept the last would have been to reject the most
powerful philosophical movement of Hutcheson's age. It was
not until later in the century, when the power of Locke had
been somewhat blunted by philosophical criticism, that Locke's
tutelage was thrown off by British aesthetics.

(6) Now if the term "sense" is so basically innocuous that six
or seven aesthetic senses are not to be boggled at; that "sense"
is to be considered roughly equivalent to "pleasure of the imagination" in its aesthetic setting; that even a sense of humor is
to be included in the list of inner senses; we are led inevitably to
the conclusion, it seems to me, that the notion of innate aesthetic senses must be understandable in terms more familiar to the
modern reader, and less suggestive of a rather crude faculty
psychology. What, then, are we committing ourselves to when
we speak of a sense of humor, a sense of beauty, and departing
now from ordinary linguistic usage, senses of grandeur, imitation, novelty, fitness, and so on? More particularly, what are we
committing ourselves to when we call these senses "innate"?

To say that there is in man an innate sense of humor, or of
beauty, or of grandeur, or of imitation is merely to say that
sometimes we enjoy humor, or beauty, or grandeur, or imitation for its own sake. Many beautiful things may indeed be

useful, as many actions which are beneficial to others may also be beneficial to the agent who performs them; and we may sometimes admire beautiful things for their utility, as we may sometimes pursue courses which are beneficial to others out of interest to ourselves. But if we sometimes admire things merely for their beauty, then it is appropriate to say that we have an innate sense of beauty; and *this* is merely to say that sometimes we must answer the question *Why do you admire x?* not with *Because it can do y*, but merely with *Because I enjoy it* (in some special way). To be an innate aesthetic sense of *x* simply means that enjoyment (of some special kind) of perceiving *x* is sometimes the terminus of our interest in *x*. Hutcheson writes: "Hence it plainly appears, that some Objects are immediately the Occasions of this Pleasure of Beauty, and that we have senses fitted for perceiving it; and that it is distinct from that Joy which arises from Self-love upon prospect of Advantage . . . ." [32]

If we now cast our eye back over the list of aesthetic senses which Hutcheson is willing to countenance, we will perhaps feel less that we are being saddled with some bizarre and archaic faculty psychology. We have an *innate, internal, implanted sense* of beauty; but all this means is that sometimes we enjoy things (in a special way) with nothing else in view, just as we sometimes want to do something for others with no other end in view. We have an *innate, internal, implanted sense* of grandeur; but all this means is that sometimes we enjoy things (in another special way) with nothing else in view: likewise the *innate, internal, implanted senses* of humor, or imitation, or fitness, or novelty. They are innate because they are the endpoints of arguments. We do no essential injustice to Hutcheson if we think of the various aesthetic senses as names for various kinds of enjoyment; and, furthermore, the innateness of these senses amounts simply to saying that we sometimes treat these enjoyments as *final* answers to the question *Why?*

(7) We have so far discussed two of the four marks which Hutcheson, like many of his predecessors, took to be infallible signs of sense perception; namely, independence of will and

innateness. We come now to the third: independence of knowledge. Thus, Hutcheson writes of the sense of beauty: "This
superior Power of Perception is justly called *a Sense*, because of
its Affinity to the other Senses in this, that the Pleasure does
not arise from any Knowledge of Principles, Proportions,
Causes, or of the Usefulness of the Object; but strikes us at first
with the Idea of Beauty . . . . "[33] The perception of beauty, like
the perception of color, and unlike, say, the perception that 2
plus 2 equals 4, requires no knowledge of meanings, operations,
first principles, purposes, or anything else of the kind.[34]

And, finally, the sense of beauty, as a consequence, apparently, of its independence of knowledge, is immediate. So "the
Ideas of Beauty and Harmony, like other sensible Ideas, are
necessarily pleasant to us, as well as immediately so . . . ."[35] The
contrast here is to discursive reason, working step-by-step from
premise to conclusion. Reason plods — sense perception leaps.

(8) In sum, then, Hutcheson conceives of sense perception as:
(i) independent of the will; (ii) innate; (iii) independent of
knowledge; (iv) immediate. These four marks distinguish it from
reason; and the perception of beauty (and other aesthetic qualities) being independent of will, innate, independent of knowledge, and immediate, must in consequence be sense perception,
not rational perception.

Apart from whether aesthetic perception really is all of these
things, the question arises as to whether, even if it is, it must by
consequence be sense perception. Indeed, it is very questionable
whether the four "exclusive" marks of sense perception are
exclusive at all.

The contrast between nonvolitional sense perception and volitional reason is suspect to begin with because it is not as
obvious as it might at first appear that sense perception is independent of the will. I can, of course, refuse to look at something; and in that sense what I see is subject to my will. This is
dismissed by Hutcheson as a trivial case; for what he means to
say is that *under certain conditions* — eyes open, facing toward
object, unobstructed view, sufficient lighting, eyes healthy — my
will can have no effect upon what I see. Yet Hutcheson, like

Locke, acknowledges that *attention* plays a crucial role in perception (and by attention is meant, here, not merely a physical,
but a "mental" stance): one can look at something without
seeing it. Indeed, we do say things like "He doesn't see because
he doesn't want to." To what extent is this a metaphorical
expression? And to what extent can it be taken literally? I am
not suggesting that there are no unequivocal cases in which we
would want to say categorically that what we see (or hear, or
touch, or taste) is not subject to our wills or desires. But the
conditions governing these cases are not perhaps as trivially easy
to state as Hutcheson apparently thought. We are much more
aware today of the *activity* of perception than was Hutcheson,
who on more than one occasion speaks of sense perception as
entirely passive. And if all possible counterexamples to the nonvolitional character of sense perception are to be ruled out, not
merely the admittedly trivial ones of "not looking," we will
want a very careful statement as to what the conditions *are*
under which sense perception is not subject to the will. These
conditions may not be very easy to state; and in lieu of such a
statement, there will remain a suspicion that the counterexamples are being ruled out by fiat to protect a favored hypothesis.

But let us grant, as I think we must, that there are paradigm
cases of perception which occur regardless of whether we will
them or no. Does this distinguish them from "reason"? Are
rational "perceptions" any more subject to the will than sensible ones? I hardly think so. In this respect, sense perception and
reason are on all fours, the one with the other. I can choose not
to consider an argument, or look at the evidence, just as I can
close my eyes or avert my head. I cannot, however, choose not
to "see" that a conclusion follows from premises if I apprehend
the argument.[36] That "Socrates is mortal" follows from "All
men are mortal and Socrates is a man" is something I cannot
choose to see or not see at will, any more than I can choose to
see or not see a color under the proper conditions. If being
independent of will were a mark of sense perception, we would
have to conclude apprehending the validity of arguments or
mathematical proofs is sense perception as well. Rational "per-

ceptions" are no more subject to the will than sensible ones —
but they are no less. For just as it makes sense to say "He
doesn't see because he doesn't want to", it makes sense as well
to say "He doesn't believe because he doesn't want to." In short,
being or not being subject to the will provides no basis on which
to found a distinction between sense and reason. Thus, Hutcheson's first mark of sense perception fails completely to partition
off what we ordinarily call "sensation" from what we ordinarily
call "reason."

Whether sense perception is independent of knowledge is
tricky. The weight of opinion today certainly rejects the view
(seemingly suggested at times by eighteenth-century British em-
piricists) that sense perception is raw and conceptless data. On
the contrary, it is seen to be concept laden. And whether we
can describe a concept-laden process like sense perception as
independent of knowledge seems to me very doubtful, although
full of hidden complications. Perhaps we are not conscious of
the knowledge relevant, say, to our color perception. But are we
any more conscious of what knowledge comes into play when
we perceive that 2 plus 2 equals 4? Frege, and Humpty Dump-
ty, for reasons of their own, might like to work that out on
paper. For the rest of us, it is perceived as effortlessly and as
apparently untroubled by reflection as is the color of a lemon.
However, you will say, the *way* knowledge participates in our
perception that 2 plus 2 equals 4 is very different from the way
it participates in our perception of the yellowness of lemons or
the shapes of coins, unconscious though they both may be.
Doubtless you are right. Yet it will not help Hutcheson out. For
the game he is playing has by that admission already been lost.
We cannot help distinguish sense perception from reason merely
by the absence of knowledge from the former; and that is just
what Hutcheson seems to be claiming we can do.

Nor is the fourth mark of sense perception, *immediacy*, any
more successful in distinguishing sense from reason. Immediacy,
I take it, can be understood here in two senses, although
Hutcheson does not make this clear. We might call the "perceiving" that A plus B equals B plus A immediate in the temporal
sense, if only a negligible period of time elapses between our

attending to the equation and our acquiescing to it. Or we might call the "perceiving" immediate in an epistemological or methodological sense if what we are saying is that no logical step intervenes; if, that is, there is no proof. In Hutcheson's day, I suppose, this would be called intuitive or axiomatic. Thus, it might take some time for me to see that A plus B equals B plus A, yet I would nevertheless want to call my apprehension immediate in the methodological sense. Conversely, a Gallois or a Gauss might see instantly that some very complicated equation follows from some other, whereas it might cost a lesser man considerable time and effort; and yet we would not want to call the apprehension immediate in the methodological sense even in the case of the temporally immediate apprehension of Gallois or Gauss if there were a proof — a discursive series of steps — from one to the other. But in whichever sense we take "immediate," the immediacy of apprehension fails to be an exclusive mark of sense perception. If we take Hutcheson to be saying that no steps can intervene between the perception of an object and the perception of its beauty, this would not rule out the possibility that the perception of beauty is a rational intuition. And if we take him, on the other hand, to be saying that the perception of beauty is always instantaneous, it would, again, not rule out the possibility of the perception being rational as there are instantaneous rational perceptions even of the methodologically non-immediate kind.

Perhaps, however, Hutcheson is saying that sense perception in general, and aesthetic perception in particular, are *always* immediate whereas rational perception is sometimes immediate and sometimes not; and for this reason aesthetic perception cannot be rational but must be sensate. It is obvious, I think, that this ploy must fail as well. For in neither sense of immediate does it appear that aesthetic perception is *always* immediate, or that sense perception in general is *always* immediate.

To begin with, it is clear that the perception of beauty is not always immediate in the temporal sense. I may perceive the beauty of a rose instantaneously, but not the beauty of a three-volume novel or an opera in four acts. It does, after all, take time to read *Middlemarch* or listen to *The Marriage of Figaro*.

But surely it is clear as well that perceiving the beauty of
Middlemarch or *The Marriage of Figaro* consists in steps involving, among other things, the perception of the beauties of
various parts. Thus, to perceive that *Middlemarch* or *The Marriage of Figaro* is beautiful, other perceptions of beauty must
intervene, just as to perceive that one theorem follows from
another, intervening rational perceptions may be necessary.
Again, there does not seem to be any ground here for distinguishing sense perception from reason and identifying aesthetic
perception with the former.

With regard to *innateness*, the picture is not so clear because
the concept is a difficult one to pin down. However, we argued
previously that for Hutcheson the sense of beauty is innate in as
much as we cannot resolve our aesthetic interest into any *other*
kind of interest. And what this means is that there is a natural
terminus to our aesthetic reasoning. I may point out to you the
features that an object possesses, to try to get you to see its
beauty. But a point comes when, if you do not acquiesce, I
simply conclude that you lack "taste," aesthetic sensibility, an
"ear for music," or something of the kind. In other words, I
treat you as I would a color-blind person: someone with a
"sense" lacking or impaired.

But if this is what we mean by a faculty being innate, innateness, like Hutcheson's other three marks, fails to distinguish
sense perception from reason. For it is clear that rational argument, too, has its terminus: the point at which we appeal to
self-evidence or intuition. And if someone fails ultimately to
grasp a rational argument, we conclude that he lacks rational
insight (or what have you). What else can we do but treat someone who cannot be gotten to "see" a proof as a rationally
"blind" man?

Hutcheson, to be sure, saw the innateness of the aesthetic
senses as a psychological or physiological innateness and conceived of the possibility of creatures having aesthetic perceptions vastly different from our own. "Other *Minds*," he writes,
"may possibly be so framed as to receive no [aesthetic] Pleasure from *Uniformity* [as we do], and we actually find that the
same regular Forms do not seem equally to please all the Ani-

mals known to us . . . . " [37] Here, it might be claimed, the symmetry between reason and sense perception breaks down; for reason is not "innate" in this psychological or physiological sense. A creature who did not share our rational "perceptions" would not be said to have different rational perceptions from our own. Rather, he would be said to be "irrational" — to not have rational perceptions at all.

This may be true enough; but it will not help Hutcheson's argument. For what Hutcheson is trying to do is to show aesthetic distinctions are sensation-like rather than reason-like by showing that they are, among other things, innate. However, innateness alone will not do the job. He must assume further that they are innate in the way in which sense perception is innate and not the way in which reason is innate. And that would be begging the question at issue.

III

THE SENSE OF "BEAUTY"

(1) It was established in Chapter II that Hutcheson acknowledges the existence of (at least) six "internal senses" which might fairly be described as "aesthetic senses": they are the senses of *beauty, grandeur, imitation, novelty, fitness,* and *humor.* What I want to establish now are the "objects" of these "senses," or, what Hutcheson takes to be equivalent, the references of the terms "beauty," "grandeur," and so on. I will concern myself in this chapter exclusively with the object of the sense of beauty, or, the reference of the term "beauty," as the sense of beauty and its object are discussed at length by Hutcheson. If we find out anything about the objects of the other senses, it will have to be mostly by inference from what we find out about the sense of beauty and its object.

It might be thought that we already have in our hands what we are seeking. For we already know that the sense of beauty is a disposition to receive pleasure. Surely, then, *pleasure* (of some special kind) must be the object of the sense of beauty.

This may indeed be what we ultimately conclude about the matter. But a moment's reflection will reveal that the road is not by any means so direct. The sense of hearing, after all, is (among other things) a disposition to receive pleasure; but the object of the sense of hearing is sound as well as pleasure. So we cannot conclude merely from the fact that the sense of beauty is a disposition to receive pleasure, that pleasure is its sole object, or that the term *beauty* refers to a pleasure (of some special kind). The passage which holds the key to our puzzle is the following:

Let it be observ'd that in the following Papers, the word Beauty is
taken for the Idea rais'd in us, and a Sense of Beauty for our
Power of receiving this Idea. Harmony also denotes our pleasant
Ideas arising from compositions of Sounds, and a good Ear (as it is
generally taken) a Power of perceiving this Pleasure. [1]

Our difficulty here involves the term "idea" as it is used by
Hutcheson and Locke. For on the Lockean model of perception, which Hutcheson adopts, the term "idea" refers (at least)
to the following kinds of sensations: pleasures (and pains), sensations of secondary qualities (for example, "sweet" or "red"),
sensations of primary qualities (for example, "square") — all of
which are at least prima facie candidates for the referent of the
term "beauty." Beauty is said, in the passage quoted, to refer to
an idea; and harmony — the beauty of sound — is called, more
specifically, a pleasant idea. But an idea need not be a pleasure;
and a pleasant idea need not be a pleasure either; witness the
fact that the idea of my girlfriend is a pleasant idea though it is
not a pleasure.

These difficulties can be resolved only by examining closely
what Hutcheson has to say further about the idea of beauty.
And before we do this we must have at least a rough outline
before us of Locke's perceptual model *as it was understood by
Hutcheson*. (I add this proviso as Hutcheson's interpretation of
Locke on these points may not be the one that a careful contemporary reading of the *Essay Concerning Human Understanding* would support.) [2]

(2) I do not intend to present anything like a systematic
account of Locke's theory of perception. This would lead us
too far afield. What I wish to do, rather, is to present some
crucial passages from Locke which very obviously provided
Hutcheson with his philosophical foundations. With these passages before us, we will then be able to carry forward our interpretation of Hutcheson. And to assure ourselves that these passages do indeed express views of Locke which Hutcheson
shared, I will, whenever possible, set them alongside Hutcheson's own words.

Locke's primary philosophical goal, as he states it, is to "inquire into the *original* of those *ideas*, notions, or whatever else you please to call them, which a man observes, and is conscious to himself he has in his mind; and the ways whereby the understanding comes to be furnished with them."³ That Hutcheson shared this goal is perfectly clear; in fact, this passage seems to have given him the title for his first book, *An Inquiry into the Original of Our Ideas of Beauty and Virtue*. And this kind of title continued, throughout the eighteenth century, to be used by those who shared the empiricist approach to aesthetics; witness, for example, Edmund Burke's later *Philosophical Enquiry into the Origin of Our Ideas of the Sublime and Beautiful*.

What, then, is the "original" of our ideas? Locke's answer, as every student of philosophy knows, is *experience*; and experience is *perception*: either "external" or "internal," that is, by the five senses, or "introspection." "Our observation employed either about external sensible objects, or about the internal operations of our minds perceived and reflected on by ourselves, is that which supplies our understandings with all the materials of thinking."⁴

What kinds of ideas does perception deliver? Locke is not altogether clear.⁵ Ultimately, the mind becomes furnished with two kinds of ideas, "simple" and "complex" (or "uncompounded" and "compounded"). Simple ideas are always the direct result of perception: either the "outer" perception of the five external senses, or the "inner" perceptions of introspection. Thus, "These simple ideas, the materials of all our knowledge, are suggested and furnished to the mind only by those two ways above mentioned, vis. sensation and reflection."⁶ And *one* meaning that "simple" seems to have for Locke is the *given*. The opposite of the given — that is, *given in perception* — is that which is constructed (or otherwise arrived at) by the mind subsequent to perception. "When the understanding is once stored with these simple ideas, it has the power to repeat, compare, and unite them, even to an almost infinite variety, and so can make at pleasure new complex ideas."⁷ Hutcheson, following Locke, recognizes this power (or powers) of the mind, and hence this version of the distinction between simple and complex ideas: "The Mind has a Power of compounding Ideas that were received separately. . . ."⁸ So, for Locke and Hutcheson, there are simple ideas and complex ideas; and sometimes they seem to mean by this ideas given in perception and ideas "constructed" out of the given (or otherwise arrived at from the given), but not themselves given.

However, there are times when Locke seems to mean by "simple" idea something like irreducible or atomic, and by "complex" idea, the idea analyzable into simple ideas, thus suggesting that the complex idea *can* be given in perception, and is complex in the sense that it can, subsequent to perception, be broken down into its constituent parts. Hutcheson shares this confusion, speaking not only of the mind's power of constructing complex ideas out of simple ones, but of analyzing *given* complex ideas into simples, by "considering separately each of the simple Ideas, which might perhaps have been impress'd jointly in the Sensations."⁹

Ideas can further be distinguished as either of primary or of sencondary qualities. As Hutcheson interpreted Locke, the distinction is one between ideas which resemble qualities in the external world and ideas which do not. Locke's most unequivocal statement of the distinction in these terms reads:

> [T]he ideas of the primary qualities of bodies are resemblances of them, and their patterns do really exist in the bodies themselves, but the ideas produced in us by these secondary qualities have no resemblance of them at all. There is nothing like our ideas, existing in the bodies themselves. They are, in the bodies we denominate from them, only a power to produce these sensations in us: and what is sweet, blue, or warm in idea, is but the certain bulk, figure, and motion of the insensible parts, in the bodies themselves, which we call so.¹⁰

Finally, we must add to the ideas of primary and secondary qualities the ideas of pleasure and pain. "Amongst the simple ideas which we receive both from sensation and reflection *pain* and *pleasure* are two very considerable ones."¹¹

Our course now is clear. Hutcheson accepts these distinctions of Locke's down the line. Like Locke, he distinguishes among simple and complex ideas, ideas of primary and ideas of secon-

dary qualities, and ideas of pleasure and of pain. The word
"beauty," he tells us, "is taken for an Idea rais'd in us . . . . "
Our task, then, is to determine whether that idea is, for Hutcheson, simple or complex, the idea of a primary or secondary
quality, or a pleasure.

(3) The first question before us is whether the idea of beauty
was a complex idea for Hutcheson. It was for Locke in fact one
of his paradigm cases: "Ideas thus made up of several simple
ones put together, I call *complex;*— such as are beauty, gratitude, a man, an army, the universe; which, though complicated
of various simple ideas, or complex ideas made of simple ones,
yet are, when the mind pleases, considered each of itself, as one
entire thing, and signified by one name."[12] Complex ideas can
be divided into three kinds, according to Locke: those of *sub-
stances*, *modes*, and *relations*, the term "mode" signifying some
attribute of substance. Modes can further be subdivided into
simple and *mixed*, the idea of beauty falling into the latter category.

> Of these *modes* there are two sorts which deserve distinct con-
> sideration: First, there are some which are only variations, or dif-
> ferent combinations, of the same simple idea, without the mixture
> of any others . . . . Secondly, there are others compounded of
> simple ideas of several kinds, put together to make one complex
> one: v.g. beauty, consisting of a certain composition of colour and
> figure, causing delight in the beholder . . . .[13]

It is here that Hutcheson parts company with his mentor and
strikes out on his own. He does not seem to follow Locke in
making beauty a complex idea; had he done so, indeed, there
would have been no need to postulate a *sense* of beauty. That
there is a sense of beauty implies that the idea of beauty is a
simple idea. Locke himself allowed the possibility of there being
more than the generally acknowledge five senses: "I have here
followed the common opinion of man's having but five senses;
though, perhaps, there may be justly counted more . . . . "[14]
And it is this suggestion of Locke's, perhaps, which put
Shaftesbury and Hutcheson on their way. It is Locke's precept

that for every distinct kind of simple idea there must be an appropriate sense. Hutcheson cleaved to it: "When two Perceptions are entirely different from each other, or agree in nothing but the general Idea of Sensation, we call the powers of receiving those different Perceptions, *different* Senses."[5] Thus, that Hutcheson believed it necessary to postulate a sense of beauty, together with his acceptance of the above precept, leads us to the conclusion that beauty, for Hutcheson, was a simple idea.

It is worthy of some mention, however, that we must discover the simplicity of the idea of beauty in Hutcheson inferentially; it is nowhere stated explicitly in the first *Inquiry* (or elsewhere, so far as I know). Hutcheson, in fact, seems to reserve the name *simple idea* exclusively for the sensations of the external senses. And the hypothesis of a sense of beauty is treated in one place, quite cavalierly, as rather a matter of choice and convenience than of necessity. Thus, he writes:

> It is of no consequence whether we call these Ideas of Beauty and Harmony, Perceptions of the External Senses of Seeing and Hearing, or not. I should rather choose to call our Power of perceiving these Ideas, an *Internal Sense*, were it only for the Convenience of distinguishing them from other Sensations of Seeing and Hearing which men may have without Perception of Beauty and Harmony.[16]

That Hutcheson never explicitly stated the simplicity of the idea of beauty leaves open the bare possibility that, like Locke, he thought of it as a complex idea and invoked a sense of beauty because the *pleasure* which *accompanies* the idea of beauty requires it, aesthetic pleasure presumably being itself a simple idea and thus requiring a sense to perceive it. But this is, at best, an awkward and left-footed reading of Hutcheson; nor will it produce, in the long run, a coherent interpretation. I shall assume, therefore, with every commentator on Hutcheson known to me, that, unlike Locke, Hutcheson believed the idea of beauty to be a simple idea; and that because the postulating of a sense of beauty would make this palpable to any student of Locke, he never felt it necessary to make the premise explicit. Beauty, then, is a simple idea; and this conclusion brings us to our next task: deciding whether Hutcheson thought of beauty as the idea of a primary quality, the idea of a secondary quality, or a pleasure.

(4) The question now before us is: Does the term *beauty* refer to the idea of a primary quality, the idea of a secondary quality, or a pleasure (of some special kind)? The passage in which Hutcheson provides most of the materials for such a determination is full of difficulties, and must be quoted at some length.

> Beauty is either Original, or Comparative; or if any like the Terms better, Absolute or Relative: Only let it be noted, that by Absolute or Original Beauty, is not understood any Quality suppos'd to be in the Object, that should of itself be beautiful, without relation to any Mind which perceives it: For Beauty, like other Names of sensible Ideas, properly denotes the Perception of some Mind; so Cold, Heat, Sweet, Bitter, denote the Sensations in our Minds, to which perhaps there is no resemblance in the Objects that excite these ideas in us, however we generally imagine that there is something in the Object just like our Perceptions. The Ideas of Beauty and Harmony being excited upon our Perception of some primary Quality, and having relation to Figure and Time, may indeed have a nearer resemblance to Objects, than these Sensations that seem not so much any Pictures of Objects, as Modifications of the perceiving Mind; and yet were there no Mind with a Sense of Beauty to contemplate Objects, I see not how they could be call'd beautiful. We therefore by Absolute Beauty understand only that Beauty which we perceive in Objects without comparison to any thing external, of which the Object is suppos'd an Imitation, or Picture; such as that Beauty perceiv'd from the Works of Nature, artificial Forms, Figures, Theorems. Comparative or Relative Beauty is that which we perceive in Objects, commonly considered as Imitations or Resemblances of something else.[17]

Let us begin by listing the claims made here which we must somehow absorb into a coherent interpretation.

i. "Beauty" is not the name of a quality in objects.

ii. No object would be called "beautiful" if there were no mind (with a sense of beauty) to perceive it.

iii. "Beauty" is the name of a "perception" or "sensible idea"

in the mind of a perceiver, *like* "cold," "heat," "sweet," "bitter."

iv. Ideas like "cold," "heat," "sweet," "bitter" do not resemble any qualities in objects which excite these ideas.

v. The ideas of beauty and harmony can be aroused in the
mind by some *primary* quality (or qualities).

vi. The ideas of beauty and harmony, because they can be
aroused by (the primary qualities of) figure and time, may resemble objective qualities somewhat more than ideas such as
"cold," "heat," "sweet," "bitter," which do not resemble any
objective qualities at all. (I interpret Hutcheson as holding here
that arrangements both of primary and secondary qualities, as
well as combinations of the two, can give rise to the idea of
beauty. The quoted passage perhaps suggests, out of context,
that *only* arrangements of primary qualities can. But this is not
consistent with what Hutcheson says elsewhere.)

Now Locke, and Hutcheson, following Locke, held to a
causal and representational theory of perception: *causal* in that
what we are directly aware of in perception are "ideas in the
mind" caused to be there by qualities of objects of which we
are not directly aware; *representational* in that some of the
ideas are said to resemble or represent some of the qualities
which cause them. And this being the case, we may rule out any
"naively realistic" interpretation of Hutcheson: that is, any interpretation in which beauty is a quality of objects which we
perceive directly.[18]

We may also rule out the possibility that the idea of beauty is
the idea of a primary quality, for two reasons. First, beauty is
said to be relative to some perceiving mind; but primary qualities are not — they exist independently of any perceiving mind.
To be sure, secondary qualities exist objectively in a certain
sense: as "powers" of certain arrangements of primary qualities
capable of causing certain ideas (e.g., "cold," "heat," "sweet,"
"bitter") in our minds, but they have no objective existence
apart from that. Second, the idea of beauty may be more like
the quality in objects which arouses it than the ideas of secondary qualities are, but this relation is not considered to be the
strong relation of resemblance which holds between the ideas of

primary qualities and the corresponding qualities themselves. (I
discuss this point at greater length toward the end of this chapter.) Hence, beauty is the idea of something very like a secondary quality, or it is a pleasure: these two possibilities alone
remain.

(5) What case can we make for beauty as the idea of a secondary quality? To begin with, the crucial passage which we
quoted at length above leaves the distinct impression that beauty is the idea of something very like a secondary quality: it does
so by likening beauty *only* to the ideas of secondary qualities
("cold," "heat," "sweet," "bitter") when spelling out its subjective, mind-dependent status. If beauty were a pleasure, why
not use the concept of pleasure in explicating this point? Pleasure, after all, is subjective and mind-dependent, too.

But we need not rely on the above passage alone to support a
construal of beauty as the idea of a secondary quality. For
passages abound in which the idea of beauty is sharply distinguished from the pleasure to which it is said to give rise. Thus,
Hutcheson writes in one place: "the Ideas of Beauty and Harmony, like other sensible Ideas, are necessarily pleasant to us, as
well as immediately so . . . ,"[19] clearly suggesting that the idea
of beauty gives rise to a pleasure, and thus that it is not itself a
pleasure (although it is a pleasurable idea). Again, in discussing
the beauty of scientific and mathematical theorems, Hutcheson
writes that "we discern a sort of Beauty, very like, in many
respects, to that observ'd in sensible Objects, and accompany'd
with like pleasure . . . "[20] Here, too, the idea of beauty is said to
give rise to or accompany a pleasure and cannot, therefore, be
identical to it.

We have already eliminated the possibility that beauty is the
idea of a primary quality. If, then, the idea of beauty is not
identical with a pleasure, but as the two passages quoted above
seem to suggest gives rise to, or is accompanied by, a pleasure,
two possibilities alone remain: either it is a complex idea, or it
is the idea of something like a secondary quality. There is strong
reason to believe that Hutcheson did not take beauty to be a
complex idea because there would, in this case, have been no

reason to postulate a *sense* of beauty. By elimination, then, we seem to be left with but one remaining possibility: the idea of beauty is the idea of a secondary quality like "red" or "warm" or "bitter."

(6) There seem, then, to be passages which can be interpreted only as sharply distinguishing between the idea of beauty and pleasure. Yet, there are passages, too, which seem unequivocally to identify beauty with pleasure. Hutcheson often expresses the distinction between a man who can and a man who cannot perceive beauty as the distinction between a man who can and a man who cannot experience pleasure (of some special kind). Thus, he writes:

> [M]any Men have, in the common meaning, the Senses of Seeing and Hearing perfect enough; they perceive all the simple ideas separately, and have their pleasures .... And yet perhaps they shall relish no pleasure in Musical Compositions, in Painting, Architecture, natural Landskip; or but a very weak one in comparison of what others enjoy from the same Objects. This greater Capacity of receiving such pleasant Ideas we commonly call a fine Genius or Taste...[21]

Here, it appears to me, the distinction between aesthetic and nonaesthetic rests squarely on the concept of pleasure or enjoyment. The difference between a man who does and a man who does not have the sense of beauty is the difference between a man who does and a man who does not enjoy, take pleasure in, "Musical Compositions, ... Painting, Architecture, natural Landskip." Surely the implications of this are that the idea of beauty is identical with a pleasure (of some special kind); the experience of a certain kind of pleasure is said to be identical with the having of the capacity to perceive beauty.

Another passage which points unequivocally to an identification of beauty with pleasure is the following, added by Hutcheson to the fourth edition of the *Inquiry*, perhaps indicating that he was aware of the ambiguity of his text and was inclining more in his later years toward the identification of beauty with pleasure. It reads, in part: "The bare Idea of the Form is something separable from Pleasure, as may appear from the different *Tastes* of men about the Beauty of Forms, where we don't imagine that they differ in any Ideas, either of Primary or Secondary Qualities."[22]

Hutcheson, I believe, is here contrasting individuals with and individuals without the sense of beauty. Let us say that two such people, one with and one without the sense of beauty, are looking at X. Now the fact that their disagreement about the beauty of X is not a disagreement about primary or secondary qualities does not rule out the possibility that beauty is *like* a secondary quality; and that is really what our alternative to the beauty-as-pleasure interpretation maintains. What Hutcheson is saying here is that when an individual with and an individual without the sense of beauty disagree about the beauty of X, they are not disagreeing about the normal, acknowledged, garden-variety qualities of objects — those that are perceived by the universally recognized five senses. What rules out the beauty-as-secondary quality interpretation in this passage is the further claim that when we disagree about the beauty of X, we are revealing differences in our perceptions of pleasure. We can all perceive the same primary and secondary qualities of X, says Hutcheson, and yet not all perceive the beauty of X, because we can all perceive the primary and secondary qualities of X and yet not all experience pleasure (of a certain kind) in perceiving X. Thus, perceiving pleasure (of some special kind) is identical with perceiving beauty; and the idea of beauty, then, must be identical with pleasure since the perception of beauty is the having of the idea of beauty.

(7) We have examined some passages which seem amenable only to the interpretation of beauty as the idea of something very like a secondary quality, as well as passages amenable only to the interpretation of beauty as a pleasure. There are, in addition, passages which seem amenable to either interpretation; and it would be well to look at some of these in the bargain.

The passages I have in mind are all of the same kind and are best described as phrases; for example: "this Pleasure of Beauty:"[23]; "the Pleasures of Beauty"[24]; and so on.

The phrase "pleasure (or pleasures) of beauty" is clearly susceptible of being interpreted in the same way as a phrase like "the pleasure of his company." His company is not identical with pleasure (or a pleasure), but gives pleasure, is enjoyed. His company, and the pleasure of his company, are two different things. Likewise, it might be argued, beauty is no more identical with pleasure in the phrase "the pleasure of beauty" than is his company identical with pleasure in the phrase "the pleasure of his company." Thus, both phrases quoted above are compatible with the view that the idea of beauty is pleasant, gives rise to pleasure, but is not identical with pleasure: they are both compatible, in other words, with the interpretation of beauty as something like the idea of a secondary quality.

But the phrase "the p of q" often means something like "the p that is called q" (as in "the state of Washington") or "the p (genus) that is q (species)" (as in "a state of inebriation"). So we may also construe the phrase "the pleasure of beauty" as "the pleasure that is called 'beauty' " or "the pleasure (genus) that is beauty (species)." And this, of course, makes the phrase (and others like it) perfectly compatible with the notion of beauty as pleasure (or a pleasure).

(8) We have before us now three classes of statements about the idea of beauty: (i) the class of statements to the effect that it is very like the idea of a secondary quality; (ii) the class of statements to the effect that it is pleasure (or a pleasure); (iii) the class of statements that are compatible with both (i) and (ii). We have five choices: we can conclude that Hutcheson is simply too vague to be interpreted one way or the other; we can conclude that he is self-contradictory; we can plump for (i) and sweep (ii) under the carpet as lapses in language; we can plump for (ii) and carpet (i); we can, finally, take the heroic line and try to find a position that is compatible with both (i) and (ii).

With regard to the first alternative, it is certainly the case that Hutcheson has not made his position clear. If he had, we would not face five alternatives. But whatever he was vague about (and he was vague about something), it was not the distinction between the idea of a secondary quality and a pleasure. I think he knew that distinction perfectly well; and if he treated the idea of beauty sometimes as the one and sometimes as the other, it was not because he was unaware of the difference. Locke was clear enough on this point to make it beyond belief that his disciple should be confused.

Nor does it seem any more credible to me that Hutcheson should contradict himself in so obvious a way on so obvious a point. There may be contradictions in his position; but they are not as blatant as that.

The third and fourth alternatives are at least plausible. If I were to choose one, I would choose the fourth, plump for beauty as a pleasure, and consider any statement to the effect that beauty is like a secondary quality a *lapsus calami*. For Hutcheson's book, as he states in the preface, is committed to the examination of pleasure; and the sense of beauty is proposed to account for our experiences of a particular kind of pleasure. It is much easier to read "pleasure" for "beauty" than to describe the idea of beauty as an idea which gives rise to a pleasure. The text will support the former interpretation with fewer wrenches and groans. But this alternative does not produce anything like real conviction. It may be better than the third, yet the best that can be said for it is that it is the lesser evil. There are just too many strong and detailed passages in which beauty is likened to a secondary quality. It requires more averting of the eyes than I can manage to dismiss them as loose talk. The heroic line seems the only palatable one.

What stands in the way of a consistent interpretation is our easy acceptance of the disjunction: either a secondary quality or a pleasure. Can we not say *both*? There is an eighteenth-century precedent, with which there is no reason to think Hutcheson was not familiar, for making this move. For although Locke, as we have seen, sharply distinguished between the ideas of secondary qualities and pleasures or pains, this distinction is blurred by Berkeley in the *Three Dialogues Between Hylas and Philonous* (1713). Whereas Locke would say, for example, that when I put my hand close to a fire, I am affected with the simple idea of a secondary quality, *intense heat*, which gives rise to *another* simple idea, pain, Berkeley wants to say that there is but *one* simple idea which can be understood under two descriptions, "intense heat," and "pain." Thus, Philonous, Berkeley's mouthpiece in the dialogue, maintains that "the fire affects you only with one simple, uncompounded idea . . . this same simple idea is both the intense heat immediately perceived, and the pain; and, consequently . . . the intense heat immediately perceived, is nothing distinct from a particular sort of pain." [25] Notice, we are not attributing to Locke the view that there is any perceptible time interval between the perception of intense heat and the perception of pain: only the view that we are affected with a complex idea which can be analyzed into simple ideas of intense heat and pain. Where Locke and Berkeley differ is that whereas for Locke we are affected with a complex idea of "intense heat" plus "pain," for Berkeley we are affected with a simple idea which can be described either as "intense heat" or "pain."

Now what I want to argue is that for Hutcheson the idea of beauty as something like a secondary quality, and the idea of beauty as a pleasure are one and the same idea, just as Berkeley's idea of intense heat and his idea of pain are one and the same idea. The reason, then, why Hutcheson sometimes describes beauty as the idea of something like a secondary quality and sometimes as a pleasure is that he thinks of them as two descriptions of the *same* simple idea. That he was not altogether clear about the point is beyond dispute; for he was, I suspect, not altogether committed to the position, and vestiges of the old distinction between ideas of qualities and pleasures (or pains) still remained. Nevertheless, the recognition that Hutcheson may at least have been gravitating toward Berkeley's notion that the idea of a secondary quality and its associate pain (or pleasure, as the case may be) are not two sensations, but one, makes his seeming carelessness much more understandable: much less like carelessness, in fact, and much more like the adumbration of a novel and not yet clearly worked out position.

Furthermore, it seems to me that in making this move, Hutcheson has recognized the kind of double-aspect phenomenology of beauty which has made it seem to some both a "subjective feeling" and an "objective quality" — as the fusion theory puts it, a feeling objectified. Thus, beauty described as a pleasure emphasizes the subjective; beauty described as the idea of something like a secondary quality, even on the Lockean model of secondary qualities, emphasizes the objective "feel" of aesthetic qualities.

In any event, we can now accommodate all three classes of statements about the idea of beauty: those that take it to be the idea of a secondary quality, those that identify it with pleasure (of some special kind), and (of course) those that can be interpreted either way. We look in vain for a clear statement to the effect that the idea of beauty is one or the other because it is both: the same idea under different descriptions.

(9) One task yet remains before we can conclude that we have accommodated all of Hutcheson's statements about the idea of beauty in one consistent interpretation. For we have one crucial passage outstanding — the most puzzling of all; and at first blush it seems quite intractable. It is the statement that "The Ideas of Beauty and Harmony being excited upon our Perception of some primary Quality, and having relation to Figure and Time, may indeed have a nearer resemblance to Objects, than these Sensations [i.e., "cold, heat, sweet, bitter"] that seem not so much any Pictures of Objects, as Modifications of the perceiving Mind . . . ." How are we to reconcile Hutcheson's descriptions of beauty as the idea of something like a secondary quality, and his descriptions of beauty as a pleasure, with this unique description of beauty as the idea of a quality apparently somewhere betwixt and between the idea of a primary quality and the idea of a secondary quality?

We can approach our problem by resolving it into two questions. To begin with, Hutcheson is not saying that the idea of beauty is the idea of a secondary quality: only that it is *very like* our ideas of secondary qualities. Our first question, then, is: What is the *crucial* difference between the idea of beauty and the ideas of secondary qualities? Our second question: Can this difference be what Hutcheson is trying to get at when he describes the idea of beauty as bearing more resemblance to external qualities than do the ideas of secondary qualities (which bear none at all)? I believe we can answer "Yes" to the second question; and this will wrap up our interpretation of Hutcheson on the idea of beauty.

Hutcheson claimed that beauty is "an idea rais'd in us"; but he claimed, too, that there is an identifiable objective qual- ity — or, rather, a complex of identifiable objective qualities — which is always the cause of this idea being raised in us.

> The Figures that excite in us the Ideas of Beauty, seem to be those in which there is *Uniformity amidst Variety* .... what we call Beautiful in Objects, to speak in the Mathematical Style, seems to be in a compound Ratio of Uniformity and Variety; so that where the Uniformity of Bodys is equal, the Beauty is as the Variety; and where the Variety is equal, the Beauty is as the Uniformity.[26]

This formula is, of course, nothing new, encapsulating, as it does, the aesthetic taste of Neoclassicism.

It is worth noting that Hutcheson is referring here to *uni- formity amidst variety* as an arrangement of primary qualities; and the sort of beauty occasioned by it is the beauty of "cor- poreal form": in music, the formal arrangement of physical vibrations in air, and in visual beauty, the formal arrangement of shapes and contours. But there are other arrangements that can also be said to possess *uniformity amidst variety* and which cannot be construed as arrangements of primary qualities. Thus, mathematical, scientific, and philosophical "theorems" all can possess *uniformity amidst variety,* and give rise to the idea of beauty; yet they can hardly be described as arrangements of primary qualities. Nor is there any reason why Hutcheson could not allow that an arrangement of secondary qualities (colors, say) may possess *unity amidst variety.*[27] We will confine our- selves here, however, to a consideration of *unity amidst variety* as an arrangement always of primary qualities because it is in this context alone that the passage we are trying to explicate occurs.

We are now in a position to see what the idea of beauty has in common with the ideas of secondary qualities. On the Locke- an model of perception, the word "red," for example, refers, when we speak with the philosophically learned, to a simple sensation which is caused by an arrangement of primary qualities; and for Hutcheson, the word "beautiful" refers, when we are speaking with the philosophically learned, to a simple sensation which is caused by an arrangement of primary qualities. In this respect they are on all fours.

But we can now see, too, in what way the idea of beauty is very different from the ideas of secondary qualities. For the ideas of secondary qualities, according to Locke, are "produced in us ... by the operation of *insensible* particles on our senses."[28] So although the sensation of redness is produced in us by an arrangement of primary qualities, it is not an arrangement that can be perceived by us, independent of our sensation of redness, for it is an arrangement of *insensible* particles. The primary qualities that produce the idea of beauty are gross: we can perceive them independently and conclude such-and-such an arrangement of primary qualities causes the idea of beauty. A person who is beauty-blind (that is, who lacks the sense of beauty) can nevertheless be said to perceive the cause of the sensations which he cannot ever have. But a person who is color-blind can in no sense be said to perceive the cause of the sensation he cannot have. A person who is having the idea of beauty may indeed be in the same position as the person who is having the sensation of redness; for one can have the idea of beauty and be ignorant of the causal law that "The idea of beauty is caused by *uniformity amidst variety*" and, even if not ignorant of it, may not in this particular instance be aware of what particular *uniformity amidst variety* is causing one's idea of beauty. But there is also the case of the person who is having the idea of beauty and knows the causal law as well as the particular fact that his idea of beauty is being caused by such-and-such an arrangement of primary qualities which possesses *uniformity amidst variety*. (Hutcheson envisions both kinds of cases.) And the latter case can never arise in the perception of a secondary quality, on the Lockean model of perception. We can never both have the sensation of redness and perceive independently the arrangement of primary qualities causing it; for the arrangement is, by hypothesis, insensible.

Now an arrangement of primary qualities which has *unity amidst variety* can give rise in the perceiver to the simple idea called "beauty." But it can also give rise to the complex idea of the particular *unity amidst variety* which is causing the simple idea of beauty. If we could not have this complex idea of *unity amidst variety*, *unity amidst variety* would be as imperceptible to us as the arrangements of insensible primary qualities which cause our sensations of redness. And this complex idea of some particular instance of *unity amidst variety* resembles it: that is, resembles the complex arrangement of primary qualities which occasions the idea. If we speak with the learned, neither our idea of this particular *unity amidst variety* nor the *unity amidst variety* in objects which occasions it can properly be called "beautiful — only the simple idea of beauty can be called that. But if we speak with the vulgar, we may call the quality in objects which causes the idea of beauty, namely, *unity amidst variety,* "beauty," and call the objects which possess it "beautiful."

Locke has no compunction about speaking with the vulgar in calling objects "red," although strictly speaking, only the sensation is "red," the objects merely having the power to cause the sensation in us. Likewise, Hutcheson sometimes speaks with the vulgar in calling the quality of *unity amidst variety* "beauty," and the objects which possess it "beautiful," although strictly speaking only the simple idea of beauty is "beautiful," objects merely having the power to cause the sensation in us. When we speak with the learned, our idea of beauty, like our idea of redness, bears no resemblance to any objective quality. But when we speak with the vulgar, it can be said that our idea of beauty resembles the quality in objects which causes the idea, meaning our idea of *unity amidst variety* resembles the objective quality *unity amidst variety.* For although our simple idea of beauty does not resemble *unity amidst variety,* our complex idea of *unity amidst variety* does. But even when we speak with the vulgar we cannot say that our sensation of redness resembles the quality in objects which causes the idea. For there is no counterpart of our complex idea of *unity amidst variety* when we perceive redness. (And, thus, when Hutcheson *seems* to suggest that the idea of beauty can be aroused by arrangements of primary qualities and the ideas of secondary qualities cannot, what we must understand him to be saying is simply that the idea of beauty can be aroused by *perceptible* arrangements of primary qualities and the ideas of secondary qualities cannot, their cause being the *imperceptible* atomic structure of matter.)

When Hutcheson, then, claims that the idea of beauty bears more of a resemblance to an objective quality than do the ideas of secondary qualities, he is referring to the fact that we can have an idea of the quality which causes our simple idea of beauty, and *this* idea resembles that quality, whereas we cannot have an idea of the quality which causes, say, our simple idea of redness. In this sense, the simple idea of beauty is something like the idea of a primary quality; and so it is really a third kind of quality, somewhere betwixt and between the Lockean primary and the Lockean secondary qualities.

It is certainly difficult to know why Hutcheson chose such an obscure way of saying what he had to say on this point. Perhaps the easiest answer is that Locke's terminology forced him to frame his position in this needlessly opaque way. For he was, in a way, breaking new ground for the theory of beauty while working within a perceptual theory framed by a philosopher almost without parallel for his lack of interest in, and sensitivity for, aesthetic questions. The Lockean model of perception must have severely hamstrung Hutcheson. It is a minor miracle that he was able to achieve even the clarity he did. Shaftesbury, in his attempt to make aesthetics a respectable philosophical discipline, made even more sacrifices to the gods of unintelligibility.

IV

THE SENSE OF "BEAUTIFUL"

(1) We have established the referent of the word *beauty*: an idea which is *both* a pleasure and the idea of something like a secondary quality — not two simple ideas, but one simple idea under two different descriptions. This being the case, what do I assert when I say an object is "beautiful"? Whatever *else* I am doing, according to Hutcheson, when I say "*X* is beautiful," I am either *describing* or *expressing* some feeling; namely, the feeling which Hutcheson calls "the idea of beauty." Thus, the statement "*X* is beautiful" possesses what I shall call a "feeling moment" as part of its analysis; and it is the feeling moment which we must first determine. So when I talk about the meaning or analysis of "*X* is beautiful" in the next four sections, I will be referring throughout to the analysis of its feeling moment and to that alone.

Now I might, when I say "*X* is beautiful," be referring to my own feeling; or I might be referring to someone else's (either an individual's or a group's). I shall call the former the first-person analysis of the feeling moment of "*X* is beautiful" and the latter, the third-person analysis. We can further divide the first-person analysis into the cognitive and the noncognitive. According to the cognitive first-person analysis, "*X* is beautiful" can be understood to describe my state of mind upon perceiving *X*. It can be true or false, depending upon whether the description is accurate or not. But according to the noncognitive analysis, "*X* is beautiful" can be understood to express or evince (but not to describe) my state of mind upon perceiving *X*. As A. J. Ayer put the view, in one of its classical formulations, "Such words as 'beautiful' and 'hideous' are employed . . . not to make statements of fact, but simply to express [and not describe] certain feelings . . . . "[1] On the noncognitivist analysis, "X is beautiful" cannot be true or false, any more than "Ouch" or "Oh boy" can be.

In recent years, three commentators on Hutcheson have tried to interpret him as a noncognitivist in his ethical theory.[2] Can a case be made for a noncognitivist interpretation of Hutcheson's aesthetics? I shall argue that such a case cannot be established because Hutcheson's theory of language will not permit it. And, although I will not press the point here, I think it obviously follows that a noncognitivist interpretation of Hutcheson's ethics must founder on the same reef. Hutcheson's linguistic commitments simply will not allow of a noncognitivist analysis either of the feeling moment of "X is beautiful" *or* "X is good."

(2) What is the case for Hutcheson as an aesthetic noncognitivist? It seems to me quite clear that whenever Hutcheson talks about beauty as a pleasure, his view is compatible with a noncognitivist interpretation. For his language is vague; and we always have a choice of reading "express," rather than "describe," in the appropriate places.

But in addition there *are* passages which positively lend themselves to a noncognitivist reading. Thus, Hutcheson writes in one place of "our Approbation of any Form whatsoever as *Beautiful*,"[3] and in another of "the Constitution of our Sense [of beauty] so as to approve *Uniformity* . . . . "[4] Surely these passages suggest that I should understand "X is beautiful" not as a description of a particular kind of feeling I am having, but rather as the expression of a certain kind of approval. When I say "X is beautiful," I am saying, on this interpretation, "I aesthetically approve of X." Nor am I describing a state of my mind; namely, the state of aesthetically approving of X, when I say "X is beautiful." For to say "I aesthetically approve of X" is not to describe my approval at all, but to do something else; namely, to approve aesthetically of X.

It should be kept in mind, however, that expressing an emo-

tion and describing it are not mutually exclusive. A groan expresses my agony; and the statement "I am in agony" (said in
an anguished voice) not only describes my state; it expresses my
agony into the bargain. Thus, if we establish that for Hutcheson "X is beautiful" *expresses* my feeling of beauty, it does not
by any means follow that the same statement cannot *describe*
my feeling of beauty as well. What I argue, in the following
sections, is simply that Hutcheson did not recognize the nondescriptive use of language which Ayer and others have called
"expressing" or "evincing" emotion. Hence, although Hutcheson might very well have agreed that "X is beautiful" expresses
my aesthetic approval of X, he would not consider expressing
approval a nondescriptive use of language. And, therefore, the
possibility that "X is beautiful" *both* describes the state of
feeling I am in *and* expresses it does not exist for Hutcheson.
Expressing is describing — and that is the end of it.

(3) Having now considered briefly the case for a noncognitivist interpretation of Hutcheson, what is the case against?
Primarily, it is, as I have already said, that Hutcheson's philosophy of language will not allow for a nondescriptive interpretation of what we do when we express or evince emotion, or
approval, or any other attitude or state of mind. I shall argue
that case in a moment. But even if we could not dismiss a
noncognitive approach as being inconsistent with Hutcheson's
deep-seated linguistic commitments, we would still find impedi-
ments. For apart from the question of how Hutcheson would
construe the notion of expressing or evincing an emotion (as
opposed to describing it), there are difficulties, to begin with, in
even the first step of a noncognitivist interpretation: it is not by
any means clear that we can always substitute "express" or
"evince" for "describe" where a noncognitivist interpretation
demands it.

When Hutcheson describes the idea of beauty as a pleasure of
some special kind, it does indeed seem just as plausible to analyze "X is beautiful" in terms of expressing or evincing pleasure
as it does to analyze it as describing a state of mind of the
speaker. But when Hutcheson represents the idea of beauty as

something like the idea of a secondary quality, this plausibility vanishes; and, if our previous analysis is correct, it is *always* appropriate to describe beauty as the idea of something like a secondary quality. Our paradigm here was Berkeley's treatment of intense heat and pain: both are names of the same simple idea. And although it makes perfect sense to talk about expressing a feeling of pain, it makes no sense at all to talk about expressing a feeling of intense heat. The simple idea of beauty can always be understood under the description "pleasure (of some special kind)." But it can also be understood always under the description which construes it as the idea of something like a secondary quality.

This being the case, we cannot understand "*X* is beautiful" always as "I aesthetically approve of *X*," any more than we can understand "*X* is intensely hot" always as "Ouch" although "*X* is intensely hot" *may* both express pain and describe my idea of intense heat. "*X* is beautiful" may (when said in a certain tone of voice) be saying something like "Oh boy," just as "*X* is intensely hot" may (when said in a certain tone of voice) be saying something like "Ouch." But "*X* is beautiful" must also be a description of the speaker's state of mind on Hutcheson's model of perception, just as is "*X* is intensely hot" on Berkeley's. "*X* is beautiful," then, can no more be construed solely as "Oh boy" than "I am in pain" can be construed solely as "Ouch." Both may be expressing or evincing a pleasure or pain; but they are describing a state of mind as well. Therefore, even if evincing or expressing a state of mind were considered by Hutcheson a nondescriptive use of language, it still would not follow that his theory of aesthetic judgment is noncognitivist. For "*X* is beautiful," on Hutcheson's view, even *if* it expresses or evinces an emotion, *also* describes the emotion it is said to evince or express, just as "I am in pain," if it expresses or evinces an emotion, always also describes the emotional state of the speaker.

Nor is any of this inconsistent with Hutcheson's use of the term "approval" referred to above. Recall the question which Socrates put to Euthyphro: "Do the gods love piety because it is pious, or is it pious because the gods love it?"[5] If Hutcheson

were a noncognitivist, he would be maintaining that X is beautiful (at least in part) because it is approved, not approved because it is beautiful; for to say "X is beautiful" would mean in a
noncognitivist interpretation (in part) "I aesthetically approve
of X." But when Hutcheson speaks (for example) of "our Approbation of any Form whatsoever as *Beautiful*," he gives no
evidence of believing that our approval of forms (even in part)
makes them beautiful. He can just as well be interpreted as
believing that they are approved because they are beautiful —
because, that is, they give us the idea of beauty, which under
one of its descriptions is a pleasure of some special kind. And,
indeed, that something should give us pleasure is a perfectly
good reason to approve it (although there are also perfectly
good reasons to disapprove of something even though it gives
pleasure). In short, even if Hutcheson did allow that "I approve
of X" is a noncognitive linguistic utterance, it would not follow
that the phrase "our Approbation of any Form whatsoever as
Beautiful" supports a noncognitivist interpretation of "X is
beautiful"; for the possibility is not ruled out by Hutcheson's
text of our approval of X being subsequent to, rather than
constitutive of, our determination that X is beautiful.

(4) But suppose that we *could* always interpret "X is beautiful" in Hutcheson's text as "I aesthetically approve of X."
Could we then conclude that Hutcheson was a noncognitivist?
We could only if Hutcheson allowed that "I aesthetically approve of X" is a noncognitive utterance: that it does not express
a judgment at all; that it cannot be true or false. And that he
would allow this seems at first blush highly improbable. C. D.
Broad's sentiments, when considering the possibility of Richard
Price's being an ethical noncognitivist, coincide exactly with my
intuitions about Hutcheson's being an aesthetic noncognitivist:

> If it had been put to him, he would probably have regarded it as
> too fantastically absurd to be taken seriously. It is, indeed, the
> kind of theory which can be swallowed only after one has under-
> gone a long and elaborate process of 'conditioning' which was not
> available in the eighteenth century.[6]

Perhaps Hutcheson would have found aesthetic noncognitivism less mind-boggling than Broad believed Price would have found the ethical variety. For Price was, after all, a rationalist in ethics, and Hutcheson was in the opposite camp. Nevertheless, one gets a feel for a historical period — and noncognitive value theory just does not feel right in a pre-Humean context. But we must have something more to go on here than intuitions, especially since three reputable philosophers apparently do not share my intuitions about Hutcheson and noncognitivism. To this something more we must now turn our attention.

The deepest commitments of any philosopher, those that are most immune from his doubt, are apt to remain unexpressed. Such is almost entirely true of Hutcheson's theory of language. But it is only by knowing Hutcheson's linguistic presuppositions that we can absolutely rule out a noncognitivist reading of his aesthetics. So we must again turn to Locke for insight into Hutcheson's philosophical first principles.

It would certainly not be true to say that for Locke's theory of language, in the beginning was the word; for in the beginning was the idea; but the single word, for Locke, is the beginning of language. The theory is presented in a nutshell in Book III, Chapter ii, paragraph 1 of the *Essay,* which I shall quote in full.

> Man, though he have great variety of thoughts and such from which others as well as himself might receive profit and delight; yet they are all within his own breast, invisible and hidden from others, nor can of themselves be made to appear. The comfort and advantage of society not being to be had without communication of thoughts, it was necessary that man should find out some external sensible signs, whereof those invisible ideas, which his thoughts are made up of, might be made known to others. For this purpose nothing was so fit, either for plenty or quickness, as those articulate sounds, which with so much ease and variety he found himself able to make. Thus we may conceive how *words,* which were by nature so well adapted for that purpose, came to be made use of by men as the signs of their ideas; not by any natural connexion that there is between particular articulate sounds and certain ideas, for then there would be but one language amongst all men; but by a voluntary imposition, whereby such a word is made arbitrarily the mark of such an idea. The use, then, of words, is to be sensible

> marks of ideas; and the ideas they stand for are their proper immediate signification. [7]

Locke maintains, then, a kind of social contract theory of language, very like Hobbes's, in which the atomic bearer of meaning is the word. Most words — although this passage seems to suggest *all* — are said to be marks of, or signs of, or the names of ideas; or they are said to signify or refer to ideas. The purpose of language, Locke goes on to say, is in the main to arouse in someone else the ideas of the speaker (or writer); and this is accomplished by each word of an utterance arousing in the hearer (or reader) the idea which that word stands for in the mind of the speaker (or writer). "When a man speaks to another, it is that he may be understood; and the end of speech is that those sounds, or marks, may make known his ideas to the hearer." [8] This power of language to arouse in, or convey to, the hearer (or reader) the ideas of the speaker (or writer) arises through the unvarying conjunction, by convention, of particular sounds (or marks) and particular ideas: "there comes, by constant use, to be such a connexion between certain sounds and the ideas they stand for, that the names heard, almost as readily excite certain ideas as if the objects themselves, which are apt to produce them, did actually affect the senses." [9]

But there must be more to language than individual words: we speak and write not in single, unconnected words but in words forming larger complexes, beginning with the sentence. And Locke was well aware that we cannot form words into sentences if the only words we use are the names of ideas. Thus, Locke is forced to conclude that "Besides words which are names of ideas in the mind, there are a great many others that are made use of to signify the *connexion* that the mind gives to the ideas, or to propositions, one with another." [10] These, like "is," "is not," "but," and so on, do, however, also *refer,* though not to ideas: rather, to *operations* of the mind. "The mind, in communicating its thoughts to others, does not only need signs of the ideas it has then before it, but others also, to show or intimate some particular action of its own, at that time, relating to those ideas."

The difficulties of Locke's position are legion. To mention
but two: How do we ever come to agree upon the significations
of words if the objects they signify are ideas and operations of
the mind, both, according to Locke, private to the individual
language users? And how came Locke to conclude that single
words are the minimal bearers of meanings, when it seems obvious that sentences are? For single words can seldom, if ever,
constitute meaningful utterances. But it is not our purpose here
to evaluate Locke's theory of language or construct a better
one. Our intention is to discover whether Locke's theory, as he
construed it, can accommodate nondescriptive uses of language
required by noncognitive value theory. And this question, unfortunately, causes trouble enough.

Locke nowhere in Book III of the *Essay* discusses any linguistic unit beyond the word in any detail at all. And we can get
nothing from his discussion of words that rules out the notion
of expressing or evincing emotions. Locke claims that words
refer to ideas and operations of the mind; and there is, so far as
I can see, no objection to saying that when I express or evince
my feelings I (among other things) refer to them. Locke claims
that the main purpose of language is to make the listener (or
reader) conscious of the speaker's (or writer's) ideas; and this is
certainly sometimes my intent when I express or evince my
emotions. What we want to know, however, is how, in the
Lockean linguistic model, we are to construe *sentences* like "*X*
is beautiful"; and Locke nowhere seems to discuss sentences
with any thoroughness.

We do, indeed, get some few hints in Chapter ix of Book III
which are worth considering, although they are maddeningly
brief and desultory. Locke distinguishes between two uses to
which language as communication can be put: the civil and the
philosophical. Of the philosophical use Locke writes: "By the
philosophical use of words, I mean such a use of them as may
serve to convey the precise notions of things, and to express in
general propositions certain and undoubted truths, which the
mind may rest upon and be satisfied with in its search after true
knowledge." [11] The civil use is "such a communication of
thoughts and ideas by words, as may serve for the upholding

common conversation and commerce, about the ordinary affairs and conveniences of civil life, in the societies of men, one amongst another." The only difference between the civil and philosophical uses of language, besides their subject matter, is the rigor which we require of them: "a great deal less exactness will serve in the one than in the other . . . " (an echo of Aristotle's admonition against expecting mathematical exactitude in disciplines that will not allow of it).

From these few bits and pieces we can form some kind of a vague outline. The philosophical use of language consists in the attempt to "express in general propositions certain and undoubted truths . . . ." The philosophical use of language, therefore, leaves no room for noncognitive linguistic usage: since noncognitive expressions are not propositions at all, being neither true nor false. But the only *other* use of language that Locke recognizes is the civil use. And this differs from the philosophical use only in two respects: it treats of different subject matter and demands less exactitude. If these are the only two respects in which it differs from the philosophical use, it must agree with the philosophical use in expressing propositions. But if the only two uses of language which Locke acknowledges both express propositions and that alone, there is no way for Locke's theory of language to accommodate nondescriptive, noncognitive expressions. If Hutcheson shares these linguistic presuppositions, he cannot be read as an aesthetic noncognitivist. The presumptive evidence in favor of his sharing them is considerable, given his general Lockean position in theory of knowledge. And what other theory of language was there available to him?

This is not to say the descriptive theory of language was monolithic. Berkeley, for one, railed against Locke's linguistic views, to the extent of suggesting that "the communicating of ideas marked by words is not the chief and only end of language, as is commonly supposed," and went on to propose some nondescriptive, exhortatory uses, "the raising of some passion, the exciting to or deterring from an action, the putting the mind in some particular disposition . . . ."[12] But Berkeley himself never went on to make any real philosophical use of these insights. And in ethics and aesthetics, where the contemporary philosopher, weaned on Ayer and Stevenson, would naturally tend to look, Berkeley seems to have been, in fact, a rationalist, even further from noncognitive value theory than Hutcheson.

If, indeed, Hutcheson had adopted the noncognitive use of language, which Berkeley describes as "the raising of some passion," and applied it to the analysis of "X is beautiful," he would have been halfway to the kind of analysis Stevenson has suggested for "X is good"; namely, "I approve of this; do so as well."[13] But he would have had only the second half of the analysis, the imperative part. To say "X is good," according to Stevenson, is to express a positive attitude toward X *and* to urge others to adopt this attitude toward X. If Hutcheson had made use of Berkeley's suggestion, he would have had the "do so as well" but not the "I approve." "X is beautiful" would have been analyzed as "Approve of X," but not "I approve of X." There would be no expression of emotion, only the attempt to arouse emotion. There would be no feeling moment. And since we are already committed to the view that "X is beautiful" has, for Hutcheson, what we have called a feeling moment, that is, either an expression or description of someone's emotion, we cannot accept the hypothesis that Hutcheson was making use, in his aesthetic analysis, of Berkeley's exhortatory use of language. The most we can say is that it might have given Hutcheson the idea for *another* nondescriptive use: the evincing of emotion.

It *might have* given him the idea — but it didn't. For, as a matter of fact, Hutcheson has left us at least one fairly conclusive passage which seems to rule out any noncognitive use of language on his part: a passage which is clearly Lockean in outlook, and more clear than Locke as to the role of sentences or propositions. The passage which I have in mind occurs in an exchange of letters between Hutcheson and Gilbert Burnet in the *London Journal,* later published in book form as *Letters Between the Late Mr. Gilbert Burnet and Mr. Hutcheson Concerning the True Foundation of Virtue or Moral Goodness* (1735). Hutcheson writes in the second letter:

> [We] know that by custom words or sounds are made signs of
> ideas and combinations of words signs of judgments. We know
> that men generally by words express their sentiments and profess
> to speak, as far as they know, according to what is matter of fact,
> so that their profession is to speak truth.[14]

It should first be noted that when Hutcheson says "men
generally by words express their sentiments," he does not in
this context mean by "sentiment" either "feeling," "emotion,"
or anything else of the kind, but merely "opinion." The word
sentiment seems to have had the same double meaning in the
eighteenth century that it has today, sometimes meaning "feeling" and sometimes "opinion." (Indeed the word "feeling" has
the same double meaning.) When I send flowers I am expressing
my sentiments in the former sense; and when I give a lecture on
Hutcheson I am, for the most part, expressing my sentiments in
the latter sense. And when Hutcheson says that "men generally
by words express their sentiments," he must be understood to
mean that men express their opinions with words, a perfectly
innocent sentiment.

With this trivial misinterpretation guarded against, we can
very quickly summarize what Hutcheson is saying about language in the correspondence with Burnet:

i. Words are the signs of ideas.

ii. Combinations of words, that is, sentences, are the signs of
judgments.

iii. Judgments are expressed by men to state matters of fact,
and are either true or false.

With this summary before us, we see that there is neither a
chink nor a cranny in Hutcheson's theory of language to accommodate a noncognitive linguistic use. What men express in language is only what is susceptible of truth or falsity. A linguistic
emotive expression cannot be a nonstatement, but must be a
genuine statement, either true or false, about an emotion. In the
light of this we can conclude with some assurance, I think, that
a noncognitive interpretation of Hutcheson is out of order:

Locke's theory of language, which was Hutcheson's also, will not allow it.

But how, if this is the case, would Hutcheson interpret the phrase "I approve of X," a phrase which, as we have seen, Hutcheson himself uses in an aesthetic context? For we are told that we approve the things we find beautiful. The answer — unpalatable though it must be to the contemporary philosopher — is that "I approve" is seen by Hutcheson as a description of the speaker's state of mind, which is no *more* unacceptable, no more mind-boggling for someone to have held, than to say "I believe" is a description of the speaker's state of mind; and a better philosopher than Hutcheson, as we know, held that view in Hutcheson's time. If this is not the way it *was*, then Austin and the emotivists have taught us nothing new about language. Hutcheson, in 1725, was not writing early Austin or Ayer: he was writing early Hutcheson.

(5) We have now ruled out any noncognitive interpretation of the feeling moment of "X is beautiful." We are left with a choice between a first-person or a third-person description of a state of mind: a choice between "I have the feeling of beauty contemplating X" or "P has the feeling of beauty contemplating X" where P is some person or group of persons other than the speaker. This choice is further widened by the fact that the feeling of beauty may be (to use C. D. Broad's terms) either "occurrent" or "dispositional." When I say "I have the feeling of beauty contemplating X" I may mean either "I am having (here and now) the feeling of beauty contemplating X" (the occurrent interpretation), or "I have the feeling of beauty whenever contemplating X" (dispositional interpretation). And when I say "P has the feeling of beauty contemplating X" I may mean "P is having (here and now) the feeling of beauty contemplating X" (occurrent interpretation) or "P has the feeling of beauty whenever contemplating X" (dispositional interpretation). I adopt the first-person dispositional interpretation of Hutcheson for the following two reasons: first-person because Hutcheson, unlike Hume, does not, it would seem, analyze "X is beautiful" in terms of any kind of consensus of feelings;

dispositional because it allows for saying correctly "X is beautiful" when X is not perceived, which we would surely want on occasion to say.

We conclude, then, that the feeling moment of "X is beautiful" is to be rendered "I have the feeling of beauty whenever contemplating X." But what else is there to "X is beautiful" besides the feeling moment? What else am I asserting? And what characterizes this feeling of beauty? What makes it distinguishable from other feelings of pleasure we might get contemplating X?

(6) Let us take the second question first. What distinguishes the feeling of beauty? We have all along been referring to the feeling of beauty as some *special* feeling of pleasure. What is special about it? How do I know when I am having it? Three possible answers immediately suggest themselves: that the feeling of beauty is distinguished by its cause; that it is distinguished by its particular subjective "feel"; that it is distinguished by its being felt when the perceiver is taking a particular attitude or perceptual stance.

First, then, the feeling of beauty is caused by a particular quality: *uniformity amidst variety*. So it might be that I know I am experiencing the feeling of beauty by knowing that the pleasurable feeling I am having is being caused by *uniformity amidst variety*. But this does not appear to be a plausible answer. For according to Hutcheson, we can know that X is beautiful without knowing that *uniformity amidst variety* is the cause of the feeling of beauty: "We may have the Sensation [of beauty] without knowing what is the Occasion of it; as a Man's Taste may suggest Ideas of Sweets, Acids, Bitters, tho he be ignorant of the Forms of the small Bodys, or their Motions, which excite these Perceptions in him"[15]; and to know that "X is beautiful" is true we must know that we are experiencing, or have experienced, the feeling of beauty. Anyway, presumably the cause of the feeling of beauty is discovered by induction: "I am having the feeling of beauty contemplating X, and X has *uniformity amidst variety*, I am having the feeling of beauty contemplating Y, and Y has *uniformity amidst variety* . . . ."

therefore *uniformity amidst variety* is the cause of the feeling of beauty." So we would have to be able to identify the feeling of beauty prior to discovering its cause, and its cause, therefore, could not be the means by which we recognize it.

That the feeling of beauty may be distinguished by a felt quality of the pleasure itself is indeed suggested by one passage; but the same passage suggests equally that the feeling of beauty may be distinguished, rather, by a particular attitude of the perceiver — what later philosophers have called the attitude of "aesthetic disinterestedness."[16] Hutcheson states that "this Pleasure of Beauty . . . is distinct from that Joy which arises from Self-love upon prospect of Advantage . . . ."[17]

We might read this passage as follows. The pleasure of beauty has a different feeling quality from the pleasure called "joy," which we experience in contemplating objects with a thought to their practical advantage, rather than merely for themselves as objects of perception. (This is, of course, and is meant to be in direct contrast to the Hobbesian view that *all* pleasures, including pleasures of contemplation and perception, are pleasures from prospect of advantage to the perceiver.) The attitude we take, of ignoring the possible advantage to ourselves of an object of contemplation, puts us in the proper condition to receive a pleasure of a certain kind from the perception of *uniformity amidst variety*. But the relation of the attitude to the pleasure is a contingent one. *Uniformity amidst variety* will cause the perceiver to have the feeling of beauty if, among other things, the perceiver is in the attitude of nonattention to prospects of advantage, "entirely abstracted from [the desire of] *Possession* or *Property*."[18] The disinterested attitude of the perceiver is part of the complex of conditions under which *uniformity amidst variety* will give rise to the feeling of beauty in the perceiver. And it is not logically impossible for the feeling to arise in the absence of the attitude.

A second possible reading would make the connection between the attitude of disinterestedness and the feeling of beauty not a contingent, but a necessary, one. We might say that joy and the pleasure of beauty feel the same, but the pleasure of beauty is by definition the pleasure which we receive in contemplating an object disinterestedly. In this case it becomes self-contradictory to assert that the feeling of beauty arose and the attitude of disinterestedness did not obtain; and it is the attitude, then, not the quality of the feeling, which is the distinguishing mark.

Our choice is clear: between a feeling causally connected with the attitude of the perceiver and a feeling noncontingently connected with this attitude. And the choice, for once, is very easy to make. The latter alternative points toward an analysis of emotions, not as inner states caused by external states which in turn cause responses of appropriate kinds, but rather as related noncontingently to circumstance, symptom, and action, such that if all three are absent, the emotion (logically) must be absent, too.[19] The former alternative, however, is clearly the one which Hutcheson's historical context forces upon us. For it is the ubiquitous Cartesian model of emotions that we must assume Hutcheson to be working with; and that model unequivocally construes the relationship between emotions and their external circumstances and manifestations as a causal (contingent) one. Our conclusion, then, must be that for Hutcheson, the feeling of beauty is distinguished by a particular "inner" felt quality, *caused* in part by the attitude which the perceiver takes toward the object of his aesthetic contemplation: that attitude being one of indifference to the practical advantages of the object.

(7) We now recur to the question of what (if anything) is asserted in "*X* is beautiful" beyond the feeling moment ("I have the feeling of beauty whenever contemplating *X*"). The answer is nothing; but this answer requires some explanation.

Hutcheson tells us that the objects which cause the feeling of beauty upon contemplation are consistently those which possess *uniformity amidst variety;* this we know presumably by induction and can state in terms of a causal law: *A* causes *B* under conditions *C*, where *A* is *unity amidst variety,* *B* the feeling of beauty, and *C* a complex of conditions including the stipulations that the perceiver has the sense of beauty and takes the disinterested attitude. But we should not be led by this to the conclusion that when I assert "*X* is beautiful" I am asserting "I experience the feeling of beauty whenever contemplating *X* and *X* has *uniformity amidst variety . . .* " or anything else of the kind. For *uniformity amidst variety* is contingently connected with the feeling of beauty. I can know *X* is beautiful without knowing that *X* has *uniformity amidst variety,* just as I can know that a canary is yellow without knowing about wavelengths and spectra. Nor am I *incorrect* if I say "*X* is beautiful" even though *X* does not possess *uniformity amidst variety;* I am merely *surprising.* Although the causal law *"Uniformity amidst variety* causes the feeling of beauty in the disinterested perceiver" *might* serve as the basis for standards of correct and incorrect aesthetic judgments, it does not, and Hutcheson does not assert that it does. He indeed spends a good deal of time trying to explain *why* there is aesthetic disagreement. However, he does not treat deviation from what would be expected as deviation from the *correct,* but rather as deviation from the expected, given the fact that the hypothesis *"Uniformity amidst variety* causes the feeling of beauty in the disinterested observer" is empirically wellfounded. There are, in fact, only two possible ways in which I can be mistaken when I say "*X* is beautiful," and they are (i) if I mistake some other feeling for the feeling of beauty, or (ii) if I do not have the feeling of beauty *whenever* I (disinterestedly) contemplate *X,* for "I have the feeling of beauty whenever contemplating *X*" entails "*X* is beautiful."

What, then, accounts for the deviations (not from correctness, remember, but from the expected)? This is a question that gives Hutcheson no small amount of trouble. For if there is a sense of beauty common to men, and if there is a firmly established empirical generalization to the effect that this sense of beauty gives rise to the feeling of beauty under certain statable conditions, should we not expect universal aesthetic agreement in the family of man when these conditions obtain? Yet even an eighteenth-century Scottish divine, whose acquaintance with the exotic and bizarre could hardly be called extensive, observed the far from universal nature of aesthetic agreement; and it indeed gave him pause, so much so that he said of the *Inquiry Concerning Beauty* in the preface, *"the* Author *perhaps in some Instances has gone too far, in supposing a greater Agreement of Mankind in this* Sense *of* Beauty, *than Experience will confirm . . . ."* [20]

There are two kinds of aesthetic "disagreement" envisioned by Hutcheson: (i) disagreement about whether or not X is beautiful; and (ii) disagreement about the relative beauty of X in comparison to Y.

Suppose, then, that Mr. A experiences the feeling of beauty contemplating X and Mr. B does not; and suppose further that both are disinterested observers and X possesses *uniformity amidst variety*. It is, of course, always open to Hutcheson to claim that Mr. B lacks a sense of beauty; and, indeed, that "Many men" lack the sense of beauty is, Hutcheson tells us, "plain from Experience."[21] Just such situations of deep-seated disagreement in aesthetic or moral perception, after all, are what drive us, if we are of such a mind, to sense or intuition as the court of last appeal. That *many* men do really lack the ability to make aesthetic distinctions seems doubtful; but that some men do may very well be "plain from Experience."

Suppose, however, that both parties are known to possess the sense of beauty (by whatever means such a thing can be known), and yet Mr. B nevertheless still fails under the proper conditions to experience the feeling of beauty contemplating X, whereas Mr. A does experience it. We can treat this case at the same time as the case in which Mr. A and Mr. B disagree in the comparative aesthetic merits of X and Y — for example, Mr. A claiming that X is more beautiful than Y and Mr. B claiming that Y is more beautiful than X. We are supposing, then, the following two cases:

i. X has *uniformity amidst variety*. Mr. A gets the feeling of beauty contemplating X and Mr. B does not. Both possess the sense of beauty. The proper conditions for aesthetic perception obtain.

ii. X and Y have *uniformity amidst variety*. Both have equal *uniformity* but X has greater *variety*. Mr. A thinks X is more beautiful than Y and Mr. B thinks Y is more beautiful than X.

Both possess the sense of beauty. The proper conditions for aesthetic perception obtain.

According to Hutcheson's theory we should expect that in the first case both Mr. A and Mr. B will experience the feeling of beauty contemplating X and (therefore) agree that X is beautiful. And we should expect that in the second case Mr. A and Mr. B will both think X is more beautiful than Y, for " . . . The Variety increases the Beauty of equal Uniformity" and "The greater *Uniformity* increases the *Beauty* amidst equal *Variety* . . . . "[22] Hutcheson's explanation is the same in both cases. Mr. A and Mr. B are not perceiving the *same* objects at all, and hence they are not *really* having a disagreement at all. This needs spelling out. Hutcheson writes:

> The [simple] Ideas rais'd in different Persons by the same Object, are probably [some way] different, when they disagree in their Approbation or Dislike . . . .
> . . . there does not seem to be any Ground to believe such a Diversity in human Minds, as that the same Idea or Perception should give pleasure to one and pain to another . . . not to say that it seems a Contradiction that the same Idea should do so.[23]

Now, on the Lockean model of perception there are two things we might mean if we said that Mr. A and Mr. B are perceiving the "same" object. We might mean that they are both receiving sense impressions from the same group of primary qualities (that is, the same external object), or we might mean that they are both experiencing the same group of sense impressions (that is, the same internal object — "in the mind"). Thus, it might at times be the case that two people were perceiving the same object in the former sense and not in the latter. In more contemporary terms this would be a situation in which they were perceiving the same "ontological" or "stimulus" object, but different "phenomenological" objects.

What Hutcheson means by "simple ideas" in the above paragraphs are the sense impressions (other than pleasure and pain) of the five garden-variety senses. And what he is claiming is that when Mr. A and Mr. B, under proper conditions, disagree about whether X is beautiful or not (in spite of the fact that X pos-

sesses *uniformity amidst variety*), they may be perceiving the
same primary qualities, the same ontological or stimulus object,
but they are not perceiving the same ideas, the same phenomenological object; and when Mr. A and Mr. B disagree whether X
is more beautiful than Y, under proper conditions (in spite of
the fact that X and Y have equal *uniformity* and Y has less
variety), they may be perceiving the same primary qualities, the
same ontological or stimulus objects, but they are not perceiving the same ideas, the same phenomenological objects.
They are each perceiving a different group of sense impressions,
each attributing or denying beauty to a different phenomenological object.

There is, hence, no real disagreement at all. What Mr. A Calls
X possesses or lacks at least one simple idea not possessed or
lacked by what Mr. B calls X; and what Mr. A calls Y possesses
or lacks at least one simple idea not possessed or lacked by what
Mr. B calls Y. The sentences "X is beautiful" and "X is more
beautiful than Y" refer to groups of simple ideas; and if the
group of simple ideas which Mr. A takes to be X or Y differs
from the group Mr. B takes to be X or Y, even in respect of one
simple idea, then Mr. A and Mr. B are not disagreeing when Mr.
A says "X is beautiful" and Mr. B says "X is not beautiful," or
when Mr. A says "X is more beautiful than Y" and Mr. B says
"Y is more beautiful than X."

Those familiar with some recent discussions of whether we
can properly say that music is "sad" or "happy" (and the like)
may find an echo in Hutcheson's position. It has often enough
been pointed out that if emotive words really do characterize
music in the same way that color words, say, characterize the
objects to which they apply, there should be substantial agreement among language users, in any given case, as to what emotive word is the appropriate one; and such agreement, it is argued, is manifestly absent from discussions of music. To which
objection it has been replied: "The assumption that persons
whose sense of the [emotive] meaning of a piece of music
differs can yet have the very same sense perception of the
sounds is, so far as I know, devoid of all evidence."[24] In other
words, if Mr. A thinks a piece of music is "happy," and Mr. B

thinks that it is "sad," we may assume that they are disagreeing
about the "same" piece of music, and use this disagreement as
evidence against the notion that words like "sad" and "happy"
have any objective criteria of application in a musical context.
But there is no evidence for this assumption; and if we wish to
defend the view that emotive words do have objective criteria of
application in musical contexts, we may claim that in some
sense or other those who disagree about the emotive character
of a piece of music are not talking about the "same" piece of
music, do not "have the very same sense perceptions of the
sounds," although they are in the presence of the "same" physical vibrations.

But Hutcheson goes even further than this. He does not merely *suggest* that Mr. A and Mr. B *may* be perceiving different
phenomenal objects. He does not claim that there is no evidence
that they *are* perceiving the same phenomenal objects. Rather,
he claims that their disagreements about X and Y *imply* that
they are not perceiving the same phenomenal objects: "it seems
a contradiction . . . that the same Idea or Perception should give
pleasure to one and pain to another." We have adequate evidence for the claim that Mr. A and Mr. B do not mean the same
things by X and Y if they do not agree about the beauty or
deformity of X and Y; X and Y are as described above; and the
conditions for aesthetic perception obtain. In short, Hutcheson
has made it true by definition that there can be no real aesthetic
disagreement. His theory is immune from falsification, but at
the price of analyticity.

(8) Why should two normal observers not perceive the same
phenomenal object in the presence of the same ontological object; or, in Lockean terms, why should two normal observers be
aware of different groups of ideas in the presence of the same
primary qualities? Hutcheson offers two explanations. We will
conclude this chapter with a consideration of them. Both stem
from the diversity of human experience, not innate human differences, and both were readily available to Hutcheson in
Locke's *Essay*.

First, it is manifest even to philosophers like Locke and

Hutcheson, who speak of the *passivity* of perception, that *attention* is an activity necessary for perception and that increased attention can increase the ideas derived from the external object. Locke recognized that the presence of an object to the normal observer, even under optimal viewing conditions, does not guarantee perception of all there is to perceive: "that which uses to produce the idea, though conveyed in by the usual organ, not being taken notice of in the understanding, and so imprinting no idea in the mind, there follows no sensation." [25]

Along similar lines, Hutcheson emphasized the tendency of education and habit to increase one's power of perception by increasing the length and breadth of attention. *"Custom,"* he wrote, "may make us capable of extending our Views further, and of receiving more complex Ideas of *Beauty* in Bodys, or *Harmony* in Sounds, by increasing our Attention and quickness of Perception." [26] And again: "This *Education* and *Custom* may influence our *internal Senses,* where they are antecedently, by enlarging the Capacity of our Minds to retain and compare the Parts of complex Compositions . . . . " [27] By these means Mr. A, for example, in the presence of the same ontological object as Mr. B, may nevertheless perceive a very different phenomenological object; or, in Lockean terms, in the presence of the same primary qualities, be aware of a very much larger group of ideas. This being the case, what arouses the idea of beauty in Mr. A's mind is not the "same" object that fails to arouse it in Mr. B's (or whatever). It is not, notice, the sense of beauty itself that is sharpened by custom and education: it is the attention capacity of the five garden-variety senses that gives the sense of beauty more complex phenomenal objects to perceive. Where Mr. A and Mr. B differ is not in sensitivity (or lack of it) of their respective senses of beauty, which are by nature equal. But it is the acquired capacities of their five bodily senses which make Mr. A's phenomenal objects different from Mr. B's, and his aesthetic judgments *seemingly* different because they are, in fact, judgments about different objects.

Second, and more important, is the influence of the association of ideas, which was to play an even more prominent part in later British philosophy. Custom and education, Hutcheson claims, can increase our capacity for attending to the stimulus present before our senses and therefore increase the sense impressions one can gain from the stimulus object. More of the stimuli present end up affecting Mr. A than Mr. B; hence, Mr. A's phenomenal object is different from Mr. B's. But there is another stage at which the phenomenal object is being formed: the stage at which all of the physical stimuli present have had (or have failed to have) their effects, and what we would now perhaps call the psychological makeup takes over. At this point the psychological machinery of the association of ideas comes into play, adding to the phenomenal object ideas which have been in the past associated with the ideas aroused by the physical stimuli, but which are not directly aroused by the now present physical stimuli. Examples here will be instructive; and it would be historically appropriate to get them from Locke.

In the fourth edition of the *Essay Concerning Human Understanding* (1700) Locke added to Book II a chapter which he called "Of the Association of Ideas." The topic had already been treated by Hobbes and was to gain more momentum as the Enlightenment waned. The following examples are taken from Locke's *Essay:* [28]

[i] A grown person surfeiting with honey no sooner hears the name of it, but his fancy immediately carries the sickness and qualms to his stomach, and he cannot bear the very idea of it . . . .

[ii] The ideas of goblins and sprites have really no more to do with darkness than light: yet let but a foolish maid inculcate these often on the mind of a child, and raise them there together, possibly he shall never be able to separate them again so long as he lives, but darkness shall ever afterwards bring with it these frightful ideas, and they shall be so joined, that he can no more bear the one than the other.

[iii] Many children, imputing the pain they endured at school to their books they were corrected for, so join these ideas together, that a book becomes their aversion, and they are never reconciled to the study and use of them all their lives after; and thus reading becomes a torment to them, which otherwise possibly they might have made the great pleasure of their lives.

All of these examples follow the same general pattern: A is experienced with B at time t, and at the time $t+1$ A is experienced by itself and, because of the past association with *B, B* is called to mind as well. *A* may be a simple or complex idea which then brings with it another simple or complex idea which in turn brings with it a third idea, "pleasure" (or "pain"): *B,* that is, is either a "pleasant" or "painful" idea. (*B* may, of course, be neither pleasant nor painful, but indifferent. However, the ideas which we are interested in here are pleasant or painful ones, and we shall restrict ourselves to them.)

Sometimes, Locke's examples, as we can see, omit the intermediary idea: that is, as in example [iii], we are told that *A* (reading books) has been associated with pain, so that when *A* is now experienced, pain is experienced along with it. But on Hutcheson's view, and I suspect on Locke's, too, this would be a kind of associational enthymeme; for each simple idea, according to Hutcheson, is naturally either pleasant or unpleasant (or indifferent). No simple idea can ever *itself* become pleasurable, if it is originally unpleasant or indifferent; and no simple idea can ever *itself* become painful, if it is originally pleasant or indifferent. No complex idea can, either, since it is merely a sum of simple ideas. Thus, when we say that the complex idea of "reading," which is pleasant, became painful by being associated with pain, we are speaking loosely. What we mean, for Hutcheson, would be this: those that find reading unpleasant may find it so because reading was associated in the past with beatings and scoldings; and beatings and scoldings are painful. Those who find reading pleasant lack this association with painful ideas. Thus, those who find reading unpleasant perceive a complex idea when they contemplate reading different from that perceived by those who find it pleasant. And because this complex idea contains some unpleasant ideas, they find reading unpleasant. But two people who are perceiving the *same* complex idea, or the *same* simple idea, must both experience pleasure, or both experience pain. As Hutcheson puts the view, when some simple or complex idea ceases to be pleasant, for example, "we shall generally find that there is some accidental Conjunction of a disagreeable Idea, which always recurs with the Object . . . ."[29]

Let us return, now, to the matter of aesthetic disagreements.

Mr. A finds X beautiful and Mr. B does not. Both have the sense of beauty and both are disinterested observers. Both have equal powers of attention and are both, hence, getting an equal share of ideas from the stimulus object. Yet they may still not be perceiving the same phenomenal object because one may have different associations from the other. So Mr. A's X may, because of the nature of his associations, indeed lack *uniformity amidst variety* and Mr. B's X may, because of the nature of his associations, indeed possess it. And the same argument will apply, *pari passu*, to a disagreement about the relative aesthetic merits of X vis-à-vis Y.

A further effect of the association of ideas is to make it easier to mistake some other pleasurable idea for the idea of beauty. "The *Association* of Ideas . . . often makes men have an aversion to Objects of beauty, and a liking to others void of it, but under different Conceptions than those of *Beauty* and *Deformity*." [30] Thus, Mr. A may mistake his pleasant feeling of security which, through the association of ideas, he has come to connect with a particular house, for the feeling of beauty and think the house beautiful when it is not; whereas Mr. B, free of this association, sees immediately that the house is totally lacking in beauty. The house lacks *uniformity amidst variety* and causes the idea of beauty neither in Mr. A nor in Mr. B. But it causes *another* pleasant idea in Mr. A which he mistakes for the idea of beauty. In this case, too, the association of ideas is responsible for Mr. A's and Mr. B's perceiving different phenomenal objects in response to the same primary qualities. There is, however, no idea of beauty involved in the case at all. The various permutations and combinations of this case also can, of course, apply *pari passu* to a disagreement about the relative aesthetic merits of two or more aesthetic objects.

(9) If, then, Mr. A and Mr. B disagree about the beauty of X, or about the relative beauty of X vis-à-vis Y, we are to assume, when all else fails, that they are perceiving different phenomenal objects even though they both say X and Y in the presence of the same stimulus objects; and all else fails when we determine that Mr. A and Mr. B both have the sense of beauty, both

are disinterested observers, and neither is mistaking some other feeling for the feeling of beauty. Now we should expect to find, if we examine such cases closely, that either Mr. A or Mr. B, due to varied experiences, has more or less power of attention or different trains of associations connected with the same stimulus object (or both) — for these are the factors which determine that different phenomenal objects will be perceived in the presence of the same stimulus object.

But suppose we do examine the cases closely, and suppose we do not turn up anything of the kind. Suppose that we find no appreciable difference in perceptual training, no appreciable difference in power of attention, no appreciable difference in trains of association. Suppose, indeed, that Mr. A and Mr. B are identical twins. Are we then to conclude that they are not, as previously thought, perceiving different phenomenal objects? Clearly not: for, as we have seen, that hypothesis is above empirical refutation. Any unexpected aesthetic judgment that is not the result of mistaking some other feeling for the feeling of beauty is, by stipulative definition, a judgment about some other aesthetic object than the one it seems to be about. Thus, no aesthetic judgment can ever cause embarrassment to Hutcheson. What *should* have caused him embarrassment was his means of achieving this result; namely, defining aesthetic disagreement in such a way as to make nothing answer to the description. To which the obstinate will doubtless reply: "But nevertheless there *is* aesthetic disagreement, for all of that; and if we must give up the name, we will invent another."

V

VARIETIES OF AESTHETIC
EXPERIENCE

(1) In Chapters II-IV we have been examining what might be called Hutcheson's aesthetic "first philosophy", the basic tenets of his position regarding the epistemological status of aesthetic perceptions and judgments. In this chapter, and the next, we shall be concerned with first, fleshing out some of the more important details of the position, including what we would call Hutcheson's philosophy of art (as something at least logically distinct from his aesthetics); and, second, the uncovering of the theological underpinnings. The first task, that of limning in the details, itself divides naturally into two parts: the distinguishing of the varieties of feelings that we might call "aesthetic," and Hutcheson's age tended to call the "pleasures of the imagination"; and the distinguishing of the varieties of objects that, according to Hutcheson, normally produce such feelings or ideas in us. (It is in the latter inquiry that we shall come to grips with Hutcheson's somewhat sketchy reflections on art.)

We can begin by listing once again the senses which Hutcheson acknowledged as falling under the general head of "pleasures of the imagination," and which I shall not scruple to call at times "aesthetic." They are, in Hutcheson's most generous mood, the senses of *absolute beauty, relative beauty* (or *imitation*), *harmony, design* (or *fitness* of means to ends), *grandeur* (or *sublimity*), and *novelty,* to which we must add the sense of *humor,* which Hutcheson wrote of in his *Reflections Upon Laughter,* but which appeared only once in his other works when he was enumerating the internal senses.

86

These senses must be examined one by one and brought into the framework of Hutcheson's general aesthetic theory. In so doing, we will make clear perhaps why Hutcheson seems rather ambivalent as to whether he is talking about different distinct senses or merely different manifestations of the same sense; and why he says next to nothing about *novelty* or *grandeur* in the *Inquiry Concerning Beauty,* except to throw a rather terse remark in their direction and refer the reader to Addison for further enlightenment.

(2) The aestheticians of the eighteenth century spent a great deal of effort on the problem of distinguishing among the various pleasures of the imagination by trying to describe their "feel." It is worthy of some note that Hutcheson never did this sort of thing. The reason, I suspect, is that he saw the difference, at least vaguely, between philosophy and psychology. Having made the logical point that aesthetic judgments are judgments about feelings, he considered his work as a philosopher finished.

The judgment "*X* is beautiful," we have seen, is a judgment about a *particular* feeling, identifiable of itself, without reference to the objects that occasion it. But by induction we can conclude that the objects which do occasion it possess *unity amidst variety;* hence, we have good inductive grounds for believing that *unity amidst variety* causes the idea of beauty. There are, then, two ways of telling whether a feeling is *the* feeling of beauty: first by its "quality"; and second by whether or not the object which occasions it possesses *unity amidst variety*. But there is this important difference between them: the subjective "quality" is noncontingently connected with the feeling, whereas the cause, of course, is contingently connected. Therefore, it is logically impossible for any feeling to have the subjective "quality" of the feeling of beauty and yet fail to be the feeling of beauty, whereas it is logically possible for the feeling of beauty to be aroused in the absence of *unity amidst variety*.

"*Grandeur* and *Novelty*," Hutcheson tells us, "are two Ideas different from *Beauty*, which often recommend Objects to us."[1]

The reason is to be found, he adds, in *Spectator* No. 412, part
of the series which Addison called *The Pleasures of the Imagination.*

Addison, unlike Hutcheson, was very much concerned with
describing the subjective experiences of beauty, grandeur, and
novelty. And it seems clear that Hutcheson was reasonably content with Addison's descriptions. Of the feeling of grandeur (or
sublimity), Addison wrote: "We are flung into a pleasing aston-
ishment . . . and feel a delightful stillness and amazement in the
soul . . . . "[2] The novel, on the other hand, "fills the soul with
an agreeable surprise, gratifies its curiosity, and gives it an idea
of which it was not before possessed."[3] And beauty, in contrast
to both, "diffuses a secret satisfaction and complacency
through the imagination . . . "; it "strikes the mind with an inward joy, and spreads a cheerfulness and delight through all its
faculties."[4] Now whatever the adequacy (or inadequacy) of
these descriptions (and, as I have said, Hutcheson was not particularly interested in this aspect of aesthetics), it is clear that
Addison was attempting to characterize what he believed to be
widely different subjective states. Thus, the ideas of novelty and
grandeur do not fulfill the first criterion: they do not have the
same subjective "quality" as the idea of beauty. This being the
case, they did not appear to Addison or Hutcheson as merely
species of the same genus as the idea of beauty.

Nor is the second criterion fulfilled, for the qualities of objects which occasion the ideas of grandeur and novelty are
neither of them *unity amidst variety,* the former being "the
largeness of a whole view, considered as one entire piece," the
latter "Every thing that is new or uncommon . . . . "[5] (And,
clearly, an object can be large or new or uncommon without
possessing *unity amidst variety.*)

The ideas of grandeur and novelty, then, are different from
the idea of beauty in the two crucial respects enumerated
above: they are different in felt quality, and they are not occasioned by the same objective quality. Why, then, does
Hutcheson place them, along with the idea of beauty, under the
same rubric, i.e., "The Pleasures of the Imagination"? Hutcheson insists that the "*grandeur* and *novelty* of objects excite

some grateful perceptions not unlike the former [i.e., beauty, harmony, and imitation] . . . . "[6] But if they are not unlike, in what way are they like? For, as we have seen, they *are* unlike in two important ways. Hutcheson's answer is that they, like the idea of beauty, are appreciated not for their possible consequences but for their own sake alone. Grandeur and novelty qualify to be numbered among the pleasures of the imagination because "Whatever is grateful to any of these perceptive powers is for itself desirable, and may on some occasions be to us an ultimate end."[7]

What, then, of the sense of humor? Is the feeling of amusement a variety of the feeling of beauty? Or is it, like the feelings of grandeur and novelty, a separate feeling in its own right? And is its cause *unity amidst variety* or some other quality? Finally, does it even qualify as a pleasure of the imagination? Hutcheson, after all, never specifically refers to it as such. To answer these questions, we will have to give the subject of humor a separate and more extensive hearing; for unlike grandeur and novelty, humor is a subject on which Hutcheson has something to say.

(3) Hutcheson'a account of comedy, in the three papers that were later to be published as *Reflections Upon Laughter,* begins as do most of his writings, with his *bete noire,* Hobbesian egoism. Hobbes, steady to his usual text, had presented a selfish interpretation of laughter. It was, he maintained, the expression of "sudden glory," an immediate feeling of superiority. "*Sudden Glory,* is the passion which maketh those *Grimaces* called LAUGHTER; and is caused either by some sudden act of their own, that pleaseth them; or by the appreciation of some deformed thing in another, by comparison whereof they suddenly applaud themselves."[8]

Hutcheson's task, in the first of his three papers on laughter, is to refute Hobbes. He does so by adducing counterexamples to show that the feeling of sudden glory is neither the necessary nor the sufficient condition of laughter; that laughter sometimes arises in the absence of sudden glory, and sometimes does not in its presence. For, he argues,

> If Mr. Hobbes's notion be just, then, first, there can be no Laugh-
> ter on any occasion where we make no comparison of ourselves to
> others, or of our present state to a worse state, or where we do not
> observe some superiority of ourselves to others, or of our present
> state to a worse state, or where we do not observe some superior-
> ity of ourselves above some other thing; and again, it must follow,
> that every sudden appearance of superiority over another must
> excite laughter, when we attend to it. [9]

In the second and third papers, Hutcheson presents his own
views on laughter, based upon his own familiar strategy: identification of the "quality" in objects which arouses the mental
state in question; denial that the mental state is always desired
for the sake of something else — namely, self-interest; the related assumption that the mental state is at least sometimes
desired for its own sake; and, finally, the assumption which
must for Hutcheson follow from this, that there is a "sense"
appropriate to that mental state.

The cause of laughter — the quality in "objects" that arouses
it — is very like *unity amidst variety,* although Hutcheson never
mentions the similarity. If we think of *unity amidst variety* as a
harmonious composition of parts, then laughter is aroused when
this harmony is gently disturbed by an overemphasis of the
variety. The *slightly* inappropriate metaphor; the *slightly outre*
simile; this, for Hutcheson, is the essence of comedy.

> That then which seems generally the cause of laughter is the bring-
> ing together of images which have contrary additional ideas, as
> well as some resemblance in the principal idea: this contrast be-
> tween ideas of grandeur, dignity, sanctity, perfection, and ideas of
> meanness, baseness, profanity, seems to be the very spirit of bur-
> lesque; and the greatest part of our railery and jest is founded
> upon it. [10]

Thus, for example, if I call an airplane a "silver eagle," my
metaphor is entirely appropriate (if not very original) and a-
rouses no laughter; and if I call it a "silver sloth," my metaphor
is entirely inappropriate and therefore perhaps silly — but not
humorous. If, however, I call it a "tin goose," my metaphor is
not altogether inappropriate, since aluminum looks like tin, and

geese fly. Yet what we associate with tin are homey and trivial items of daily use, not sleek modern machines; and geese, unlike eagles, are served for Sunday dinner. This *variety* of extraneous and slightly inappropriate associations upsets the *unity* of the metaphor without totally destroying it. Herein lies the comic. That humor results in a pleasurable state is obvious; and being a special kind of pleasurable state, distinct from all others and desired at times for its own sake, Hutcheson's epistemology requires a "sense" of humor for it. But Hutcheson observes, too, that laughter is a peculiarly social phenomenon; and if at times humor is desired merely for the special kind of pleasure it gives rise to, it more often serves a further useful purpose in society: the puncturing of overinflated intellectual balloons. When we stand in worshipful awe of some molehill which we ourselves have made into a mountain, or when we even cower before it, comedy is the antidote. "Nothing is so properly applied to the false grandeur, either of good or evil, as ridicule . . . . "[11]

We are now in a position to place the "sense" of humor in Hutcheson's overall scheme. It bears the following affinities to the sense of beauty. It gives rise to a special kind of pleasure. This pleasure is aroused by a quality in "objects" somewhat (but not entirely) like *unity amidst variety;* and it is sometimes desired for its own sake. The last characteristic marks out humor as one of the pleasures of the imagination. Why Hutcheson did not specifically classify it as such in his systematic works is not clear. Perhaps he did not because the practical, moral purpose of comedy predominates, in Hutcheson's view, which would have made it unwelcome in the company of pleasures that were supposed to owe their worth to no purpose at all, and were, in fact, achieved by putting one's self out of gear with purposes altogether. In any case, comedy seems to straddle the fence between the aesthetic and the nonaesthetic in Hutcheson's thought.

(4) Working our way up the list of aesthetic senses, we come to the sense of *design*, or *fitness* of means to ends. It made only one appearance in Hutcheson's writings: in the posthumous

System of Moral Philosophy (1755). Hutcheson stated there: "As we are endued with reason to discern the fitness of means for an end, and the several relations and connexions of things; so, there is an immediate pleasure in [the] knowledge, distinct from the Judgment itself, tho naturally joined with it."[12]

But although fitness was not named in the first *Inquiry,* it was not ignored either. For in discussing the various objects that arouse the idea of beauty, Hutcheson there described the very same thing that he later called "fitness of means for an end," ascribing the beauty of fitness to *unity amidst variety.* Thus, he wrote with regard to the beauty of animals:

> And how amazing is the *Unity* of Mechanism, when we shall find that almost infinite diversity of Motions, all their Actions in *walking, running, flying, swimming;* all their serious Efforts for *Self-preservation,* all their freakish *Contortions* when they are gay and sportful, in all their various Limbs, perform'd by one simple Contrivance of a contracting *Muscle,* apply'd with inconceivable Diversitys to answer all these Ends! Various Engines might have obtain'd the same Ends; but then there had been less *Uniformity,* and the *Beauty* of our Animal Systems, and of particular Animals, had been much less, when their surprising *Unity* of Mechanism had been remov'd from them."[13]

Hutcheson's progress here is interesting: from fitness as simply another variety of beauty, to fitness as a separate "aesthetic" feeling with a separate sense appropriate to it. The reason for this progress lies, I think, in the observations of Edmund Burke and others, that fitness is certainly not a sufficient condition for beauty. The connection between fitness and beauty is indeed reflected in our language; as Hogarth remarked, "When a vessel sails well, the sailors always call her a beauty; the two ideas have such a connexion."[14] But (going from the shipyard to the barnyard) Burke argued, "on that principle the wedgelike snout of a swine, with its tough cartilage at the end, the little sunk eyes, and the whole make of the head, so well adapted to its offices of digging, and rooting, would be extremely beautiful."[15] Clearly, though, we do praise fitness in a way very like the way we praise beauty; and if the snout of the pig is not beautiful, it is, nevertheless, "beautifully adapted" to its end. How, then, to reconcile our use of "beautiful" to express our approval of fitness with the fact that fitness is not sufficient condition for beauty? Hutcheson's way, I suggest, was finally to reject fitness as a species of the beautiful, but to allow it "aesthetic" status as one of the pleasures of the imagination. In so doing, he blunted Burke's counterexample and yet could provide (although he never did so explicitly) a plausible explanation of why we praise fitness as beautiful; it may not, strictly speaking, be beautiful, he could argue, but it is, like beauty, a pleasure of the imagination.

(5) With the senses of *absolute beauty, relative beauty,* and *harmony,* we come to the sense of beauty proper. For all are excited by *unity amidst variety,* and Hutcheson gives no evidence of believing that they give rise to three separate ideas rather than one. Hence, there is no compelling reason to call them three senses, rather than one, which seems to be why Hutcheson never did so in the *Inquiry* and why, even when he started to in his subsequent works, he tended to treat the distinction merely as a *façon de parler.*

What mainly distinguishes these three species of beauty is the diversity of objects which excite them. The sense of harmony, of course, involves a completely distinct external sense, the sense of hearing, as it is the sense appropriate to beauty of sound. The sense of relative beauty, or imitation, is not distinguished by being proper to any one particular external sense, although a large portion of imitations will, of course, be conveyed through the sense of sight in the form of paintings, drawings, statues, plays, and dances. But theater is a mixed art: we hear as well as see the actors — and both literature and music are thought of by Hutcheson as having representational aspects.

The sense of absolute beauty encompasses, for Hutcheson, any perception of *unity amidst variety* that is not aural and does not involve perceiving something as a representation of something else. In the *Inquiry,* as we have seen, this included the perceiving of fitness; and it included, too, the perceiving of the "beauty" of scientific and other systems of thought.

To these objects of the aesthetic senses we must now turn our attention. They can conveniently be distributed among three classes: (i) natural objects; (ii) intellectual "objects" (by which is meant theories, or parts of theories, such as laws or theorems); (iii) art "objects."

(6) Hutcheson writes far more extensively on the beauties of nature than would be fashionable today; and this is true of most eighteenth-century authors. "Aesthetics" to the contemporary mind is philosophy of art almost exclusively; but in Hutcheson's time the priorities were, if anything, reversed. Thus, Hutcheson draws almost all of his examples of absolute beauty from nature; works of art provide nearly none. Absolute beauty, it will be recalled, is the beauty resulting from the perception of *unity amidst variety*, where there is no relation between the object perceived and any other object aesthetically relevant. *Comparative*, or *relative, beauty* is the beauty which results from the perception of some *unity amidst variety* existing in virtue of a correspondence between two objects, or between an object and an idea. The most common form which relative beauty takes is the beauty of imitation. Thus, Hutcheson writes:

> [W]hat we call *relative* [beauty] is that which is apprehended in any *Object*, commonly consider'd as an *Imitation* of some Original: And this *Beauty* is founded on a *Comformity*, or a kind of *Unity* between the Original and the Copy. The Original may be either some Object in *Nature*, or some *establish'd Idea*; for if there be any known *Idea* as a Standard, and Rules to fix this Image or *Idea* by, we may make a *beautiful Imitation*.[16]

One would expect that natural objects provide examples only of absolute beauty. For comparative beauty presupposes the intervention of a maker who contrives to fashion an object in imitation of another, or in correspondence with some preconceived idea. But being an unabashed Deist, Hutcheson sees nature as the work of art *par excellence;* and where we can read God's intentions, we can perceive the admirable way in which He has fashioned nature after His plan. So:

> This Beauty arising from Correspondence to *Intention*, would open to curious Observers a new Scene of Beauty in the Works of NATURE, by considering how the Mechanism of the various Parts known to us seems adapted to the Perfection of that Part, and yet in Subordination to the Good of the Greatest Whole, or of all Beings, to have been the Intention of the AUTHOR of Nature; and cannot avoid being pleas'd when we see any part of this Design executed in the Systems we are acquainted with.[17]

It might be thought that perhaps all such aesthetic perceptions of nature are closed to the non-Christian. Such, however, need not be the case on Hutcheson's view. For just as we can admire a statue of Hercules if it "retains that *Grandeur*, and those marks of *Strength* and *Courage,* which we imagine in that Hero,"[18] without being Greek polytheists, so, Hutcheson might argue, an atheist can admire the natural world *as if* it were an embodiment of the Christian "myth," without for a moment believing it to be anything but a myth. Indeed, it may very well be that many a nonbeliever's tastes in natural beauty are unconsciously formed by a Christian view of nature.

But although comparative beauty does, according to Hutcheson, have a place in the sun of natural beauty, it is a small place: absolute beauty is the major factor here.

Hutcheson begins his discussion of absolute beauty in nature with a discussion of the simplest geometrical forms: squares, rectangles, triangles, and so on. As we have seen, he maintains that " . . . The *Variety* increases the Beauty in equal Uniformity" and "The greater *Uniformity* increases the *Beauty* amidst equal *Variety* . . . ."[19] Before we go on to examine how the natural world is seen by Hutcheson to embody this principle, it would be well to contemplate for a moment its logical absurdity. Hutcheson clearly is treating uniformity and variety as two logically independent characteristics. We might, for example, say that we admire a chair both for its comfort and for its durability. And, since comfort and durability are logically independent, we can say that if two chairs were equally comfortable, we would (all other things being equal) prefer the more durable one; and if they were equally durable (all other things being equal) we would prefer the more comfortable one.

Hutcheson treats unity and variety in just this way; but this seems to be a logical error. Two objects cannot (logically) have equal uniformity *and* unequal variety, or equal variety *and* unequal unity. If *A* has more variety than *B*, then it follows that *A* is less unified than *B*; and if *A* is more unified than *B*, then it follows that *A* has less variety than *B*. So at least it appears to me.

As to the application of this rather suspect principle to nature, Hutcheson tends to emphasize the aspect of unity, which certainly reveals something about his taste in natural beauty, as well as the taste of his contemporaries. But as there is a good deal of excellent work in this area of the history of ideas, there is no need to pursue the subject here; nor would it be within the purview of the present study to do so. We can, however, at least glance at some examples of Hutcheson's treatment of natural beauty, for the purpose of further limning in his aesthetic theory.

For Hutcheson, nature provides an inexhaustible resource of variety in which unity presents the unexpected (but nevertheless frequent) foil. It is for this reason — because variety is expected and unity surprising — that unity is the major operator in the aesthetic enjoyment of the natural world. A second point worth noting in Hutcheson's treatment of natural beauty is his emphasis upon the universal, rather than the particular: upon the relation of individual objects to nature as a whole, rather than the beauty of these objects in themselves. Both of these points will emerge in the following illustrations. Hutcheson writes:

> [I]n every part of the World of NATURE which we call *Beautiful,* there is vast *Uniformity,* amidst almost infinite *Variety* . . . . Every particular Object in *Nature* does not indeed appear *beautiful* to us; but there is a vast Profusion of *Beauty* over most of the Objects which occur either to our Senses, or Reasonings upon Observation . . . . the Forms of all the great Bodys in the Universe are nearly spherical; the Orbits of their Revolutions generally Eliptick, and without great Eccentricity in those which continually occur to our Observation: and these are Figures of great *Uniformity,* and therefore, pleasing to us . . . .

.   .   .   .

If we descend to the minuter Works of NATURE, what vast *Uniformity* among all the Species of *Plants* and *Vegetables* in the manner of their Growth and Propagation! what exact Resemblance among all the Plants of the same Species whose Numbers surpass our Imagination! . . .

AGAIN, as to the *Beauty* of *Animals,* either in their inward Structure, which we come to the Knowledge of by Experiment and long Observation, or their outward Form, we shall find vast *Uniformity* among all the Species which are known to us, in the Structure of those Parts, upon which Life depends more immediately.[20]

It can be seen clearly in all of the above examples — the beauty of celestial bodies, of plants, and of animals — that it is the surprising uniformity among vast numbers of individuals that, for Hutcheson, provides our aesthetic pleasure in these objects. But it is hardly ever the individual object that is admired: it is nearly always the individual object as part of a system. Hutcheson's admiration of natural beauty, therefore, is for the most part concept laden. Of course, no natural object can be perceived at all without being automatically placed in some conceptual frame. We cannot see an *object* without seeing it *as* some *kind* of thing or other. We cannot admire the beauty of a green pepper without seeing it as *something,* if not as a green pepper. But it is a long way from this admiration of a green pepper to Hutcheson's, which would involve the realization that *this* green pepper is one of many green peppers, all of which resemble each other to a remarkable degree. In short, Hutcheson looked at nature, even when looking for absolute beauty, as a philosopher and scientist. If he looked at it as a poet, it was as a Lucretius or a Dante, not a Keats or a Shelley.

(7) In the chapter of the *Inquiry Concerning Beauty* which he calls "Of the Beauty of Theorems," Hutcheson breaks ground in a place where no one seems ever to have taken up the task after him. Scientists, mathematicians particularly, speak of the beauty or elegance of their theories and demonstrations; yet little serious work, so far as I know, has ever been done by philosophers to investigate these linguistic uses. Few, I think,

share Collingwood's view that the word "beautiful" has no particular aesthetic significance at all and can simply be thought of as synonymous with "good" or "praiseworthy" or something of the kind.[21] But many, I suspect, think this of the scientist's use. Perhaps they are right, but the topic might well repay further inquiry. And Hutcheson deserves some credit for broaching it, although what he comes up with is not very satisfactory.

Quite predictably, Hutcheson finds the beauty of theorems to be in their subsumption of variety under a unifying principle. "For in one *Theorem*," he states,

> we may find included, with the most exact Agreement, an infinite Multitude of particular Truths; nay, often an Infinity of Infinites . . . . Thus for instance, the 47th Proposition of the first Book of EUCLID'S Elements contains an infinite Multitude of Truths, concerning the infinite possible Sizes of right-angled *Triangles*, as you make the Areas greater or less; and in each of these Sizes you may find an infinite Multitude of dissimilar *Triangles*, as you vary the Proportion of the Base to the *Perpendicular;* all which Infinitys of Infinites agree in the general *Theorem.*[22]

Thus, the *variety* of Euclid's forty-seventh proposition lies in its universality: for it is a proposition about *all* right triangles; and there is an infinite number of them. Its *unity* of course lies in the fact that *all* of these triangles fall under one proposition.

But generality, as I think Hutcheson correctly observes, is not the only determiner of beauty. For if the particulars brought under the generalization are too diffuse — that is, if there is an excess of variety — the general proposition will not be as beautiful. So, for example, in the proposition *every whole is greater than its part,* "we shall find no *Beauty* in the Contemplation: Because howsoever this proposition does contain many Infinitys of particular Truths; yet the *Unity* is inconsiderable, since they all agree only in a vague, undetermin'd Conception of Whole and Part, and in an indefinite Excess of the former above the latter, which is sometimes great and sometimes small."[23] Furthermore, Hutcheson observes in later editions of the *Inquiry* that trivial propositions are not admirable, "even where the *Unity* is sufficiently distinct and determinate," for they give us no "*Surprize* in the Discovery." [24] This latter is not a lack of beauty, however, but a lack of novelty.

Hutcheson recognized, at least vaguely, too, although not as fully as he ought to have done, that the beauty or elegance of a proposition must somehow lie not just in itself, but in its relation to a system of other propositions. "There is," Hutcheson said, "another Beauty in Propositions, which cannot be omitted; which is this, When one *Theorem* shall contain a vast Multitude of Corollarys easily deducible from it." [25]

Hutcheson was certainly on the right track here; but what he failed to see was that it must be a double track. For the richness of a logical system, the number of theorems provable within it, is just one mark of its elegance. The economy with which this richness is achieved is the other. As a recent author has remarked in this regard:

> [A] system is more elegant the simpler is its list of primative terms and the simpler is its list of axioms. On the other hand, neither our list of primative terms nor our list of axioms can just be cut arbitrarily short, for if the axioms selected are too few and too weak or contain too meager an array of primative terms, then the theorems deducible will be insufficient to make the system interesting. [26]

We are correct, I think, in seeing an *aesthetic* argument here. For the richness and economy of an uninterpreted logical system (where the values of truth or utility cannot yet cloud the issue) seem to me directly analogous to the richness of thematic development with economy of thematic material that a Beethoven, say, achieves in his best symphonic structures. Nor do I see why this should not be thought of as a genuine aesthetic experience. There are times when the mathematician and logician are just as unequivocally enjoying their creations aesthetically as the composer. And it may be that the scientist, too, sometimes must fall back on a basically aesthetic judgment, when all else fails, as, for instance, in the decision to interpret the Michelson-Morley experiment relativistically. Einstein often expressed his own theoretical intuitions in distinctly aesthetic terms. It would be well worth the effort of aestheticians to determine how far such expressions are metaphorical and how far literal.

(8) Hutcheson's reflections on art are in one major respect a disappointment. His position is one that would have lent itself to a formalist philosophy of art; and any movement in that direction in the eighteenth century would have been a healthy antidote to the ubiquitous theory of art as imitation. But in this Hutcheson was of his time and his place; and the principle of *unity amidst variety* is bent, as we have already seen, out of its formalist orbit to accommodate the mimetic paradigm. This is not to say that Hutcheson was so blind as to ignore completely the formal element in the arts, in spite of what we feel was a missed opportunity to redress the balance in its favor. And it is to the absolute beauty, the purely formal, in art that we must first turn our attention.

Hutcheson's remarks concerning the nonimitative, that is, absolute, beauty of the arts are distressingly few. The most extended of them, not surprisingly, concern music and architecture, the arts which have always been most recalcitrant to imitation theories. What Hutcheson thought about the formal properties of the other arts will have to be extrapolated, for the most part, from these.

The passage in which Hutcheson outlines his musical speculations is worth quoting at some length; it is revealing of the two ways in which the principle of *unity amidst variety* is treated; namely, as cause of the idea of beauty after the manner of the secondary qualities, and as cause of the idea of beauty, where the observer actually perceives, is aware of, the cause — which borders on quite another notion of aesthetic quality. Hutcheson writes:

> *Harmony* often raises Pleasure in those who know not what is the Occasion of it: And yet the Foundation of this Pleasure is known to be a sort of *Uniformity*. When the several Vibrations of one Note regularly coincide with the Vibrations of another, they make an agreeable Composition; and such Notes are called *Chords*. Thus the Vibrations of any one Note coincide in Time with every second Vibration of its *Octave;* and two Vibrations of any Note coincide with three of its *Fifth;* and so on in the rest of the *Chords*. Now good Compositions, beside the Frequency of these *Chords,* must retain a general *Unity* of Key, an *Uniformity* among the Parts in *Bars, Risings, Fallings, Closes.*[27]

Music, of all the arts, presented to a thinker of Hutcheson's stripe the most promising data. For here, surely, one might argue, is an exact aesthetic analogue of the secondary-quality model: a correlation between perceptions and mathematically measurable minute properties of matter. Just as certain arrangements of the "insensible atoms" produce the sensation of redness, certain arrangements of sound waves produce the pleasurable sensations of the third, fifth, and octave. Indeed, in the musical case we can go even further — express with mathematical exactitude the musical intervals and correlate them with a preference ranking of the resultant musical sensations. When we do this we find that the most consonant intervals have the simplest arithmetical ratios, or, in Hutcheson's view, the most *unity*.

That the relationship between the work of art and the aesthetic experience is not a cause-and-effect relationship, at least of the simple kind Hutcheson has in mind, we will leave until a future chapter. Suffice it to say here, even the modest claim of a correlation between the arithmetical simplicity of the musical intervals and their preference ranking will not wash: certainly not now, and not even in Hutcheson's day. It is true that there was a time when the fifth, octave, and unison were considered the only consonant intervals, and the third, a dissonance. But that time was long past when Hutcheson was writing. Indeed, the third was basic to the music of Hutcheson's era, and (to look ahead a few years), if Mozart's sister is to be trusted, the infant prodigy's first signs of talent were attempts to pick out the thirds on the harpsichord, clearly preferring them to the other, more arithmetically simple intervals. If Hutcheson had ever heard music based on the pure intervals of unison, octave, and fifth (for example, the organum of the Notre Dame school) he would have found it crude and "dissonant" in comparison with the music of 1725, rich in passages of parallel thirds. His own preference ranking would have favored music with an abundance of thirds; yet his own theory would predict a preference for music with an abundance of unisons, octaves, and fifths, the more "unified" intervals.

But Hutcheson saw that there must be more to the absolute

beauty of music than this. We do, after all, hear many patterns in sound; and we never *hear* the arithmetic ratios of unison, octave, and fifth at all. We can hear, for example, as Hutcheson points out, "a general *Unity* of Key, an *Uniformity* among the Parts in *Bars, Risings, Fallings, Closes,*" in other words, what we would call the formal aesthetic features of music. It is Hutcheson's view, as we have seen, that the idea of beauty is caused in us by *unity amidst variety*, either unperceived (as, for example, in the arithmetical proportions of sound waves), or perceived (as, for example, in the audible patterns of sound, like *"Unity* of Key"). Music, then, provides a paradigm case of this dualism. It also brings into focus what is so unsatisfactory about construing the relationship between the idea of beauty and the work of art as a causal one. Perhaps it *is* plausible to say that certain unperceived properties cause us to have aesthetic perceptions. But we surely would not want to say that the audible "large" formal features of music, like key or rhythm, cause us to have aesthetic perceptions. Rather, the perceiving of these *constitutes* our aesthetic perceptions.

The absolute beauty of architecture provides, for Hutcheson, further evidence that the basis of beauty is in *unity amidst variety*. And Hutcheson makes it clear that architecture serves here merely to exemplify what is universal to all of the fine arts. "As to the Works of Art, were we to run thro the various artificial Contrivances or Structures, we should find the Foundation of the [absolute] Beauty which appears in them, to be constantly some kind of *Uniformity,* or *Unity* of Proportion among the Parts and of each Part to the Whole."[28] Nor is the principle of *unity* merely characteristic of British, even Continental, taste in art. Thus, Hutcheson writes of architecture:

> In that kind of Architecture which the EUROPEANS call *Regular,* the *Uniformity* of Parts is very obvious, the several Parts are *regular Figures,* and either *equal* or *similar* at least in the same Range .... And tho other Countrys do not follow the *Grecian* or *Roman* Proportions; yet there is even among them a Proportion retained, a *Uniformity,* and Resemblance of corresponding Figures; and every Deviation in one part from that Proportion which is observ'd in

the rest of the Building, is displeasing to every Eye, and destroys
or diminishes at least the *Beauty* of the Whole.[29]

Architecture, and the other visual arts, as well as literature,
do not provide the ready analogy with secondary qualities
which music does. Yet if Hutcheson had been familiar with
some of the Renaissance writers on architecture, he might have
attempted, as they had done, to relate the architectural forms
with the proportions of the consonant musical intervals.[30] But
in his discussion of the absolute beauty of Architecture, and, we
must assume, in his thinking about all of the other arts (with, of
course, the exception of music), Hutcheson dealt with *unity
amidst variety* as a relation holding only between macroscopic
proportions. Nevertheless, we cannot, even here, think of these
properties as constituting our aesthetic perceptions. Rather, we
must treat them, as we have seen before, as the *causes* of our
aesthetic perceptions, if we are to be faithful to Hutcheson's
teaching. As such, however, they can be either conscious or
unconscious. That is, the man whose idea of beauty is being
caused by *unity amidst variety* may or may not be aware of the
unity amidst variety; and may or may not be aware that it is the
cause of his idea. Unfortunately, Hutcheson never made explicit
the distinction between *unity amidst variety* as a cause and as a
constitutive feature of our aesthetic perceptions. As we shall
see, this chicken came home to roost when the rationalists criticized his theory, although they scarcely were more clear about
it.

(9) We can conveniently subdivide Hutcheson's treatment of
the nonformal in art into those nonformal elements that are
appropriate to the "aesthetic" senses and those that are appropriate to the "nonaesthetic" ones. And for all practical purposes
this comes down to a subdivision between those elements appropriate to the sense of relative beauty (or imitation) and
those appropriate to the moral sense.

In discussing relative beauty, Hutcheson mentions but two of
the fine arts: painting and poetry. Of painting he has little to
say, perhaps because in his eyes painting is so obviously the

paradigm case of imitative art that it requires no lengthy argument to establish the fact. In spite of his formalistic bent, he is as far from Clive Bell as Hogarth from Cezanne.

In regard to poetry, Hutcheson is somewhat more lavish with his comments. But the thrust is basically the same; art imitates nature: "The same Observation holds true in the Descriptions of the Poets either of *natural* Objects or Persons; and this *relative Beauty* is what they shou'd principally endeavour to obtain, as the peculiar *Beauty* of their Works." [31]

Two points are worth making with regard to Hutcheson's treatment of imitation (i.e., relative beauty) in the arts. The first has been made before, but is worth especially emphasizing. For Hutcheson, the content of art is, in a certain sense, purely formal. We do not find Dürer's portrait of his aged mother beautiful because of any significance that we attach to the subject matter: motherhood, age, humanity, or anything else of the kind. It is beautiful because of a formal relationship that holds between the painting and Dürer's mother, or our idea of what such a person as Dürer's mother might look like. Because there is a unity, an isomorphism between Dürer's mother, or our idea of her, and Dürer's picture, our sense of beauty responds, just as it would to the formal unity of any nonobjective pattern or design. From the purely aesthetic point of view, then, there is nothing to choose between Dürer's picture of his mother and Harnett's pheasants and fruits. For both fulfill — the latter perhaps even more satisfactorily — the formal requirement of unity which must hold between the object of imitation and the object imitated. And so, for all of his talk of imitation in art, Hutcheson in a peculiar sense remains a formalist in principle; and content, as we understand it, is for him peculiarly irrelevant.

The second point that deserves notice concerns the role of morality in art. It is an odd thing to find a moralist encouraging the representation of the immoral in art. But this is exactly what we find Hutcheson doing in the name of greater realism. For, after all, we live in what even a Leibnizian must admit *appears* to be an immoral world, or, at least, a world in which the immoral appears to have more than just a supporting role. And were the artist to make his world too morally perfect, it would be a poor representation of the real one. Therefore

> [A] Poet should not out of choice draw the *Finest Characters*
> possible for *Virtue;* these Characters indeed abstractly consider'd
> might give more Pleasure [to the moral sense], and have more
> *Beauty* than the *imperfect* ones which occur in Life with a mix-
> ture of Good and Evil: But it may suffice at present to suggest
> against this Choice, that we have more lively Ideas of *imperfect*
> *Men* with all their Passions, than of *morally perfect Heroes,* such
> as really never occur to our own Observation; and of which con-
> sequently we cannot judge exactly as to their Agreement with the
> Copy. And further, thro Consciousness of our own State, we are
> more nearly touch'd and affected by the *imperfect Characters;*
> since in them we see represented, in the Persons of others, the
> *Contrasts* of Inclinations, and the *Struggles* between the Passions
> of *Self-Love* and those of *Honour* and *Virtue,* which we often feel
> in our own Breasts. [32]

Hutcheson seems to portray here a kind of dilemma which
the artist must juggle in his representations. If he chooses to
gratify the moral sense, and does so by presenting an excess of
virtue, then the sense of beauty will be offended by the lack of
realism. If, on the other hand, he panders to the sense of beauty
wholly, the result may well be so offensive to the moral sense as
to make for an equally unpalatable extreme. Nor can this dilemma be represented wholly as one with the aesthetic on one horn
and the nonaesthetic on the other, for Hutcheson is not altogether free of Shaftesbury's tendency to blur the distinction
between the aesthetic and the moral. Notice that a *virtuous*
character is described by Hutcheson interchangeably as a *beautiful* one. Is the artist not, then, on Hutcheson's view, making an
aesthetic judgment when he considers the effects his characters
will have on the *moral* sense of his audience?

It should be remarked, too, in reference to the passage just
quoted, that Hutcheson's notion of realism might better be described as a notion of *credibility;* in art the realistic is the believable, and the believable is the verifiable. The artist must depict
what his audience has experienced. Otherwise, the audience cannot make a judgment of its realism, for it cannot make a comparison of the object imitated with the object of imitation.

Artistic realism for Hutcheson, then, must be relative to the experience of the perceiver: a position which is quite in line with the most recent writings on the subject of representation by such as E. H. Gombrich and Nelson Goodman.

(10) It is appropriate that we terminate our discussion of Hutcheson's reflections on art by returning again to his musical views; appropriate at least in the way a Beethoven coda is: introducing new and slightly discordant material, not altogether integrated with what has gone before. For Hutcheson introduces into his observations on music what to him, and his age, was a commonplace, but what, if not inconsistent with his general aesthetic theory, is certainly not provided for by it.

Hutcheson's major aesthetic category, the beautiful, is subdivided, as we have seen, into two major divisions: *absolute* and *relative*. Consistency demands that each of the fine arts reflect this dichotomy. With regard to absolute beauty, this demand is readily satisfied. For each of the fine arts is realized in some perceptual medium or other. And every such medium is susceptible of being organized in a pattern that exhibits to the perceiver *unity amidst variety* — the prerequisite for absolute beauty. In respect to relative beauty, however, the situation is problematical. For music resists any obvious treatment in imitative or representational terms. How can music be brought into line with the rest of the fine arts? This must be a problem for any representative interpretation of art.

Three alternatives were current in the literature when Hutcheson wrote the first *Inquiry*. I shall call them the *imitative* theory, the *representational* theory, and the *arousal* theory.

If we take painting as our paradigm case of an *imitative* art, we can express the relation between art and its object as one of *resemblance*. The portrait of Dürer's mother resembles, looks like, Dürer's mother. If music is imitative in this sense, it must resemble, *sound* like, its object.[33] For example, the flute obligatto in Handel's aria "Sweet bird that shuns't the noise of folly" quite literally sounds like a bird's song.

By *representation* is meant something more general of which *resemblance* is a special case. A symbol need not, and indeed in some cases cannot, resemble its object of *representation*. Music can *resemble* only what is heard. It may, however, *represent* what is perceived by some sense other than the sense of hearing. Thus, for example, Bach *represents* the Christian "following" Jesus (in the *St. John Passion*) with a canonic phrase in which the flute "follows" the singer. And, I have argued elsewhere, it was the view of a contemporary of Hutcheson's and Bach's, Johann Mattheson, that music *represents* the passions of the soul, that is, the emotions, by presenting an isomorphic structure — a view that anticipates, in certain crucial respects, the more recent theories of Carrol Pratt and Susanne Langer.[34]

But, finally, the connection between music and the emotions was more often expressed, in Hutcheson's day, as a causal one. Music was thought of as able not merely to represent the emotions, but thereby to *arouse* the emotions represented in the listener. "What passion cannot Music raise and quell?" Dryden asked in the *Ode for St. Cecilia's Day*. His answer, and the answer of many others in Hutcheson's day, was "None."

There were three options with regard to musical "content" that his age left open to him, and Hutcheson might easily have absorbed either of the first two into his general theory. Music-as-imitation would, of course, have received the same treatment as was given the visual arts. And music-as-representation would surely have been close to Hutcheson's treatment of literature, which after all is imitative only in a very loose sense. What Hutcheson was really maintaining was not that literature is imitation, but that it is representation. A description in a poem does not literally resemble what it describes. Hutcheson might have maintained the same for music. But he did not.

Oddly enough, Hutcheson plumped for the one theory of musical content that his position was not prepared to accommodate — the *arousal* theory. He wrote, on this regard,

> There is also another Charm in *Musick* to various Persons, which is distinct from the *Harmony,* and is occasion'd by its raising agreeable Passions. The *human Voice* is obviously vary'd by all the stronger Passions; now when our *Ear* discerns any resemblance between the *Air* of a *Tune,* whether sung or play'd upon an Instrument, either in its *Time* or *Key,* or any other Circumstance, to the

sound of the *human Voice* in any Passion, we shall be touch'd by
it in a very sensible manner, and have *Melancholy, Joy, Gravity,
Thoughtfulness* excited in us by a sort of *Sympathy* or *Conta-
gion.*[35]

During the eighteenth century the arousal theory of musical
expression usually comprised two basic premises: (i) music in
some way either resembles or represents some entity which ordinarily arouses emotions in human beings; and (ii) therefore,
music is also capable of arousing emotions in human beings. In
later eighteenth-century Britain (in Daniel Webb's *Observations
on the Correspondence Between Poetry and Music,* for example) music was thought of as isomorphic with something like
Descartes' *esprit animaux,* the physiological cause of the emotions. Hutcheson here has adopted an earlier version of the
arousal theory, dating back at least to the Florentine *Camerata,*
in which the rise and fall of the melodic line is likened to the
rise and fall of the human voice in impassioned speech.[36] Since
the human voice is able to arouse emotions in human beings, so
too, it is argued, can music, through this averred affinity of
melody to speech.

Had Hutcheson adopted only the first premise of this theory
(as Mattheson was to do with the later one), it would have
resulted in a purely representational theory of musical expression, completely compatible with his representational theory of
literature. But in adopting the second premise, he located the
"content" of music in its ability to arouse emotions in the
perceiver. And we find no hint in Hutcheson as to *why* the
arousal of emotions should be of any aesthetic significance; nor
does there seem to be any facet of his aesthetic theory which
promises help in this direction. Among Hutcheson's contemporaries, DuBos, Hume, and Burke, most notably had evolved
explanations of how the arousal of emotions can result in an
aesthetic experience. There is no hint of such an explanation in
Hutcheson.

VI

GOD AND AESTHETICS

(1)About one-third of Hutcheson's first *Inquiry* is taken up with theological topics: the existence of God, and the theological underpinnings of aesthetic perception. If sheer bulk is any measure of intellectual interest, then we must conclude that for Hutcheson the most interesting and compelling aesthetic problems were theological ones. But for us, alas, they are the least likely to arouse curiosity of any other kind than the antiquarian. I shall not, therefore, devote anywhere near the space to Divine speculations in my book that Hutcheson devotes to them in his. For the judgment of history is that what Hutcheson had to offer to philosophy in general, and aesthetics in particular, did not that way tend.

Hutcheson raised three questions which fall under the head of aesthetic theology: (i) To what extent does the fact of aesthetic perception (as Hutcheson construes it) provide evidence for the existence of God? (ii) What *other* evidence can be adduced for the existence of God? (iii) What is the final cause of the aesthetic sense (or senses)? The first two questions are answered by appeal to what we call the argument from (or to) design, and comprise Section V of the first *Inquiry:* "Concerning our Reasonings about *Design* and *Wisdom* in the *Cause,* from the *Beauty* or *Regularity* of *Effects.*" The third comprises Section VIII, the concluding one: "Of the *Importance* of the *internal Senses* in Life, and the *final Causes* of them."

(2) Hutcheson placed little stock in the a priori proofs of the existence of God available to him, either the ontological and

causal proofs of Descartes, or those of his countryman Samuel
Clarke. Of the former, he wrote, "I do not use the Cartesian
arguments, [which are] obviously full of manifest fallacies."[1]
And of his attitude to the latter, his first biographer, the Rever-
end William Leechman tells us:

> Tho' he most heartily approv'd of the Doctor's conclusions, and
> had the highest sense of his singular abilities and virtues, yet after
> the most serious and attentive consideration of his arguments, he
> did not find that conviction from them which he wished and
> expected . . . . After all the enquiry he could make, he still con-
> tinued extremely doubtful of the justness and force of all the
> metaphysical arguments, by which many have endeavoured to
> demonstrate the existence, unity, and perfections of the
> Deity . . . . It was his opinion in this early part of his life, and he
> never saw cause to alter it, that as some subjects from their nature
> are capable of demonstrative evidence, so others admit only of a
> probable one . . . .[2]

Given this aversion to a priori arguments, it is not surprising
that Hutcheson should turn to the most popular (or soon to be)
a posteriori proof, the backbone of Natural Religion in the
eighteenth century. I shall consider two versions of that argument here: one an aesthetic version, claiming that the aesthetic
nature of the universe demands a rational cause (i.e., God); the
other a nonaesthetic version, claiming that the regularity of the
universe demands such a cause. As we shall see presently, the
former is simply a special case of the latter. Let us determine
first, then, why Hutcheson believes that an aesthetic universe
demands a rational creator.

(3) It is, as we have seen, a purely contingent matter of fact
that certain arrangements of primary and/or secondary qualities — namely, the arrangements exhibiting *uniformity amidst
variety* - would be called beautiful by us. For they are called
beautiful in virtue of their *causing* us to have a certain kind of
pleasurable feeling; and it is a contingent matter of fact that
these particular arrangements, and not some other, cause this
feeling (and not some other, or no feeling at all). "There
seems," Hutcheson says, "to be no necessary Connection of our

pleasing Ideas of *Beauty* with the *Uniformity* or *Regularity* of
the objects, from the Nature of things, antecedently to some
Constitution of the AUTHOR of our Nature, which has made
such Forms pleasant to us."[3]

Let us suppose, now, that there is no rational cause of the
universe; or, as Hutcheson would put it, let us suppose that the
universe is the result merely of "undirected" or "undesigning"
force, "That Force with which an Agent may put Matter into
Motion, without having any Design of Intention to produce any
particular Form."[4] But that is equivalent, Hutcheson believes, to
saying that the state of the universe is the result of "chance."
And if this were indeed the case, it is extremely unlikely (the
chance is close to zero) that we would be so constituted, and so
situated, that our aesthetic nature would match our surroundings in such a way as to enable us to get pleasure from them,
considering the perhaps infinitely large number of ways we
might have been constituted aesthetically, and the equally large
number of possible situations we might have found ourselves in.
As Hutcheson puts the case:

> But then, as there are an Infinity of *Places* in which Animals may
> be situated, and an Infinity of *Relishes* or *Senses* is suppos'd pos-
> sible; that in the immense Spaces any one Animal should by
> Chance be plac'd in a System agreeable to its Taste, must be
> improbable as *infinite* to *one* at least: And much more unreason-
> able is it to expect from Chance, that a multitude of Animals
> agreeing in their Sense of *Beauty* should obtain *agreeable Places*.[5]

In other words, the only explanation for the congruence of
our taste with our environment that is probable enough to com-
mand assent is an explanation in terms of a rational agent who
fashioned this congruence. Our aesthetic situation, then, is best
explained by the hypothesis of a designing cause; that is, God.

Now what first must occur to any modern reader is that there
is no improbability at all in supposing an organism to be suited
to its environment, aesthetic or otherwise. We call this *adaptation,* and we have a scientific theory — Darwin's theory of evolution— to account for it, if not in every detail, at least in some
kind of generally accepted schema. *Of course* there may be an

infinite number of environments in which we (or our ancestors) might have found themselves. And in any one of them, we (or whatever creatures, if any, evolved there) would, by the process of natural selection, have become adapted to them, if they were suited to life in the first place. We may seem to be "made" for our surroundings; but we accept that this is as illusory as the "rising" and "setting" of the sun, both illusions having been dispelled by suitable scientific theories.

The thrust of the argument here is not to hold Hutcheson responsible for the impossible. No one supposes that he, in 1725, could have foreseen Darwinism or anything like it. Even Darwin trembled at the thought of the human eye. And a far more powerful intellect than Hutcheson, closer to the event, averred, "we may confidently assert that it is absurd for men . . . to hope that maybe another Newton may some day arise, to make intelligible to us even the genesis of but a blade of grass from natural laws that no design has ordered."[6] But Kant drew a more modest conclusion than Hutcheson: not that no natural explanation exists, merely that we can never know what it is.

> But, then, are we to think that a source of the possibility of organized beings amply sufficient to explain their origin without having recourse to a design, *could* never be found buried among the secrets even of nature, were we able to penetrate to the principle upon which it specifies its familiar laws? This, in its turn, would be a presumptuous judgement on our part. . . . On the question, therefore, whether or not any being acting designedly stands behind what we properly term physical ends, as a world cause, and consequently, as Author of the world, we can pass no objective judgement whatever, be it affirmative or negative.[7]

Hutcheson is guilty here of using the argument from design to produce what Antony Flew calls a "God of the Gaps"; that is, a theological explanation for what the theologian confidently predicts science cannot compass.[8] But that is immediately to lay the argument open to the perfectly just reply of Kant that such a judgment is presumptuous. The argument from design must concern itself with the explanation of but one unique event: the universe, governed internally by natural laws.

It should be remarked that Hutcheson himself was not completely unaware of the God of the Gaps fallacy. For in discussing the forming of crystals out of solution, he took note of the fact that the patterns into which the crystals form are adequately explained by accepted scientific theories. Here "we frequently see *regular Forms* arising, tho there is nothing in this Affair but an *undirected* Force of *Attraction* suppos'd."⁹ In other words, here is a pattern, a design in nature which can be explained without any appeal to the Deity. But this explanation itself must be in terms of more basic regularities: for "unless we suppose some preceding *Regularity* in the Figures of *attracting* Bodys, they shall never form any regular Body at all." Ultimately we will arrive at the basic system of natural laws which we see as characterizing our universe in the large. And then we will ask the question (if we wish to generate the argument from design): What caused this regular, law-governed universe? The reply of the Butlers and Paleys is, of course: Nothing could have caused such a state of affairs but a rational agent. Here we have the argument from design in its proper and strongest form.

(4) Hutcheson's various attempts to state the argument from design in the first *Inquiry* never do, in fact, really escape the God of the Gaps. For in each case, we can now point to a possible, if not an adequate, scientific explanation for what Hutcheson claimed could be the result of divine decree only. Thus, to examine them with a view to conviction is about as sensible as inviting a dead man to play chess. But as Hutcheson did place so much confidence in them, we should at least go through the ritual of setting one up and knocking it down.

Perhaps the closest Hutcheson comes to escaping the God of the Gaps and producing the classical argument from design is the following, in which he asks us to consider this example: "*a Pair of Wheels* of our ordinary Carriages; each *Circular, Spokes* equal in *length, thickness, shape; the Wheels* set *Parallel,* the *Axle-tree* fix'd in the *Nave* of both, and secur'd from coming out at either end . . . ."¹⁰ That this mechanism, simple though it is, could have been formed by "*undirected Concourses,*" we all believe so unlikely as to be not worthy of serious consideration. Wagon wheels, in our experience, are always the product of wheelwrights, not the winds and the tides. Hutcheson concludes: "What shall we say then of a *Plant*, a *Tree*, an *Animal*, a *Man*, with *such multitudes* of adapted Vessels, *such Articulations, Insertions* of *Muscles, Diffusions* of *Veins, Arterys, Nerves:* The *Improbability* that such Machines should be the Effect of *Chance* must be near the *infinitesimal* Power of *Infinite* to *Unity.*"

Clearly, the argument will have no appeal to anyone armed with the principle of natural selection. It could have been advanced only in an age when adaptation had no satisfactory explanation in terms of natural law. But that reveals again the God of the Gaps in Hutcheson's design argument. Of course, it is highly improbable that the various adaptive features of life could have evolved in a universe governed only by the natural laws known to Hutcheson's age, in the absence, that is, of biological laws, just as it is highly unlikely that a wagon wheel could be formed by the winds and the tides. However, this makes God a substitute for biological explanations, under the tacit assumption that such explanations are in principle impossible: an assumption we now have good reason to believe is false, or at least doubtful.

But although Hutcheson again falls here into the weakest form of the design argument, he is just a step away from the less palled version, "Paley's Watch" and the argument from design as formulated by Cleanthes in the *Dialogues Concerning Natural Religion.* The beginning is there. A wagon wheel is made by a rational agent: this we know by experience. But it is not to a plant or an animal, or a part of one or another of them, that the wagon wheel must be compared: rather, to the universe as a whole. Thus Cleanthes:

> Look round the world: contemplate the whole and every part of it: You will find it to be nothing but one great machine, subdivided into an infinite number of lesser machines, which again admit of subdivision to a degree beyond what human senses and faculties can trace and explain. All these various machines, and even their most minute parts, are adjusted to each other with an accuracy, which ravishes into admiration all men who have ever

contemplated them. The curious adapting of means to ends, throughout all nature, resembles exactly, though it much exceeds, the productions of human contrivance; of human design, thought, wisdom, and intelligence. Since therefore the effects resemble each other, we are led to infer, by all the rules of analogy, that the causes also resemble; and that the Author of Nature is somewhat similar to the mind of a man; though possessed of much larger faculties, proportioned to the grandeur of the work which he has executed. [11]

Now there is even in Cleanthes' refined argument a suggestion that the individual adaptations themselves require a theological explanation. But the general thrust of the argument is that the universe, viewed as a whole, is the object in need of a rational causal agent, by analogy with the machines which we all know were made by men and not by the unaided forces of nature: for the world is "nothing but one great machine"; and machines, as we all know from experience, are made by mechanics.

The universe, then, to the extent that it is like a watch or a wagon wheel, must have a cause similar to the watchmaker or the wheelwright. But, as Philo warns us, the argument from analogy is a dangerous one: it may indeed be true "that similar causes prove similar effects, and similar effects similar causes . . . . " But "Unless the cases be exactly similar, they repose no perfect confidence in applying their past observation to any particular phenomenon." [12] Yes, the cause of the universe is about as much like a wheelwright as the universe is like a wheel. We *all* can accept *that* with confidence, Lucretius and Marx, as well as Paley and Butler. A pre-Humean argument from design, or one that has not at least taken Hume's criticisms seriously, is very like a pre-war washing machine — quaint, but badly in need of overhauling.

(5) It is not my intention here to heap ridicule upon Hutcheson's theological views, but merely to call a spade a spade. Clearer heads than his have been knocked by Hume. Suffice it to say: Hutcheson believed in God. That he believed in God on insufficient grounds is not really to our purpose. The point is that he thought the existence of God has important conse-

quences for aesthetics. We must now examine what these consequences are.

Hutcheson saw the aesthetic senses as part of a teleological
system, under the direction, and the work of a wise and good
Governor. The wisdom and goodness of God are, along, of
course, with his existence, premises necessary for a satisfactory
explanation of aesthetic experience. But another seems to be
necessary as well: the assumption that the Deity works in the
most economical way possible (or else, that working in the most
economical way possible is part of acting wisely, even in an
omnipotent being). Armed with these premises, Hutcheson pro-
poses to discover (i) " . . . Reasons worthy of the Great
AUTHOR of *Nature* for making such a Connection between
regular Objects, and the Pleasure which accompanies our Perceptions of them . . . "; and (ii) "what Reasons might possibly
influence him to create the *World* as it at present is, as far as we
can observe, every where full of *Regularity* and *Uniformity*."[13]

We can now build up a case for God's endowing us with
aesthetic senses that derive pleasure from the perception of *uniformity amidst variety*. First, for creatures of limited, finite
intelligence and capabilities, universal generalizations, from
which specific statements can be deduced, are the most useful
form of knowledge, because, according to Hutcheson, "this pre-
vents Distractions in their Understandings thro the Multiplicity
of Propositions, and Toil and Weariness to their Powers of Action: and consequently their *Reason,* without any *Sense* of
Beauty, must approve of such Methods when they reflect upon
their apparent *Advantage*."[14] (Why God did not simply make us
less prone to weariness and distractions, which he could certainly have done without tampering with our finitude, Hutcheson
does not reveal.)

Second, objects that possess *uniformity amidst variety* "are
more distinctly and easily comprehended and retain'd, than *irregular Objects;* because the accurate Observation of one or two
Parts often leads to the Knowledge of the Whole. . . . "[15] That
the aesthetic pleasure we derive from well-proportioned objects
is due somehow to their being well adapted to our perceptual
faculties and, therefore, easily perceived is an old and oft-re-

peated claim. Descartes thought that a happy medium between the difficult and the easy must be struck; and he wrote in the *Compendium Musicae:*

> Among the sense-objects the most agreeable to the soul is neither that which is perceived most easily nor that which is perceived with the greatest difficulty; it is that which does not quite gratify the natural desire by which the senses are carried to the objects, yet is not so complicated that it tires the senses.[16]

And Spinoza states:

> When phenomena are of such a kind that the impression they make on our senses requires little effort of imagination, and can consequently be easily remembered, we say they are *well-ordered;* if the contrary, they are *ill-ordered* or *confused.* Further, as things which are easily imagined are more pleasing to the mind, men prefer order to confusion.[17]

But Hutcheson is not *explaining* the pleasure we take in the aesthetic here in terms of ease of perception. He would, in fact, have considered such an explanation illegitimate. For he has, after all, been arguing throughout against reductionism in ethics and aesthetics. Aesthetic perception is *sui generis;* that is the point of appealing to aesthetic senses. Hutcheson's motto might well be: "Everything is what it is, and not another thing." The pleasure we take in easy perception or conception is one thing; and the pleasure of beauty is quite another. What Hutcheson is maintaining, then, is that it is in the interest of a finite mind to seek objects that possess *uniformity amidst variety* because "it must be a long Attention to a vast Multiplicity of Parts, which can ascertain or fix the Idea of any *irregular Form,* or give any distinct Idea of it, or make us capable of retaining it . . . . "[18] (Again, Hutcheson gives us no explanation of why God chose this method of doing things. He could, after all, have made us a little less "finite." But perhaps this is the most economical way: the way that gets the most out of a given level of finitude, assuming that that level of finitude is required for other reasons.)

We are now in a position to explain why God implanted aesthetic senses in us. It is because he saw that we would be better off if our aesthetic preferences pointed in the same direction as our utilitarian ones. God, of course, could have chosen not to give us any aesthetic pleasures at all. But "supposing the Deity so kind as to connect *sensible Pleasure* with certain Actions or Contemplations, beside the *rational Advantage* perceived in them . . . , " it would have been a very bad arrangement indeed, Hutcheson thinks, to have our rational desires make us prefer objects and propositions that possess *uniformity amidst variety,* and to have our aesthetic desires be, say, for the completely disordered. For, in that case,

> . . . *Reason* and *Interest* would lead us to simple *general Causes,* while a *contrary Sense* of *Beauty* would make us disapprove them: *Universal Theorems* would appear to our Understanding the best Means of increasing our Knowledge of what might be useful; while a *contrary Sense* would set us on the search after *singular Truths: Thought* and *Reflection* would recommend Objects with *Uniformity amidst Variety,* and yet this *perverse Instinct* would involve us in Labyrinths of *Confusion* and *Dissimilitude.*[19]

In short, two parts of our nature would be at cross-purposes. To Hutcheson, who no less than Kant, saw the human faculties as constituting a harmonious teleological system, such a situation would have been unthinkable, more unthinkable still as a product of omnipotence and goodness. (One could, I suppose, reply to this that the aesthetic sense, just because it points in the same direction as utility, works at cross-purposes by being a distracting influence. Hutcheson himself avers that we often *confuse* aesthetic with rational interest. And the former can often be distracting, rather than helpful, to the latter.)

One further aspect of our aesthetic situation remains to be given its theological foundation. And that is the aesthetic richness of our surroundings, particularly the fact that the universe is governed by natural laws, all of which give aesthetic pleasure but not all of which are particularly useful to us. The question, then, arises, Why did God see fit to fill the universe with so much order and design when far less would have sufficed for the *needs* of men? As Hutcheson puts the question: "What Reason might influence the DEITY, whom no Diversitys of Operation could distract or weary, to chuse to operate by *simplest Means* and *general Laws,* and to diffuse *Uniformity, Proportion* and *Similitude* thro all the Parts of *Nature* which we can observe . . . ?"[20] He answers:

> [S]ince the *divine Goodness,* for the Reasons above mention'd, has constituted our *Sense* of *Beauty* as it is at present, the same *Goodness* might determine the *Great* ARCHITECT to adorn this *vast Theatre* in that manner which should be agreeable to the Spectators, and that part which is expos'd to the Observation of Men, so as to be pleasant to them . . . .

In other words, in for a penny, in for a pound.

Hutcheson's theology has just about run out of gas here. We are the way we are, and our world is the way it is, because God wishes to please us. Why does he not please us more? Why did he make London slums as well as Kew Gardens? Hutcheson cannot tell us. But who can? Aesthetics has run afoul of the problem of evil; and nothing more can be said that has not been said before.

(6) Hutcheson, more than any other philosopher of his time, was responsible for setting aesthetics on its way as a philosophical discipline. There is perhaps nothing we can point to and say: "Hutcheson was the *first.*" But he put it all together. There is no philosophical work of the day that treats the problems we now think of as constituting philosophical aesthetics in greater depth or at greater length than the *Inquiry Concerning Beauty.* More important still, Hutcheson recognized what the new wave in philosophy was to be, in his lifetime, and clothed his aesthetics in the new and durable cloth. He was, in a way, Locke's aesthetic half; and thus he provided for the heirs of Locke's empiricism the aesthetic dimension that Locke himself so manifestly lacked. Even, then, if his ideas came to nothing (which I do not believe for a moment), Hutcheson, by wedding the poor relation of philosophy to a man of distinction, made her at least respectable, if not always the apple of philosophy's eye.

What specifically was Hutcheson's accomplishment? The concept of an aesthetic sense, which Hutcheson, more than anyone
else, was responsible for forming, "gave to criticism an experi-
ential emphasis."[21] But more than this, it played a vital role in
the forming of aesthetic philosophy as we know it today. The
sense of beauty was instrumental in the evolution of aesthetics
as an autonomous discipline. What Ernst Cassirer has referred to
as "the leveling and blunting process which Shaftesbury's
thoughts suffer at the hands of Hutcheson,"[22] is, on the contrary, a process of winnowing and purifying which transformed
a philosophical miscellany into a systematic argument.

Jerome Stolnitz has argued — and rightly, I believe — that "it
is the British who first conceive of the aesthetic as a unique
mode of experience and carry out its systematic investigation."[23] And it is through the concept of "aesthetic disinterestedness," he claims, that aesthetics gained its autonomy:

> [T] he crucial point is that disinterestedness is peculiar to one kind
> of experience. Because the experience is disinterested, it is signifi-
> cantly different from such other experiences as garden variety
> perception or moral activity or theoretical inquiry. The concepts
> which are adequate for the study of these activities will not do for
> it. It must be studied in its own right. This is what aesthetics can
> call its own. Ultimately the subject-matter of aesthetics is taken to
> be the experience of disinterested perception and the nature and
> value of its objects.[24]

Aesthetics became an autonomous discipline when it had
marked out for itself a unique realm of experience; and "disinterestedness" is the means by which that experience was so
marked. This, I think, is a sound historical argument; but a link
in the chain of explanation is missing: that link is the sense of
beauty. The first step is the realization that beauty *is* an autonomous segment of experience, not reducible to any other. This
realization, however vague, is expressed in the concept of an
aesthetic sense: because the experience of the beautiful is a
unique experience, it must have a unique sense appropriate to
it. What the identifying mark of that experience is, the concept

of aesthetic disinterestedness reveals. But *that* such a separate realm of experience exists is made manifest by Hutcheson's sense of beauty.

Disinterestedness has, of course, turned out to be the more fruitful concept in our own day and in the recent past. But the historical importance of an idea cannot be measured only by its ability to survive. The sense of beauty as Hutcheson thought of it may not be a real option for twentieth-century aesthetics, whereas "aesthetic disinterestedness" has become for many, in one form or another, something like an axiom. Yet perhaps aesthetics owes as much, or more, to the former idea as to the latter.

Viewed in the light of this progressive aesthetic empiricism, Hutcheson's aesthetic theology seems like deplorable backsliding to me; and I have not been able to disguise my impatience with it. Sometimes a great theologian can make us feel, for a moment, that he was present at the creation. Hutcheson, alas, sounds, at best, like an eavesdropper.

Perhaps that is too hard a judgment, though. For there is, after all, much to admire in Hutcheson's attempt to provide an empirical grounding for ethics and aesthetics, while at the same time rejecting the example of Hobbes. He set himself, we can see by hindsight, an enormous task, and one that we still think it worthwhile to work at. It is not so surprising that he sometimes faltered, and grabbed instinctively at the Almighty for support.

PART II

HUTCHESON – AND SHORTLY THEREAFTER

"To multiply principles for every different appearance is useless, and unphilosophical too in a high degree."

Edmund Burke

VII

RATIONALIST AESTHETICS
IN THE AGE OF HUTCHESON

(1) In these remaining chapters I intend to trace the main theme of Hutcheson's first *Inquiry* — the sense of beauty — as it worked itself out in eighteenth-century Britain. The theme, however, is a complex one, with many variations and counter-points. And I am under no illusion that I trace them all. (Indeed, they are not all of them worth tracing.) Rather, I have been highly selective in my choice of subjects. This may reflect, to some extent at least, my own bias. But I hope (and believe) that it reflects, too, a fairly defensible judgment as to what was philosophically important in the reverberations which Hutcheson's aesthetic theory set up.

(2) In Britain, the moralists of the early eighteenth century were both united and divided: united against a common enemy and divided as to the conduct of the war. The enemy, of course, was Hobbes: "Throughout the seventeenth and the first years of the eighteenth century he represented the evil principle to moralists as well as to theologians."[1] But with what weapon was the Hobbesian egoism to be dispatched? Here the lines were sharply drawn. *Sentiment,* answered Hutcheson and his followers: we approve benevolence as we savor the sweet. *Reason,* countered Clarke, Balguy, and Price: the understanding tells us what is right and what wrong as surely as it tells us what is true and what false.

The dialogue between reason and feeling in Enlightenment aesthetics did not, at least during the first half of the eighteenth

century, possess the incisiveness of the analogous moral dispute.
Not as much, after all, was at stake, and there was, therefore,
more inclination toward compromise. The upholders of reason
in morality were not by any means completely averse to a
"sentimental" aesthetics. And the "rational" side of the dispute
was not as well represented on the philosophical level. For although the "sentimentalist" philosophers, notably Hutcheson
and Hume, took a good deal of interest in aesthetics and criticism, the rationalists did not. Nevertheless, aesthetic questions
did creep into the rationalists' writings on morality if only because of their opponents' concern with them; and these questions are important ones: they were to influence in no small
degree the future course of aesthetic theory in eighteenth-
century Britain, and on the Continent as well.

I am going to consider here three rationalist critics of the
moral sense school who also had something to say of a critical
nature about Hutcheson's (or Hutcheson-like) aesthetics. They
are John Balguy, Bishop Berkeley, and Richard Price. I use the
term "rationalist," however, with some caution; for although
Balguy and Price are clearly in the rationalist camp, Berkeley
did not write extensively enough on ethical questions for us to
know in any great detail what his views were.[2] But Berkeley
was a rationalist at least to the extent that he believed both the
Hobbists (notably Mandeville) and the moral sense theorists
(notably Shaftesbury) had undervalued the role of reason in
morality.

The position of Hutcheson and his followers has always been
acknowledged by historians of aesthetics, and rightly so; for,
with the possible exception of Baumgarten's work, it is the
most historically significant body of aesthetic thought that the
eighteenth century produced prior to Kant's *Critique of Judgment*. But the result of this just historical judgment has been to
throw the British rationalists completely into the shade and
thus distort our picture of early eighteenth-century British
aesthetics. It is my hope that the following three sketches will
help achieve a more balanced historical perspective — not, however, at the cost either of overestimating the rationalists or deni-
grating the importance of Hutcheson's accomplishment.

(3) John Balguy began as a rationalist with regard to the perception of moral goodness but as a reluctant follower of the aesthetic sense school — an attitude similar to that of another rationalist in Enlightenment morality, Kant, during the period of the first *Critique*.[3] Balguy based this "dualism" upon the contention that since there is universal agreement about what is good and what evil, but widespread disagreement about what is beautiful and what ugly, moral distinctions must be made by the understanding, whereas aesthetic judgments *may* require some such thing as a sense of beauty. Thus Balguy writes:

> *Virtue*, or moral Goodness, may be considered under the notion of *Pulchrum* or *Honestum*. As to the *Pulchrum* or *Beauty* of Virtue, it seems to me somewhat doubtful and difficult to determine, whether *Understanding* alone be sufficient for the perception of it, or whether it be not necessary to suppose some distinct Power superadded for that Purpose . . . . when I consider . . . that Perceptions of the *Pulchrum* and of the *Honestum*, seem not equally universal, or if universal, yet in very different Degrees; that while every rational Creature clearly and uniformly perceives, in all ordinary Cases, what is *fit*, and *just*, and *right;* many Men have little or no Perception of that *Beauty* in Actions, with which others are wonderfully charmed: And when I further consider, that some Actions appear to all Men more beautiful than others, tho' equally *right* and *fit;* . . . I find myself obliged to suspend, and wait for further Evidence.[4]

Even, of course, if Balguy were correct in his characterization of moral agreement and aesthetic disagreement, his conclusion would not follow: for agreement is not an infallible sign that the distinctions involved are rationally made, any more than disagreement is an infallible sign that the distinctions involved are not susceptible of a rational determination. In addition, it should be noted that the beauty he is talking about here is moral beauty, not the beauty of a flower or a poem. So what Balguy is saying is that, for example, there will be universal agreement with regard to such questions as whether the assassination of Caesar was right or wrong, but not as to whether it was a beautiful or an ugly action. All of which seems rather odd, since, one would think, when it was customary to refer to

actions as "beautiful" or "ugly" (in a moral sense), these terms
were synonymous with "right" and "wrong," or, at least, it was
logically impossible for an action to be "right" and "ugly," or
"wrong" and "beautiful." What, would we be disagreeing about,
one wonders, if I said that the assassination of Caesar was
"right" and "beautiful," and you said it was "right" and
"ugly"? About whether the knife strokes were gracefully executed? (I shall return to this question when I come to discuss
Price's views, for Price makes a similar point. I will then attempt
to answer it.)

Balguy's reluctance to subsume the perception of moral beauty under the reason was reinforced by what he took to be the
prominent role of pleasure in the experience of it. Pleasure, he
argued, must surely be perceived by sense, not intellect.

> For however *Ideas, beautiful* in themselves, may be *seen* by the
> Understanding, yet Pleasure is not seen, but *felt;* and therefore
> seems to be an Object of some other Faculty than that which we
> are used to consider as merely *visive.* If the purest Pleasures be
> *Sensations,* of some kind or other; the Mind in receiving them,
> must be looked upon, not as *intelligent,* but *sensible.* And indeed,
> Sensibility seems to be as distinct from the *Understanding* as the
> *Understanding* is from the *Will.* [5]

In *The Second Part of the Foundation of Moral Goodness*
(1729), Balguy spelled out his aesthetic position a little more
fully, this time with reference to natural beauty and art, not
merely moral beauty, and opted unequivocally for the aesthetics of sense perception.

> Between the Numbers 2, 8, 32, there is a real agreement of *Propor-*
> *tion*; and between the *Three Angles* of an *equilateral Triangle,* a
> real Agreement of Equality. Such Agreements essentially belong to
> the Ideas themselves, independently of the Faculty, and even of
> the Creator's Will. This is, in the most proper sense, *Truth*; and as
> such, can only be the Object of *Intelligence.* — Between a certain
> kind of *Food,* and a Man's Palate; between a certain *Prospect,* and
> his *Eye*; between a certain Combination of *Sounds,* and his *Ear*;
> there is only an arbitrary Agreement of the Object with the Facul-
> ty. For whatever *real Order,* or *Proportion* there may be among

the several Parts of complex sensible Objects; these, like all other
Relations, can only be apprehended by the *Understanding. Sense*
judges of nothing but its own Sensations. Hence we find an endless
Variety in Men's *Tastes* and *Fancies,* but not in their Understandings . . . . The Agreements between the *Numbers* and *Angles*
above-mentioned appear uniformly and universally the same, to all
Beings capable of understanding them. And the same may be said
of the Agreements between *Benefits* and *Gratitude,* and other
Moral Truths. In all such Cases the Agreements are not *relative* but
real, as being inherent in the Ideas themselves. A Power of perceiving these *real* Agreements I call *Intelligence;* a Power of perceiving the other, *Sense.* [6]

Balguy obviously wants to preserve some analogy between
aesthetic and moral qualities, despite the fact that the former
are perceived by sense and the latter by reason. Since he conceives of moral qualities as *relations* ("Agreements between
Benefits and *Gratitude,* and other *Moral Truths*"), it seems
natural that relations should find their way into his account of
aesthetic qualities as well. It would appear that aesthetic qualities, for Balguy, are to be thought of as relations, too: "an
arbitrary Agreement of the Object with the Faculty" of sense.
But this leads to difficulty.

If I "perceive" (feel) a pleasure upon hearing a C-major triad,
for example, there is, Balguy would say, a relation between the
triad and my sense of hearing — a relation which seems to have
for him the status of an aesthetic "quality." And, Balguy would
insist, that relation is perceived by sense, whereas the relation,
say, among the numbers 2, 8, and 32 is perceived by the understanding. Suppose we think of the aesthetic relation as "fitness-
for-giving-pleasure," or something of that kind. Do I *perceive*
such a relation when I feel the pleasure? Well, it is very much a
matter of what construction is put on the word "perceive."
Certainly I do not perceive that — I am not conscious that —
such a relation holds between the C-major triad and my sense of
hearing until I have reflected on the question; and that reflection is, I presume, as much an operation of intelligence or
understanding as is the perception of relations between numbers. One could experience pleasure from hearing C-major triads
without ever perceiving that there existed a relation of fitness

between such sounds and one's sense. On the other hand, if by "perceiving" a relation Balguy means something like "perceiving the result of a relation," then it is proper to say that the relation of "fitness-for-giving-pleasure," which obtains between the C-major triad and the sense of hearing, is perceived by sense. But this is certainly not what we ordinarily mean when we talk about perceiving qualities.

It is not without significance that the difficulty here involves the question of whether relations can or cannot be perceived by sensation. For it is just this question that Balguy puts to the aesthetic sense school in his next work, *Divine Rectitude* (1730). He has now come to the conclusion, on theological grounds which need not concern us, that aesthetic qualities are objective qualities; that is, they are not merely relations obtaining between some object and a faculty of sense, but between objects and qualities independent of senses or other faculties of perception. And he argues, they are objective relations for Hutcheson, too; namely, relations of *uniformity* to *variety*. Therefore, Balguy concludes, Hutcheson must be mistaken in ascribing the perception of the beautiful to an inner sense. The *"Grounds of Beauty,"* Balguy writes,

> . . . are not to be sought for among our *Senses*, or the *Agreements* between those *Senses*, and their respective *Objects*; but in the *Objects* themselves, and the *Relations* interceding between them. And by consequence that *Beauty* is of an *absolute* Nature, and a real, *objective Perfection*. The ingenious Author of the *Enquiry into the Original of our Ideas of Beauty and Virtue* [i.e., Hutcheson], tho' he professedly maintains the contrary Opinion, yet has nevertheless fixed Beauty on such a Foundation, as seems to me entirely inconsistent with his own Notion. For are not *Uniformity* and *Variety* real *Relations* belonging to the *Objects* themselves? Are they not independent on us, and our Faculties; and would they not be what they are, whether we perceived them or no? — And if they have no Dependence on any of our Faculties, much less on *Sense*: However Sense may convey to us the Ideas of external *Objects*, yet the Relations between them no *Sense* can reach. [7]

Balguy has obviously misunderstood Hutcheson's position here.

It is an instructive midunderstanding: but a misunderstanding nevertheless.

Hutcheson claims, as we have seen, that *uniformity amidst variety* causes us to have certain pleasurable feelings. He does not assert that we perceive *uniformity amidst variety* by the sense of beauty, or any other sense wholly, anymore than Locke would claim that we perceive with our eyes the atoms which cause us to have color-sensations. It is the feeling of beauty that we perceive by sense, not *uniformity amidst variety*. Reason finds out the *cause* of beauty, as it finds out the cause of color-sensation. We can indeed perceive *uniformity amidst variety* in a way we cannot perceive atoms. But Hutcheson, with perfect consistency, can claim that we perceive beauty by sense and *uniformity amidst variety,* the cause of beauty, in part by reason. One can perceive *uniformity amidst variety* without perceiving beauty, and beauty without perceiving *uniformity amidst variety*. They are not identical, as Balguy seems to think.

In what way, then, is Balguy's misreading of Hutcheson instructive? It suggests, I think, one of the places in which Hutcheson is drastically mistaken. Balguy has unconsciously assumed, in his misreading of Hutcheson, that *uniformity amidst variety* is an *aesthetic* quality, not merely the cause of one, as Hutcheson maintains. But here Balguy is entirely right and Hutcheson wrong. To perceive the world as possessing *uniformity amidst variety* is already to perceive it aesthetically: no further perception is needed to make it so. Nor is it the cause of beauty, as the properties of pepper are the cause of sneezing. The perceiving of *uniformity amidst variety* does not in its turn cause me to perceive beauty; it is, in part, constitutive of my aesthetic perception.

I shall revert to this subject again when we come to compare Hutcheson's position with Hume's in Chapter VIII. Suffice it to say now: Balguy's belief that aesthetic qualities are relational qualities and, by consequence, perceivable by reason only, provided the principal argument for Berkeley and Price in their subsequent attacks on the aesthetic sense doctrine.

(4) Berkeley chose Shaftesbury rather than Hutcheson as the representative of "sentimental" value theory and the butt of his criticism in the dialogue *Alciphron* (1732). T. E Jessop, co-editor of the definitive edition of Berkeley's philosophical works, remarks that Alciphron — the principal spokesman, in the dialogue, for the moral sense school — "faithfully outlines the philosophy of Shaftesbury," at least with regard to the perception of visual beauty.[8]

But just how faithful is the outline really, is a question well worth considering. Alciphron does indeed hold forth with what, at least on the surface, appears to be a plausible version of Shaftesbury:

> [T] here is an idea of Beauty natural to the mind of man. This all men desire, this they are pleased and delighted with for its own sake, purely from an instinct of nature. A man needs no arguments to make him discern and approve what is beautiful; it strikes at first sight, and attracts without reason. And as this beauty is found in the shape and form of corporeal things, so also is there analogous to it a beauty of another kind, an order, symmetry, and comeliness, in the moral world. As the eye perceiveth the one, so the mind doth, by a certain interior sense, perceive the other; which sense, talent, or faculty is ever quickest and purest in the noblest minds. Thus, as by sight I discern the beauty of a plant or an animal, even so the mind applauds the moral excellence, the beauty and decorum of justice and temperance.[9]

What is missing in Alciphron's account of aesthetic perception (of the nonmoral kind) is *mind;* and it is mind that Berkeley attempts to reinstate. But if mind is absent from Alciphron's aesthetics, it is by no means absent from Shaftesbury's. And to this extent Berkeley's Shaftesbury is a straw man.

Of course there can be no doubt but that Shaftesbury's writings lend themselves to the interpretation Berkeley has given. In addition, the rhapsodic tone which Shaftesbury wallows in makes interpretation such an exasperating and seemingly impossible task that one is driven finally to oversimplification if only to escape the mire of Shaftesbury's style. Berkeley himself expressed the frustration of the severely logical mind in the face of

Shaftesbury's enthusiasms when he wrote elsewhere, "it be not always easy to fix a determinate sense on such a loose and incoherent writer." [10] Yet the fact remains that Shaftesbury was far more of a rationalist than Berkeley thought — a fact that emerges with even greater clarity as Berkeley's argument progresses.

Alciphron is manipulated by Euphranor, Berkeley's mouthpiece, into defining beauty as "a certain symmetry and proportion pleasing to the eye." Euphranor then takes charge of the argument, easily compelling Alciphron to admit that proportion — and, hence, beauty — can be perceived by the mind only and never by sense.

> EUPHRANOR. Is proportion one and the same in all things, or is it different in different kinds of things?

> ALCIPHRON. Different, doubtless. The proportions of an ox would not be beautiful in a horse. And we observe also in things inanimate, that the beauty of a table, a chair, a door, consists in different proportions.

> EUPHRANOR. Doth not this proportion imply the relation of one thing to another?

> ALCIPHRON. It doth.

> EUPHRANOR. And are not these relations founded in size and shape?

> ALCIPHRON. They are.

> EUPHRANOR. And, to make proportions just, must not those mutual relations of size and shape in the parts be such as shall make the whole complete and perfect in its kind?

> ALCIPHRON. I grant they must.

> EUPHRANOR. Is not a thing said to be perfect in its kind when it answers to the end for which it was made?

> ALCIPHRON. It is.

EUPHRANOR. The parts, therefore, in true proportions must be
    so related, and adjusted to one another, as they may best
    conspire to the use and operation of the whole?

ALCIPHRON. It seems so.

EUPHRANOR. But the comparing of parts one with another, the
    considering them as belonging to one whole, and the
    referring this whole to its use or end, should seem the
    work of reason: should it not?

ALCIPHRON. It should.

EUPHRANOR. Proportions, therefore, are not, strictly speaking,
    perceived by the sense of sight, but only by reason
    through means of sight.

ALCIPHRON. This I grant.

EUPHRANOR. Consequently beauty, in your sense of it, is an
    object, not of the eye, but of the mind.[11]

Euphranor's conclusion, that "Proportions . . . are not, strictly speaking, perceived by the sense of sight, but only by reason
through means of sight," is meant as a denial of Shaftesbury's
doctrine; yet it is, in fact, very close to the doctrine that we
ascribed to Shaftesbury in Chapter I. But if Euphranor's critique is wide of the mark where Shaftesbury is concerned,
Hutcheson is by no means immune to it: the same vulnerable
point has been struck at which Balguy aimed. Berkeley argues
that proportion — one of the most commonly accepted neoclas-
sical definitions of beauty — implies a relation of parts, and that
the *comparing of parts* which the perception of such a relation
would necessitate is clearly the province of reason, not sensation. And it makes little difference whether the sense involved
be the eye, as in Berkeley's example, or an "inner sense" such as
Hutcheson's sense of beauty which, after all, is modeled on the
external sense organs.

Of course, the crucial question in Berkeley's critique, as in
Balguy's, is just what construction is to be put on the term
"perceive" when one talks about perceiving relations. If the

relations between the parts of an object are such as to make it well proportioned, we may take pleasure in it; and this pleasure is due, in some sense or other, we would want to say, to the "perceiving" of these relations. Now it is clear that we can perceive these relations by sense if by "perceive" we mean sense the pleasure in which such relations result when we look at the object. Or, if we already know that such relations give pleasure, it can be said that we perceive the relations by sense in that their presence is signaled to us by the feeling of pleasure. And it is only in these two senses that Hutcheson maintains we perceive the relation of *uniformity amidst variety* by sense. But there is another sense of "perceive" — and this is the sense in which Berkeley seems to be using the term — where the relations are *discovered* by an examination and comparison of parts. Surely Berkeley is correct in insisting that perception in this sense is, in part, *rational* perception. Which, however, Hutcheson need not deny.

Now if one argues that the perception of *uniformity amidst variety* involves the comparison of parts, and if, in addition, one takes Hutcheson to be saying that *uniformity amidst variety* is the aesthetic quality perceived by the sense of beauty (which is not Hutcheson's view), one might then be inclined to reject Hutcheson's view for the same reasons Euphranor rejects Alciphron's. And, indeed, an increasing number of critics followed this line of reasoning. It misrepresented Hutcheson's teaching; but it continued to expose the basic weakness of his position: the construal of qualities like *uniformity amidst variety* as causally, rather than noncontingently, connected with the perception of beauty.

(5) We come, now, to the last of our critics. Richard Price has recently regained a philosophical reputation that had become somewhat tarnished. Once characterized by Leslie Stephen as a "curious" writer, lacking in "intrinsic merit,"[12] he has since become a precursor of G. E. Moore[13]; and C. D. Broad lauds his *Review of the Principal Questions and Difficulties in Morals* (1758) as the finest "rationalistic" ethics prior to Ross's *The Right and the Good*[14] — high praise indeed from British moral-

ists. We close, then, with the aesthetic obiter dicta of a first-rate rationalist.

Is virtue a quality of the external world or merely of the perceiving mind? In Lockean terms, is it a primary or a secondary quality? *That,* for Price, was *the* principal question in morals. Nor was there any doubt where the rationalist stood: "*right* and *wrong,* or *moral good* and *evil,*" Price wrote, "signify somewhat *really true* of actions, and not merely sensations." [15] But although Price was willing to fight for an "objective" morality, he conceded beauty to the opposition, as Balguy at first had. The term "beautiful," for Price, had reference to feelings only, both with respect to moral and natural beauty (and, it would seem, the beauty of art, at least in some cases). Hence he was, here, in accord with Hutcheson.

Price distinguished, then, between the use of "good" and "beautiful" in moral judgment, again following Balguy's early views. "Good" and "evil," Price maintained, have reference to an objective state of affairs, discerned by reason. "Beautiful," and its opposite, on the other hand, "denote the *delightful;* or on the contrary, the *horror* and *detestation felt* by ourselves; and, consequently, signify not any real qualities or characters of actions, but the *effects in us,* or the particular pleasure and pain, attending consideration of them." [16]

It would seem, then, that for Price, as well as for Balguy, it makes some kind of sense to talk about two people agreeing that action X is right, say, but disagreeing that it is beautiful. What kind of sense *does* it make? "Right," Price is claiming, refers to some objective quality of X found out by reason; "beautiful" refers to our *feeling* of delight in X. And Price is maintaining that two people can recognize (and hence agree) that X is right, while one feels delight in X and the other does not. What Price is driving at, I suggest, is that feeling delight in X means something like feeling delight in the contemplation of doing X; that is, feeling some desire, or having some motivation for doing X. He then must think that it is logically possible for someone to recognize that X is right and yet not have any desire or motive for doing X. If that is the case, then Price is what has been described recently as an "externalist" with regard to moral obligation; that is, one who holds it logically possible for a moral agent to recognize his obligation of doing X and yet have no motivation whatever for doing X. This is in contrast to "internalism," the view that to recognize an obligation to do X is, at the same time, to acquire at least some, if not an overriding, propensity to do X.[17]

There are, it must be acknowledged, passages in Price which are incompatible with an externalist interpretation. Thus he writes, on one occasion:

> I cannot perceive an action to be right, without *approving* it; or *approve* it, without being conscious of some degree of *satisfaction* and complacency. I cannot perceive an action to be wrong, without *disapproving* it; or *disapprove* it, without being *displeased* with it.[18]

The strength of the "cannot" here seems, I think, logical rather than merely empirical; and its strength is reinforced rather than diminished as the passage progresses. Yet in the very next breath Price has slipped back into language which clearly indicates a causal, and hence contingent, relation between rightness and pleasure, and wrongness and displeasure, and provides a psychological explanation why one might fail to experience the appropriate feeling in contemplating moral qualities:

> It should be remembered here, that the effects produced by the consideration of virtue and vice, must be different in different beings, and in the same being in different circumstances of his existence. The pleasure received from virtuous actions, (that is the sense of *beauty* in them) must be varied by numberless causes both in the circumstances of the actions, and in the understandings and conditions of the percipient beings.[19]

In any case, the distinction made here by Price, and, less incisively, by Balguy, joins one of the deep issues in moral theory, but one which we must leave merely stated, and not explored, as it carries us to a topic of no special relevance to our present concerns.

In describing natural beauty, too, we have objective as well as subjective terms: Hutcheson's *uniformity amidst variety* has an objective signification; but natural beauty is merely its subjective concomitant.

> It seems impossible for any one to conceive the objects themselves to be endowed with more than a particular order of parts, and with *powers*, or an *affinity* to our perceptive faculties, thence arising; and, if we call this *beauty*, then it is an absolute, inherent quality of certain objects; and equally existent whether any mind discerns it or not. But, surely, order and regularity are, more properly, the *causes* of beauty than beauty itself. [20]

Thus, although moral qualities and physical proportions have an objective existence, for natural as well as moral beauty, to be is to be perceived.[21] Unlike Balguy, Price was steady to this text, and although a rationalist in ethics, remained in Hutcheson's aesthetic camp: but with an important demur.

That part of the aesthetic complex which is objective, Price maintained, can be perceived by intellect only. His argument is reminiscent of Balguy's and Berkeley's.

> Mere sense can perceive nothing in the most exquisite work of art . . . but what is painted in the eye, or what might be described on paper. It is the intellect that must perceive in it order and proportion; variety and regularity; design, connection, art and power; aptitudes, dependencies, correspondencies, and adjustments of parts so as to subserve an end, and compose one perfect whole; things which never can be represented on a sensible organ, and the ideas of which cannot be passively communicated, or stamped on the mind by the operation of external objects. [22]

For Price, as for Balguy and Berkeley, *uniformity amidst variety, design, proportion, fitness,* all of the commonly accepted objective correlates of the aesthetic — accepted not only by the rationalists but by the school of "sentiment" as well — demanded a rational perception, involving a comparison of parts and a recognition of their fitness and proportion. It was a process, the rationalists argued, beyond the powers of sense perception alone. Where they differed was with regard to the aesthetic status of the objective correlate. For Balguy and Berkeley it was the aesthetic itself; for Price, merely the cause.

The external cause of natural beauty for Price, as for Hutcheson, is *uniformity amidst variety.* It, not the idea of beauty
which it causes, can be brought to awareness only by intellect — a conclusion Hutcheson need not deny. Where Hutcheson
and Price part company is in the explanation of how the idea of
beauty arises. In regard to natural beauty, Price remarks,

> The general source of it, as observed by Dr. *Hutcheson,* is UNI-
> FORMITY AMIDST VARIETY. If we ask, why this *pleases?* The
> proper answer, I think, is, that by its nature it is adapted to
> please. — There seems no more occasion in this case to have re-
> course to an *implanted sense* than in the former [i.e., the case of
> moral beauty]. — Some objects, I have shewn, are necessarily satis-
> factory to our thoughts, and carry in themselves a power to give
> pleasure when surveyed. [23]

Price, then, although he ascribes the perception of beauty to
sense, wishes to dispense with the notion of a special sense of
beauty. In this he is prophetic of things to come in eighteenth-
century British aesthetics. He substitutes for it three psychological explanations of the pleasure we take in *uniformity amidst
variety,* all encrusted with tradition, and two, as we have seen,
quite familiar to Hutcheson, who used them in his theological
explanation of our aesthetic dispositions. (i) Unity makes for
ease of comprehension; objects in which variety is reduced to
some unity "are more easily viewed and comprehended by our
minds." (ii) Unity is connected with utility; "Order and symmetry give objects their stability and strength, and subserviency
to any valuable purpose." (iii) Regularity and order are evidence
of a rational designing mind; "The objects in which they appear
bear the impresses of intelligence upon them; and this, perhaps,
is one of the principal causes of their agreeableness." [24]

(6) In substituting for the sense of beauty a psychological
reduction to principles of perceptual ease, utility, and the agreeableness of intelligence, Price was negating, in effect, the most
basic premise of Hutcheson's aesthetic theory: that experience
of the beautiful, and other aesthetic qualities, is *sui generis,* and
not explainable in terms of other more basic human faculties,

pleasures, or perceptions. In so doing, Price created anew for those who came after the problem of isolating the aesthetic dimension. The absence of a true Hutchesonian sense of beauty left a void which eventually was filled by various ersatz senses — either, as in the case of Thomas Reid, sense made rational, or, in the cases of Alexander Gerard, Archibald Alison, and Dugald Stewart, sense made metaphorical. But before we turn to these developments, we must examine the sense of beauty as it survived in Hutcheson's most illustrious "follower," David Hume.

VIII

HUTCHESON AND HUME

(1) A philosophical doctrine influences its immediate posterity in diverse ways. There are disciples and there are critics; and there are those who, though the architects of their own thoughts, nevertheless accept what they can to build upon. Hutcheson's sense of beauty influenced in all these ways: it found discipleship and criticism, and, in the work of Hume, transformation and a kind of immortality that the great mind can give even to the occupations of a moment.[1]

There can be no doubt but that Hume's moral theory had roots in the writings of Hutcheson. An examination of the respective positions reveals it clearly enough; but Hume has left us even more substantial historical evidence in the form of letters to Hutcheson, written between 1739 and 1741 — the period which saw publication of the *Treatise of Human Nature*.

Hume was explicit with regard to what he obviously considered a meeting of minds in ethics: "Morality according to your Opinion as well as mine," he wrote Hutcheson, "is determin'd merely by Sentiment . . . . "[2] An analogous agreement existed in the realm of aesthetic theory, as Hume made manifest throughout his writing and particularly in the essay "Of the Standard of Taste" (1757).

There are, it will be recalled, two premises fundamental to Hutcheson's moral and aesthetic theory: (i) the value terms "good" and "beautiful" are applied to moral and aesthetic objects which occasion in the perceiver particular kinds of Lockean "ideas"; and (ii) these ideas are perceived by "internal senses." Hume accepts the first of these premises, although he substitutes "sentiment," "pleasure," and the like, for the more general term "idea." The second premise, for Hume, coalesces with the first: all that can be said about the moral sense and sense of beauty is contained in the contention that "good" and "beautiful" are applied in virtue of our having moral and aesthetic "sentiments." The position is summarized in the *Treatise:*

> An action, or sentiment, or character, is virtuous or vicious; why? because its view causes a pleasure or uneasiness of a particular kind. In giving a reason, therefore, for the pleasure or uneasiness, we sufficiently explain the vice or virtue. To have the sense of virtue, is nothing but to *feel* a satisfaction of a particular kind from the contemplation of a character. The very *feeling* constitutes our praise or admiration . . . . We do not infer a character to be virtuous, because it pleases; but in feeling that it pleases after such a particular manner, we in effect feel that it is virtuous. The case is the same as in our judgments concerning all kinds of beauty, and tastes, and sensations. Our approbation is imply'd in the immediate pleasure they convey to us. [3]

For a thoroughgoing empiricist, the moral sense and sense of beauty are extra philosophical baggage. We are aware of the *sentiments,* not the *senses;* to say that we have a moral sense or sense of beauty can be only an elliptical way of saying that we have moral and aesthetic feelings.

Having chosen the path of "sentiment" in aesthetics, Hume was faced, as were others before him, with the specter of a subjective relativism. But no previous thinker had perceived the possible consequences of the "new aesthetics" more acutely or expressed them more forthrightly than the "dispassionate" sceptic who, in Kant's words, was "so peculiarly fitted for balanced judgment."[4] Yet Hume recognized that if relativism in taste seems an unimpeachable fact, so, too, does the existence of critical standards.

> Beauty is no quality in things themselves: it exists merely in the mind which contemplates them; and each mind perceives a different beauty. One person may even perceive deformity, where another is sensible of beauty; and every individual ought to acqui-

esce in his own sentiment, without pretending to regulate those of
others . . . .

But though this axiom, by passing into a proverb, seems to have
attained the sanction of common sense; there is certainly a species
of common sense, which opposes it, at least serves to modify and
restrain it. Whoever would assert an equality of genius and elegance between Ogilby and Milton, or Bunyan and Addison, would
be thought to defend no less an extravagance, than if he had
maintained a mole-hill to be as high as Teneriffe, or a pond as
extensive as the ocean. [5]

The resolution of this paradox, this "antinomy" of taste, was
Hume's task as it is ours; and the resolution he essayed merits
the most serious consideration.

(2) Hume believed that a standard of taste could be saved
only by a strong commitment to the rational. Nor did the Enlightenment look upon feeling and reason as necessarily incompatible. Hume was echoing a host of eighteenth-century moralists and critics when he wrote in the *Inquiry Concerning the
Principles of Morals* (1757), "*reason* and *sentiment* concur in
almost all moral determinations and conclusions," and specifically with regard to the problem of taste, "in many orders of
beauty, particularly those of the finer arts, it is requisite to
employ much reasoning, in order to feel the proper sentiment;
and a false relish may frequently be corrected by argument and
reflection."[6] Thus, the principal goal of criticism, Hume believed, must be "to mingle some light of the understanding with
the feelings of sentiment . . . . "[7]

If I make an empirical statement, it is judged true or false on
the basis of whether what I assert is or is not the case. This
judgment is the province of reason. The touchstone of any such
reasoning process is some external state of affairs; the "standard" of reason here consists in correspondence to the facts of
the case. "In the operation of reasoning," Hume tells us,

the mind does nothing but run over its objects, as they are supposed to stand in reality, without adding any thing to them or
diminishing any thing from them . . . . To this operation of the
mind, therefore, there seems to be always a real, though often

unknown, standard, in the nature of things; nor is truth or false-
hood variable by the various apprehensions of mankind.[8]

But aesthetic judgments are not of this kind according to
Hume. We do not, when we pronounce the judgment "beautiful," or the reverse, merely "run over" the "objects" of thought
"as they are supposed to stand in reality, without adding any
thing to them." We do add something; we add our feelings —
our emotional reactions to the objects we perceive.

> [T]he case is not the same with the qualities of *beautiful and
> deformed, desirable and odious,* as with truth and falsehood. In
> the former case, the mind is not content with merely surveying its
> objects, as they stand in themselves: it also feels a sentiment of
> delight or uneasiness, approbation or blame, consequent to that
> survey; and this sentiment determines it to affix the epithet *beau-
> tiful or deformed, desirable or odious.*[9]

Now our feelings vary with our subjective natures: "nor can the
same object, presented to a mind totally different, produce the
same sentiment." We lack, in our aesthetic judgments, the "external standard" which our factual judgments possess. The quest
for a standard of taste, then, is a quest for such an external
standard. The Humean program in aesthetics is the translation
of value judgments into factual judgments — judgments of sentiment into judgments of reason. This is what Hume intends
when he speaks of mingling "some light of the understanding
with the feelings of sentiment."

The standard of taste is determined by judgments based on
sentiment; but not all men are equal in their fitness to judge by
sentiment: "few are qualified to give judgment on any work of
art, or establish their own sentiment as the standard of beauty."[10] The standard of taste, then, is set by those qualified to
give judgment on the basis of sentiment. And thus the question,
What is good art? is easily answered. Good art is the art which
good critics — those who are fit to judge by sentiment — approve. But now a new series of questions arises involving the
nature of good critics: "where are such critics to be found?"
queries Hume. "By what marks are they to be known? How

distinguish them from pretenders? These questions seem to throw us back into the same uncertainty from which . . . we have endeavoured to extricate ourselves." Yet we have made some progress. For, Hume maintains, questions concerning good critics "are questions of fact, not of sentiment"; and such questions, "submitted to the understanding," are susceptible, at least in principle, of a rational determination.

If, however, a rational judgment is to distinguish good critics from bad, it must find its criteria, its "standard," in the *facts* of the case; there must be some enumerable set of characteristics whereby the sheep may be separated from the goats. Hume provides five such distinguishing qualities:

> [i] When the critic has no *delicacy,* he judges without distinction, and is only affected by the grosser and more palpable qualities of the object: the finer touches pass unnoticed and disregarded. [ii] Where he is not aided by *practice,* his verdict is attended with confusion and hesitation. [iii] Where no *comparison* [between different kinds of beauty] has been employed, the most frivolous beauties, such as rather merit the name of defects, are the object of his admiration. [iv] Where he lies under the influence of *prejudice,* all his natural sentiments are perverted. [v] Where *good sense* is wanting, he is not qualified to discern the beauties of design and reasoning [i.e., the mutual relation of the parts of the work of art, and the purpose of the work], which are the highest and most excellent.[11]

(3) Now it has often been maintained that Hume is involved here in a vicious circle whereby good art is defined in terms of the good critic and the good critic in terms of good art.[12] And it is in fact easy enough to generate just such a circular definition simply by asking ourselves how it is to be determined whether or not an individual possesses the five qualities of the good critic enumerated above. If the answer forthcoming is that we know a good critic to possess these qualities because he approves of good art, then we have certainly moved in a circle. To wit: (i) good works of art are works of art approved by good critics; (ii) good critics are critics possessing five requisite qualities; and (iii) critics possessing the five requisite qualities are critics who approve good works of art.

Is this a fair representation of what Hume has to say concerning aesthetic judgment? In part, I am afraid, it is, but only in part. For there are after all *five* qualities which, according to Hume, distinguish the good critic, and they are not all of a piece. Some end us in a circular definition; others, I believe, do not. Thus, we must examine these qualities more closely if we wish to do Hume justice in this matter.

Practice Hume thinks of as "the frequent survey or contemplation of a particular species of beauty."[13] *Use of comparisons* requires juxtaposing "the several species and degrees of excellence."[14] But we must be able to recognize the beautiful before we are able to determine whether a critic has or has not been engaged in "the frequent survey or contemplation of a particular species of beauty." We must know what is excellent before we are able to determine whether or not a critic has compared "the several species and degrees of excellence." Thus, (i) the beautiful (or excellent) is defined in terms of the good critic; (ii) the good critic is defined in terms of *practice* and *use of comparisons;* and (iii) *practice* and *use of comparisons* are defined in terms of the beautiful (or excellent). Obviously, in these two cases the definition of beauty is circular.

If, however, we examine the remaining three qualities — *delicacy, lack of prejudice, good sense* — we will find quite another situation obtaining. What I wish to argue is that these qualities have, for Hume, certain crucial features in common: all are qualities not limited to critics alone; all are qualities requisite not only for aesthetic judgment but for other activities as well; and, hence, all are identifiable by marks other than the critic's approval of good art. This being the case, the circle is broken; having defined good art in terms of good critics, Hume need not, with respect to these qualities, ultimately define good critics in terms of good art.

Hume describes *delicacy* in the following way: "Where the organs are so fine as to allow nothing to escape them, and at the same time so exact as to perceive every ingredient in the composition, this we call delicacy of taste, whether we employ these terms in the literal or metaphorical sense."[15] How are we to determine whether or not a critic possesses *delicacy of taste* in

the aesthetic sense? In "Of the Standard of Taste" the implication seems to be that such *delicacy* is determined on the basis of
the critic's ability to distinguish aesthetic qualities in *good art*.
And this of course leads us again to a circular definition:
(i) good art is art approved by good critics; (ii) good critics are
critics possessing *delicacy;* and (iii) *delicacy* is the ability to distinguish the aesthetic qualities of good art.

But in an earlier essay, "Of the Delicacy of Taste and Passion" (1741), Hume relates aesthetic sensibility to emotive
sensibility in general, implying in one place that those individuals characterized by the latter are likely to possess the former
as well. He writes,

> How far the delicacy of taste, and that of passion are connected
> together in the original frame of the mind, is hard to determine.
> To me there appears to be a very considerable connection betwixt
> them. For we may observe that women, who have more delicate
> passions than men, have also a more delicate taste of the orna-
> ments of life, of dress, equipage, and the ordinary decencies of
> behaviour. Any excellency in these hits their taste much sooner
> than ours; and when you please their taste, you soon engage their
> affections.[16]

Thus, *delicacy of taste* can be identified (although perhaps not
in all cases) by a nonaesthetic quality; namely, *delicacy of passion*. One could reasonably suppose an individual to possess
delicacy of taste not on the basis of his critical judgments, but
rather on the basis of his general emotional reactions to nonaesthetic situations. With this qualification in view, we can define good art in terms of *delicacy* and yet avoid the previous
circularity. Our revised definition will be: (i) good art is art
approved by good critics; (ii) good critics are critics possessing
delicacy of taste; and (iii) *delicacy of taste* is a concomitant of
delicacy of passion.

As for Hume's requirement that the critic be free from bias,
its relevance seems obvious enough; we expect fairness in judgments, whether they be aesthetic, moral, or any other kind. "It
is well known, that, in all questions submitted to the understanding, prejudice is destructive of sound judgment, and per-

verts all operations of the intellectual faculties: it is no less contrary to good taste; nor has it less influence to corrupt our sentiment of beauty."[17]

However, there is a special sense in which an aesthetic judgment must be free from bias. Hume makes this demand of himself as a critic: "considering myself as a man in general, [I must] forget, if possible, my individual being, and my peculiar circumstances."[18] In passing critical judgments we must shed our private skins. By means of a mental exercise we take the point of view of "a man in general" and disregard our "individual being" and "peculiar circumstances." This is essentially an aesthetic version of what in Hume's moral theory has come to be known as the "disinterested spectator." Hume writes in the *Treatise,* for example: "Nor is every sentiment of pleasure or pain which arises from characters and actions, of that *peculiar* kind which makes us praise or condemn . . . . 'Tis only when a character is considered in general, without reference to our particular interest, that it causes such a feeling or sentiment as denominates it morally good or evil."[19] We attempt, both in our moral and aesthetic judgments, to separate in thought that which varies with our own personalities and times, and attend only to the common element in all human sentiment. Only thus,

free

From taint of personality,

can we hope to make judgments on the basis of sentiment that are not merely expressions of personal preference but universal judgments.[20]

As in the case of *delicacy,* the crucial point here for our purposes is that *lack of prejudice,* even in its special application to value judgments, is not a quality unique in the critic. It is, therefore, a quality that need not be determined solely on the basis of the critic's approving or recognizing good art. An individual who is generally fair-minded or able to take the point of view of the disinterested spectator in moral situations would likewise be able, one supposes, to take the point of view of "a man in general" when exercising critical judgment. Here again is a quality of good critics that can be recognized prior to any knowledge of the critic's aesthetic performance. So, having defined good art in terms of approval by good critics, and good critics in terms of *lack of prejudice,* there is no need to close the circle and define *lack of prejudice* in terms of good art.

Finally, it seems abundantly clear that *good sense,* the last of Hume's critical qualities, can hardly be considered solely an attribute of critics. Indeed, it is precisely Hume's point here that intelligence is as much a part of criticism as it is of rational inquiry: "the same excellence of faculties which contributes to the improvement of reason, the same clearness of conception, the same exactness of distinction, the same vivacity of apprehension, are essential to the operation of true taste, and are its infallible concomitants."[21] Fools do not make good critics; clever people do — nor need we make any reference to critical ability in separating the two. Again, good art can be defined in terms of approval by good critics, and good critics in terms of *good sense;* but *good sense,* having wider application than merely to good critics, need not be defined in terms of good art.

(4) Hume's definition of good art, or beauty, then, although circular in some instances, is not so in all. Good art, or the beautiful, is that approved by good critics; and good critics are characterized by five qualities: *delicacy, practice, use of comparisons, lack of prejudice,* and *good sense. Practice* and *use of comparisons* lead, as we have seen, to the vicious circle of which Hume has often been accused. For both are defined in terms of the beautiful. But *delicacy, lack of prejudice,* and *good sense,* being qualities not unique to critics, are free from this circularity; they are identifiable by marks other than the critic's approval of aesthetic objects and need not be defined in terms of good art.

But if Hume's definition of good art is free from the charge of circularity, the general argument of the essay on taste is not totally unblemished. Hume seems, in fact, to be involved in (among other things) an infinite regress.

Let us imagine that Smith and Jones disagree about a poem: Smith approves and Jones does not. Smith supports his judgment by reference to the favorable verdict of a critic, to which Jones replies that the critic in question lacks *good sense*. This might at least be one sort of dispute in aesthetics envisaged by Hume; and he would claim here, as he apparently did at times with regard to ethical disputes, that (to use C. L. Stevenson's terminology) disagreements in evaluation are to a large extent "rooted in disagreement in belief." This is what Hume means in maintaining that a critical judgment based on "sentiment" can be reduced to a rational judgment involving "facts." If Smith and Jones are thoroughly apprised of the facts, they will agree with regard to the now disputed poem — the facts, in this instance, being the credentials of the critic whom Smith invokes as his authority.

But suppose we scrutinize the facts (so-called) of the case; the *good sense,* for example, which the critic is said to possess. The phrase *good sense* may describe; it also *approves*. What has happened is that in his attempt to reduce disagreements about aesthetic values to disagreements about facts, Hume has simply pushed the value judgment a step back: the question, Is X a good poem? has become: Does Y have *good sense?* And both are evaluative questions, questions of "sentiment," not (solely) questions of fact. Smith and Jones do not (to use Stevenson's terminology again) merely disagree in "belief" about the critic, as Hume would have us think, but in "attitude" toward the critic. Thus, we are now faced with the task of reducing *good sense* to matters of fact; and the result of this reduction will doubtless require a reduction of its own.

Many would claim that the Humean attempt to reduce matters of aesthetic sentiment to matters of fact is doomed from the start: there just is no guarantee to be had that agreement about facts will result in agreement about what is beautiful. And Hume himself seems in the last analysis to have been of the same mind. For although he did maintain that *some* aesthetic disputes are rooted in disagreement about facts, he did not, it appears, believe that all are. Very near the conclusion of the essay on taste Hume wrote:

The general principles of taste are uniform in human nature:

where men vary in their judgements, some defect or perversion in
the faculties [a matter of fact] may commonly be remarked; pro-
ceeding either from prejudice, from want of practice, or want of
delicacy; and there is just reason for approving one taste, and
condemning another. But where there is such diversity in the internal frame or external situation as is entirely blameless on both
sides, and leaves no room to give one the preference above the
other [where, in other words, there is substantial agreement with
regard to the facts]; in that case a certain degree of diversity in
judgement [disagreement in attitudes] is unavoidable, and we seek
in vain for a standard, by which we can reconcile the contrary
sentiments. [22]

When an aesthetic dispute arises, the facts of the case, which for
Hume are the credentials of the critic, are relevant; and agreement about them *may* lead to a resolution of the dispute. This
will occur when the facts either clearly condemn or clearly
authorize the critic in the eyes of the disputants. But when the
critic's credentials have been thoroughly examined, or when
two rival critics present equally authoritative credentials and yet
still disagree in their judgment, the facts of the case have been
exhausted. If the dispute continues, it is now one of sentiment,
not reason; it is a disagreement in attitudes, not beliefs, and "no
reasoned solution of any sort is possible."[23] We have done all we
can *rationally* do when we have laid bare the facts of the
case. If disagreement still remains — and, for Hume, we have no
assurance that it will not — it is a disagreement not susceptible
of resolution by rational methods.

Hume, then, held out no absolute guarantees of resolution in
aesthetic questions; and for an age that pursued such guarantees
with the tenacity of a Grail Quest, this was a disappointment.
As an anonymous reviewer of the essay on taste sadly remarked
shortly after its publication, "instead of fixing and ascertaining
the standard of taste, as we expected, our author only leaves us
in the same uncertainty as he found us: and concludes with the
philosopher of old, that all we know is, that we know nothing."[24] Hume might well have replied with the words of another
"philosopher of old": "a well-schooled man is one who searches
for that degree of precision in each kind of study which the
nature of the subject at hand admits . . . . "[25]

(5) It would be instructive at this juncture, I think, to contrast Hume's position with Hutcheson's, for the purposes of bringing out more clearly the general outlines of both, and determining the comparative weaknesses and strengths of each. Both construe aesthetic judgment on the model of *perceptual* judgments like "*X* is red"; but each emphasizes a different aspect of that model and, as a result, each approaches the question of justification, of what we are doing when we support our aesthetic judgments, in a very different way.

There are two distinctive features of the perceptual model worth noting here. They are (i) that there is a standard of normalcy which, when deviated from, licenses us to declare the deviation *incorrect;* and (ii) that there is a theory which correlates our perceptual reports with certain scientifically measurable properties such that we feel confident in supposing that the properties *cause* us to have the sensations which occasion our reports. Thus, (i) if Mr. A says that *X* is red and Mr. B that it is grey, it will be prima facie evidence that Mr. B is incorrect if his eyes differ from those which have been determined to be "normal," and/or if he has viewed *X* under conditions that differ from those which have been determined to be favorable or optimal ones; and (ii) there is a very successful scientific theory that correlates certain measurable properties of light and reflecting surfaces with the sensation of redness and which accommodates our notions of normal perceiver and favorable or optimal conditions. Mr. A can *defend* or *justify* his assertion "*X* is red" by appeal (in part) to what the normal perceiver would say under favorable or optimal conditions; and he (or a scientist) could explain what causes him to have the sensation that occasions the assertion "*X* is red." Both of these features of the perceptual model we must assume to have been known to Hutcheson and Hume, although not in as well-developed a form as we know them today.

We can now see quite clearly that although they both presented a perceptual model of aesthetic judgment, Hutcheson was drawn to the second feature and Hume to the first, although both paid some attention to the feature he did not emphasize. Hutcheson, as we have seen, was convinced that he knew what "property" of objects causes the sensation of the beautiful; namely, *uniformity amidst variety*. And it is this causal feature of his perceptual model which he continually pushes to the fore, and which the casual reader of Hutcheson always remembers, although Hutcheson was aware of the part that the notion of the normal perceiver plays. Hume, on the other hand, defines the standard of taste in terms of the perception of the normal perceiver; that is, the good critic. There is indeed some evidence that he made at least a desultory effort to determine the cause of the sentiment of beauty or aesthetic approval. If, for example, Hume classified beauty as a *value,* then the following passage from the *Inquiry Concerning the Principles of Morals* implies that he believed the sentiment of beauty to be caused by the perception of the useful or agreeable in objects. He writes: "Whatever is valuable in any kind, so naturally classes itself under the division of useful or agreeable, the *utile* or the *dulce,* that it is not easy to imagine why we should ever seek further, or consider the question as a matter of nice research or inquiry."[26] It is by no means clear whether Hume really does have a firm opinion in this regard.[27] But there can be no doubt that he wrote little about it, and that he wrote extensively and carefully in the essay on taste about the first feature of the aesthetic perceptual model. We may fairly conclude, then, that Hutcheson markedly emphasized the causal explanation in the perceptual model of aesthetic judgment, and that Hume markedly emphasized the notion of normal perceiver; and herein lies the source both of their strengths and their weaknesses as aestheticians.

Let us now consider the following two conversations in which first Hutcheson, and then Hume, applies his theory.

Mr. Hutcheson. X is beautiful.
Mr. Quibble. Why do you say that?
Mr. Hutcheson. Because *X* has *uniformity amidst variety.*

Mr. Hume. X is beautiful.
Mr. Quibble. Why do you say that?

Mr. Hume. Because X is (or would be) approved by the
majority of good critics.

Now Hutcheson's answer, I suggest, sounds altogether plausible, *until* we recall what he is up to; until we remember what
the function of "Because . . . " is in Hutcheson's answer. For
what we naturally take Hutcheson to be doing is *justifying* his
assertion, giving a reason in support of it. And "*X* has *uniformity amidst variety*" seems quite acceptable as a justification
of, a reason for, "*X* is beautiful," although perhaps it is not the
only justification or a *sufficient* one. Having unity and/or variety is quite often advanced as a reason for believing that a work
of art or some other aesthetic object is beautiful or aesthetically
satisfactory. But, of course, Hutcheson is *not* offering a justification. He is offering a causal explanation. The "Because . . . "
is explanatory not justificatory. And once we realize this, the
plausibility of Hutcheson's answer vanishes. It is as if we asked
someone why he killed his wife, expecting him to tell us what
his motive or intention was, to justify his act in some way, and,
instead, he gave us a physiological explanation of what caused
his neurons to fire, his muscles to contract, and the blunt instrument in his hand to describe the arc that it did. We do not care
that the explanation may be correct; for it is the answer to the
wrong question; it completely misses the point.

Hume, however, shows, I think, that he knows the philosophically important question when he gravitates toward the first
feature of the perceptual model: the feature which embodies
justifying reasons. And Hutcheson, in gravitating toward the
second feature, the causal explanation, leads aesthetics astray.
Hume, in that he *is* trying to support or justify his assertion,
rather than causally explain it, is answering the right question.
But he is giving an entirely unsatisfactory answer to it. He is
saying, essentially, "I think that *p* because *he* thinks that *p*,"
which carries no weight in the context in which it is said. We do
indeed think it plausible to believe that *X* is red because the
normal perceiver under favorable or optimal conditions believes
that it is red. "I think so because *he* thinks so" is a satisfactory
supporting reason for "*X* is red" where "*he*" is the normal

perceiver. Why is it not satisfactory in the aesthetic context?

The answer to this question lies, I think, in the special character of perceptual qualities like redness. They are simple qualities, whereas beauty and other aesthetic qualities are complex. By this I mean merely that in the case of redness we can never point to any feature of an object except its redness by virtue of which it is red; whereas we can defend our assertion that X is beautiful by pointing out other features — its unity, or variety, or color, or proportion — and saying: "It is beautiful because it is this, that, or the other." To say "X is red because *he* says it is" is plausible because there is nothing else to say. But to say "X is beautiful because *he* says it is" carries no weight because there *is* a great deal more to say, and thus the answer becomes the least persuasive of all, the argument from authority — even less persuasive in an aesthetic context than anywhere else because, many would say, *here,* my word, rather than anyone else's, is the last word.

There is real irony here. For had Hutcheson asked Hume's question, his answer would have been a plausible one; and had Hume given Hutcheson's answer, his answer would have been a plausible one. But somehow the wires got crossed. Hutcheson asked the wrong question, but gave at least a partially correct answer to the right question. Hume asked the right question, but paid the price of giving the wrong answer. Hume, I think, is justly admired because it is usually harder to ask the right question than to give the right answer.

IX

COMMON SENSE AND THE
SENSE OF BEAUTY

(1) The path that Hutcheson's sense of beauty had to travel in Britain in the waning years of the eighteenth century lay in two directions: an attempt at epistemological reconciliation with rationalism in the work of Thomas Reid; deflection and (finally) extinction in the work of the associationist aestheticians, most notably, Alexander Gerard, Archibald Alison, and Dugald Stewart. In this chapter, at the cost of becoming slightly out of phase chronologically, I examine Reid's version of the internal sense doctrine in aesthetics: the final flowering. In Chapters X-XII, I will backtrack a bit, take a brief look at the rise of associationist psychology, discuss its integration into the aesthetic sense doctrine by Gerard, and, finally, hear the associationist litany for the sense of beauty read by Alison and Stewart.

(2) Aberdeen, Glasgow, and Edinburgh spent the post-Humean decades of the eighteenth century doing philosophical penance for the fact that Hume was a Scot. This atonement took the form of a philosophical movement known today as the Scottish Common Sense School. It was dedicated to the refutation of Humean scepticism and those doctrines of Hume's predecessors, especially Locke, Berkeley, and Hutcheson, which were considered either as contributions to the Humean view or as obnoxious in their own right. The philosopher generally acknowledged to be the founder and principal spokesman of the

common sense philosophy was Reid, who himself traced the movement, in its contemporary form, to Shaftesbury. And it was Reid who forged the last important link in the evolutionary chain of Hutcheson's seventh sense.

Reid's aesthetics is a special case of a general theory of perception; and the general theory itself arises from a critique of the Lockean perceptual model. It is, therefore, with Reid's animadversions on Locke that we must begin. The basic tenet of Locke's theory of perception Reid took to be the notion that "mind . . . perceives nothing but a world of ideas in itself." Because of this axiom, as interpreted by Reid and many others, the principal problem for British empiricism became, to use Russell's phrase, our knowledge of the external world; for if we perceive the external world at all, it is through a glass darkly, mediated always by the ideas. "Mr. Locke was aware, no less than Des Cartes, that the doctrine of ideas made it necessary, and at the same time difficult, to prove the existence of the material world without us . . . . " [1] Above all else, Reid wished to strengthen our grasp on the "material world," from which, he thought, the successive onslaughts of Locke, Berkeley, and Hume had pried us loose.

Reid's approach is straightforward: if the notion that ideas are directly perceived, but objective qualities are not, leads to difficulties, then it must be revised. If this axiom stands between man and the external world, then the axiom, not the world, must be denied. Thus, Reid insists that the objective qualities of the external world are direct objects of awareness. But it is, I think, in a quite different sense of "awareness" than would be understood by the naive realist. Naive realism was characterized by Broad as a doctrine which maintains that the quality of an object is identical with the content of the sensation:

> [T] he objective correlate just is that quality of sensible yellowness which, according to that theory, is spread out over the surface of the thing ready to be presented whenever the appropriate revelatory conditions are fulfilled. The subjective correlate just is the power of prehending the yellowness of yellow things when such conditions are fulfilled. [2]

This is not the position Reid is espousing, although his statements out of context sometimes seem to suggest it; and, in fact, Berkeley is much closer to such a view than Reid.

Reid does not discard the Lockean idea (which he calls a "sensation") as a mental entity. On the contrary, the idea, or sensation, is a necessary element in the process by which the external world is made known to us; but it is not the only element. It is coupled with what Reid at times calls "perception." With regard to a sensation, to be is to be perceived:

> Its very essence consists in being felt; and, when it is not felt, it is not. There is no difference between the sensation and the feeling of it — they are one and the same thing. It is for this reason . . . that, in sensation, there is no object distinct from the act of the mind by which it is felt — and this holds true with regard to all sensations. [3]

Thus far, then, Reid is a thorough empiricist in the Locke and Berkeley stamp — with the suggestion, however, that sensations are processes, rather than objects, since "in sensation, there is no object distinct from the act of the mind by which it is felt . . . . "

Perception as opposed to sensation is, however, on a very different footing: "Perception has always an external object . . . . " If, to use Reid's example, I smell a rose, "The agreeable odour I feel, considered by itself, without relation to any external object, is merely a sensation." But accompanying this sensation is a *belief* that the sensation is occasioned by an objective quality. "This quality in the rose is the object perceived; and that act of my mind by which I have the conviction and belief of this quality, is what in this case I call perception." [4]

We can now make out more clearly the nature of Reid's realism. As I understand the naive realist's position, "direct awareness" of objective qualities is just what Reid calls "sensation," except that for the naive realist the sensation is identical with the objective quality whereas for Reid it is not; and what Reid would call the "direct awareness" or "perception" of an objective quality is a rational, not a sensible, awareness. There is a difference between sensing and knowing an objective quality, and that is the difference between what Broad calls naive realism and the position of Reid. Reid has made of perception a rational, concept-laden activity, to an extent unheard of heretofore in the British empiricist tradition. Extended to the aesthetic, this means he can embrace Hutcheson's sense of beauty, and yet accommodate the rationalist's claim that intellect must be involved in the perception of the beautiful. He is prepared to rationalize the aesthetic sense in answer to its rational critics.

(3) The relation between sensation and perception Reid takes to be a relation of sign to significatum: "Every different perception is conjoined with a sensation that is proper to it. The one is the sign, the other the thing signified."[5] It was this notion of Reid's which, I believe, G. E. Moore was describing in one of his early papers as "the theory that one thing 'intrinsically points to,' or is 'intrinsically the sign or symbol of' the existence of another thing."[6]

William Hamilton argued in response to this part of Reid's theory that if the perception of an external quality is a *consequence* of sensation, then perception is not an immediate awareness, his implication being that Reid is guilty of a contradiction, "an explicit disavowal of the doctrine of an intuitive or immediate perception."[7] In one sense, of course, Hamilton is correct: as we have remarked, Reid is not a naive realist and does not maintain, in the manner of the naive realist, that we are directly aware of objective qualities. Hamilton construes "immediate perception" in the naive realist's sense, and is quite right in pointing out that Reid does not adhere to it. But I do not believe Reid ever suggested that he did; and can hardly be accused of disavowing a doctrine he never held. Reid contradicted Hamilton, not himself.[8] Nor, by the way, need Reid deny that perception is temporally "immediate" and experientially "simple" merely because it is in fact complex and "consequential" upon analysis. As Reid himself explains,

[I]t is with the operations of the mind, in this case, as with natural bodies, which are, indeed, compounded of simple principles or elements. Nature does not exhibit these elements separate, to be compounded by us; she exhibits them mixed and compounded in concrete bodies, and it is only by art and chemical analysis that they can be separated. [9]

The complex process can appear simple, and become temporally immediate.

What then is the exact nature of Reid's "perception"? In what way does it vouchsafe our belief in objective qualities and, hence, the external world. According to Reid,

> Every man feels that perception gives him an invincible belief of the existence of that which he perceives; and that this belief is not the effect of reasoning, but the immediate consequence of perception. When philosophers have wearied themselves and their readers with their speculations upon this subject, they can neither strengthen this belief, nor weaken it; nor can they show how it is produced. It puts the philosopher and the peasant upon a level; and neither of them can give any other reason for believing his senses, than that he finds it impossible for him to do otherwise. [10]

The appeal, then, is to the "common sense" of mankind (and the enormities that appeal to *it* has produced, in Berkeley, Moore, and Santayana, to name but a few, must give the rational man pause).

Common sense, for Reid, seems to be the rational process by which we discern immediately or, perhaps, intuit self-evident truths. He writes in one of his manuscript notes:

> As soon as this truth is understood, that two and two make four, I immediately assent to it; because God has given men the faculty of immediately discerning its truth, and if I had not this faculty, I would not perceive its truth. The truth itself, therefore, does not depend on my constitution; for it was a truth before my existence, and will be a truth, although I were annihilated: but my perception evidently depends on my constitution, and particularly upon my having, as a part of my constitution, that faculty, whether you call it reason or common sense, by which I perceive or discern this truth. [11]

Common sense is one of two elements in the rational process. "We ascribe to reason two offices, or two degrees," says Reid:

The first is to judge of things self-evident; the second to draw
conclusions that are not self-evident from those that are. The first
of these is the province, and the sole province, of common sense;
and therefore it coincides with reason in its whole extent, and is
only another name for one branch or one degree of reason.

Thus, common sense is that part of the rational machinery by
which we intuit first principles. It is an innate talent: "purely
the gift of Heaven. And where Heaven has not given it, no
education can supply the want."[12] This is, however, not what
we ordinarily mean by "common sense." We would not think
our plumber lacked "common sense" if he did not see that the
shortest distance between two points is a straight line, but we
would if he did not know to get out of the rain; yet the former,
being axiomatic, would be "common sense" to Reid, whereas
the latter would not.

Our knowledge of the external world, then, is, for Reid, rational; but we can give no reason for our belief in the external
world, any more than we can give a reason for believing a "self-
evident" truth, if by "reason" is meant some proposition or set
of propositions from which these beliefs follow, or some body
of evidence which establishes them beyond a reasonable doubt.
Such beliefs are themselves the reasons for other beliefs which
are not "common sense" beliefs; but they are themselves believed without reasons or evidence. To quote Moore again,

That for which we have no reason may, nevertheless, be certainly
true. And, indeed, one of the philosophers who hold most clearly
and expressly that we do know not only the existence of other
people but also that of material objects, is also one of those who
deny most emphatically that our own observations can give any
reason for believing either in the one or in the other. I refer to
Thomas Reid.[13]

This is, I submit, a substantially correct statement of Reid's
"common sense," although, obviously, an extremely com-
pressed one.

(4) One further aspect of Reid's general theory of perception
requires our attention before we can move on to his aesthetic

veiws: the distinction between primary and secondary qualities. Reid retains the distinction, but places it, in one important respect, on a different footing than had Locke. It will be recalled that Locke characterized the ideas of primary qualities as resemblances of the qualities themselves, whereas the ideas of secondary qualities were not so characterized. (This is, of course, not the only difference between primary and secondary qualities, according to Locke.) The theory of resemblance was immediately seized upon by Locke's critics (John Sergeant, for example)[14] long before Berkeley delivered it what many, including Reid, considered the *coup de grace*. Feeling, as he did, that Berkeley had given the resemblance theory its due, Reid dismissed it without too much ceremony, assuming that his readers were familiar with Berkeley's critique. In general, Reid considered it amply demonstrated that the notion of a resemblance between subjective and objective entities was palpably absurd. This, Reid claimed,

> was clearly discerned by Bishop Berkeley. He had a just notion of sensations, and saw that it was impossible that anything in an insentient being could resemble them; a thing so evident in itself, that it seems wonderful that it should have been so long unknown.[15]

In rejecting the notion of a resemblance between mental and physical "objects," Reid was rejecting at the same time one of the principle criteria by which Locke had distinguished primary from secondary qualities. Wishing, however, to retain the primary-secondary distinction, Reid apparently felt the need to substitute another. He found such a substitute in the older Cartesian dictum of clearness and distinctness. Descartes, as Reid well knew, had distinguished the primary from the secondary qualities, although he had not so designated them. The distinction had been adumbrated in the *Meditations* (1641) and emerged fully in Part I of the *Principles of Philosophy* (1644). According to Descartes, our knowledge of certain qualities, some of which, at least, Locke later designated secondary qualities, is not clear and distinct knowledge in that our sensations give us no information as to the objective nature of these qualities. Descartes writes in the *Principles of Philosophy:*

> [W]e have a clear or distinct knowledge of pain, colour, and other things of the sort when we consider them simply as sensations or thoughts. But when we desire to judge of such matters as existing outside of our mind, we can in no wise conceive what sort of things they are. And when anyone says that he sees a colour in a body or feels pain in one of his limbs, it is the same as if he told us that he there saw or felt something but was absolutely ignorant of its nature, or else that he did not know what he saw or felt.

But what Locke later called primary qualities are known to us clearly and distinctly:

> [S]ize in the body which is seen, or figure or movement . . . , or situation, or duration, or number, and the like, which we clearly perceive in all bodies . . . are known to us in quite a different way from that in which colour is known in the same body, or pain, odour, taste, or any of the properties which, as hitherto mentioned, should be attributed to the senses. For although in observing a body we are not less assured of its existence from the colour which we perceive in its regard than from the figure which bounds it, we yet know this property in it which causes us to call it figured, with much greater clearness than what causes us to say that it is coloured.[16]

It is this Cartesian statement to which Reid returns. His position is couched in rationalist terms:

> [O]ur senses give us a direct and distinct notion of the primary qualities and inform us what they are in themselves. But of the secondary qualities, our senses give us only a relative and obscure notion. They inform us only, that they are qualities that affect us in a certain manner — that is, produce in us a certain sensation; but as to what they are in themselves, our senses leave us in the dark.[17]

What the exact nature of the distinction between clear and obscure notions is for Descartes, vis-à-vis the primary-secondary quality distinction, can well be disputed. In the Cartesian statement one feels some kind of resemblance theory lurking. Descartes emphasizes both in the *Meditations* and in the *Principles of Philosophy:* sensations of color, odor, taste, and the like — that is, the sensations of the secondary qualities — do *not* resemble the qualities themselves. Is the implication, perhaps, that in the case of the primary qualities, there *is* resemblance between the sensation and the quality?[18] If Descartes intended this, Reid clearly did not; for, as we have seen, Reid considered the distinction between clear and confused perceptions as an alternative to the resemblance theory, not a version of it. Hamilton, however, accuses Reid of having lapsed into the resemblance heresy, despite Reid's insistence to the contrary. For if, Hamilton argues, we have a distinct notion of what the primary qualities are in themselves, "these qualities, as known, must *resemble*, or be identical with, these qualities as existing."[19] But it is not by any means obvious that a quality "as known" must be *identical with*, or *resemble*, an objective quality if we have distinct knowledge or a distinct perception of the objective quality. The former alternative smacks of naive realism, which, for reasons already given, I do not believe is the position Reid maintains. And as for the latter, it seems very odd to talk about knowledge, whether distinct or not, as "resembling" that which it is knowledge of.

We turn now, after overlong delay, to Reid's aesthetics. But we will have occasion later to return again to the distinction between primary and secondary qualities.

(5) Reid's aesthetic theory is expounded in two places: Essay VIII of the *Essays On the Intellectual Powers of Man,* which was published in 1785, and the *Lectures On the Fine Arts* (1774), which existed only in manuscript until very recently.[20] But we have an indication that one major feature of the aesthetics, namely, Hutcheson's sense of beauty, had been adopted as early as 1764. For in his *Inquiry into the Human Mind on the Principles of Common Sense,* published in that year, Reid gives us, in passing, a theory of musical perception that is clearly derived from the aesthetic sense doctrine. He writes:

Although it is by hearing that we are capable of the perception of harmony and melody, and of all the charms of music, yet it would seem that these require a higher faculty, which we call a *musical ear*. This seems to be in very different degrees, in those who have the bare faculty of hearing equally perfect; and, therefore, ought not to be classed with the external senses, but in a higher order.[21]

The "higher faculty" is, of course, Hutcheson's sense of harmony — the musical counterpart of the sense of beauty. Reid's use of it in 1764 set the pattern for the aesthetic theory that was to follow.

Reid begins his aesthetics proper with a conventional characterization "of taste in general":

That power of the mind by which we are capable of discerning and relishing the beauties of Nature, and whatever is excellent in the fine arts, is called *taste*.

The external sense of taste, by which we distinguish various kinds of food, has given occasion to a metaphorical application of its name to this internal power of the mind, by which we perceive what is beautiful and what is deformed or defective in the various objects that we contemplate.

Like the taste of the palate, it relishes some things, is disgusted with others; with regard to many, is indifferent or dubious; and considerably influenced by habit, by associations, and by opinion. These obvious analogies between external and internal taste, have led men, in all ages, and in all or most polished languages, to give the name of the external sense to this power of discovering what is beautiful with pleasure, and what is ugly and faulty in its kind with disgust.[22]

Such a statement is one that any number of aestheticians or critics might have made from before Hutcheson to the end of the eighteenth century. But it is mostly with the early eighteenth century that Reid's sympathies lie: with Hutcheson and Addison, but with Shaftesbury and the older rational tradition as well. And as Reid develops this rather conservative position, in the context of his realist theory of perception, it takes on a significance of more than passing interest and some originality.

Following Addison and Hutcheson (in the first *Inquiry*), Reid makes a tripartite division of aesthetic objects into the *novel,*

the *grand* (or *sublime*), and the *beautiful*. But these three categories do not imply three distinct senses. Reid rejects the proliferation of aesthetic faculties as merely an arbitrary matching of
qualities with "senses." He argues that the number of aesthetic
qualities acknowledged is itself arbitrary; for the number of
aesthetic qualities distinguished depends, he thinks, on the number of names a given language may have for such qualities. Thus,
the proliferation of faculties in aesthetics reduces itself to an
exercise in naming and nothing more. Says Reid,

> I conceive every division that has been made of our internal senses
> to be in some degree arbitrary. They may be made more or fewer,
> according as we have distinct names for the various kinds of beau-
> ty or deformity; and I suspect the most copious languages have
> not names for them all. [23]

We have, then, three distinct classes of aesthetic qualities and,
apparently, one "sense," or "power," appropriate to their perception, sometimes called by Reid the "internal taste" and
sometimes the "sense of beauty."

As we have seen, Reid fashioned the sense of harmony in the
Inquiry after Hutcheson's model. In the *Essays* the same model
served for the sense of beauty:

> Our external senses may discover qualities which do not depend
> upon any antecedent perception. Thus, I can hear the sound of a
> bell, though I never perceived anything else belonging to it. But it
> is impossible to perceive the beauty of an object without perceiv-
> ing the object, or, at least, conceiving it. On this account Dr.
> Hutcheson called the senses of beauty and harmony reflex senses
> [in his later works]; because the beauty cannot be perceived unless
> the object be perceived by some other power of the mind. Thus,
> the sense of harmony and melody in sounds supposes the external
> sense of hearing, and is a kind of secondary to it . . . . The like
> may be said of beauties in colouring and in figure, which can never
> be perceived without the senses by which colour and figure are
> perceived. [24]

If, in light of this passage, and the one quoted earlier, we ask
ourselves where Reid stood in the argument between aesthetic

rationalism and the aesthetic sense doctrine, the obvious answer would seem to be: with Hutcheson unequivocally. The answer is substantially correct; but it would be grossly misleading if it were left at that. Reid, as I have suggested before, opted for the sense of beauty only after he had greatly altered the empiricist account of perception, injecting into it a strong dose of rationalism. Perception acquired, in Reid's hands, a distinctly Kantian tinge; and this colored his notion of aesthetic perception as well. Thus, Reid took care to emphasize in the *Lectures On the Fine Arts* that "there is a judgment implied in every one of our perceptions," and, hence, "a judgment in every operation of taste."[25] Reid, then, was not merely a follower of Hutcheson's aesthetic sense doctrine, but one who intended, clearly, to attempt a reconciliation between that doctrine and the rationalist critique. And in making the general theory of perception the foundation of this *entente,* he showed the true philosopher's instinct for first principles.

(6) There are, it seems to me, two distinctive features that set Reid's aesthetic sense doctrine apart from Hutcheson's. The first, already discussed, is his "rationalization" of aesthetic perception. The second, now to be discussed, is the nature of the qualities that the sense of beauty is supposed to perceive.

As would be expected, Reid's realism in the general theory of perception rubs off on the aesthetic. Thus, Reid insists from the outset that the beautiful is an objective quality and not a sensation or feeling. It is a claim repeated again and again with a certain evangelical fervor.

> When a beautiful object is before us, we may distinguish the agreeable emotion it produces in us, from the quality of the object which causes the emotion. When I hear an air in music that pleases me, I say it is fine, it is excellent. This excellence is not in me, it is in the music. But the pleasure it gives is not in the music, it is in me.[26]

Now what is puzzling here is that Hutcheson, at whom this passage seems to be aimed, never denied that the feeling of beauty was caused by "the quality of the object." In fact, he insisted on it no less than Reid. Nor do Reid and Hutcheson differ merely on the question of whether the term "beautiful" names the feeling or the objective quality; Reid himself admits that it can denote either.

> In the external sense of taste, we are led by reason and reflection to distinguish between the agreeable sensation we feel, and the quality in the object which occasions it. *Both have the same name,* and on that account are apt to be confounded by the vulgar, and even by philosophers.[27]

And, Reid adds, "the internal power of taste bears a great analogy in this respect to the external."

We find this same puzzling attitude on Reid's part to his predecessors in his discussion of secondary qualities. According to Reid,

> We see, then, that Locke, having found that the ideas of secondary qualities are no resemblances, was compelled, by a hypothesis common to all philosophers, to deny that they are real qualities of body. It is more difficult to assign a reason why, after this, he should call them *secondary qualities;* for this name, if I mistake not, was of his invention. Surely he did not mean that they were secondary qualities of the mind; and I do not see with what propriety, or even by what tolerable license, he could call them secondary qualities of body, after finding that they were no qualities of body at all.[28]

Now it is simply false that Locke denied secondary qualities are "real" qualities of bodies. Secondary qualities do really exist in the external world for the Lockean. But they exist as "powers" which certain arrangements of primary qualities have of exciting certain sensations in the perceiver. The objective existence of a quality can be understood, in the Lockean tradition, in two ways. When a Lockean alludes to the objective existence of secondary qualities, he means that the secondary qualities have objective existence only as "powers" of primary qualities. "Spherical," the name of a primary quality, can refer either to the quality itself or to the idea which it arouses in the perceiver (and which resembles it). "Red," the name of a secondary quality, can refer either to an arrangement of primary qualities, or to an idea which this arrangement has the power to produce in the perceiver. In the absence of sentient beings like ourselves, the list of qualities would, on this view, certainly include the term "spherical"; but it would hardly include the term "red" because it is not the name of any single quality. "Red" might be included in a list of arrangements in which certain qualities might be found, but not in a list of those qualities themselves. As a quality term it would be redundant, not naming any quality that was not already named by other quality terms. Thus, a quality is objective, for the Lockean, in either a *weak* or a *strong* sense. A quality is objectively real in the weak sense if its objective existence can be understood in terms of other objectively real qualities, having a certain identifiable effect on the perceiver. A quality is objectively real in the strong sense if it cannot be reduced and, thus, survives the absence of the perceiver (in the way explained above).

Reid says that Locke denied secondary qualities are real qualities of bodies. But Locke did no such thing. He denied only that they are real qualities of bodies in the strong sense. Either, then, Reid did not understand one of the most elementary principles of Locke's philosophy, or he simply assumed that anyone with the slightest knowledge of Locke would understand him to be saying that Locke denied the reality of secondary qualities in the strong sense. I suggest that Reid was groping for the second alternative for the purpose of claiming, contra Locke, that secondary qualities do indeed exist in the strong sense. I suggest, further, that this has an exact analogue in Reid's critique of Hutcheson and his departure from Hutcheson's aesthetic views.

(7) Hutcheson was committed to the objective existence of aesthetic qualities in the weak sense only; although the idea of beauty is occasioned by objective qualities, these qualities are not themselves aesthetic, but are merely the primary qualities, or the primary and secondary qualities, arranged in such a way as to give rise to an aesthetic idea in sentient beings of a certain kind. Beauty does have an objective existence, for Hutcheson,

in that *uniformity amidst variety,* which occasions the idea of beauty, is a real quality of objects: an arrangement of primary or primary and secondary qualities with the "power" of arousing a particular sensation in us. But take away the perceiver and the aesthetic quality is no more, although the disposition of external qualities with the particular "power" remains.

Reid insists *continually* that the idea of beauty, which he identifies with a pleasure, is occasioned by an *objective quality.* But why should he feel it necessary to insist on something that his predecessor, Hutcheson, never denied. Clearly, this insistence makes sense only if Reid did not understand a very elementary aspect of Hutcheson's aesthetics, or if he was leaving something unsaid which he thought would be obvious to his reader; namely, that the quality he insists is the cause of the aesthetic idea is not the cause of the aesthetic but is the aesthetic itself; is not the cause of the beautiful but the beautiful itself. I can scarcely believe that Reid misunderstood Hutcheson so sophomorically, any more than he misunderstood the elements of Locke. I conclude, therefore, that Reid was insisting on the objective existence of aesthetic qualities in the strong sense, a view he was quite right in believing Hutcheson did not hold. For Reid, I suggest, the world was nondispositionally colored and aesthetic. We must now see if the aesthetic half of the conjunction will wash.

It is quite clear that novelty has no objective existence in the absence of the perceiver. Reid defines novelty as "a relation which the thing has to the knowledge of the perceiver."[29] If one is ignorant of, or unfamiliar with, the object, then it is novel; if one has knowledge of the object, then it is not. Since novelty is a relation between object and perceiver, it obviously cannot exist if one term of the relation, the perceiver, does not exist. And so it makes no sense to talk about novelty without a perceiver to whom the object can be novel. If Reid is arguing for the existence in the strong sense of aesthetic qualities, they must be qualities other than novelty. The two remaining are grandeur and beauty. Let us see how things stand with them.

"The emotion raised by grand objects," Reid tells us, "is awful, solemn, and serious."[30] The "object" most capable of exciting such an emotion is the Deity. But other objects, too, are capable, in varying degrees, of giving rise to it. The "objects" which Reid first mentions as "grand" are *minds;* and he insists, in characteristic fashion, that grandeur is predicated of these objects, and properly so, not merely of the feeling of the perceiver.

> There is therefore a real intrinsic excellence in some qualities of mind, as in power, knowledge, wisdom, virtue, magnanimity. These, in every degree, merit esteem; but in an uncommon degree they merit admiration; and that which merits admiration we call grand. [31]

There seems no room for doubt about Reid's meaning here. The grandeur of mind is an objective quality in the strong sense: a "real intrinsic excellence." If it were not, there would have been no need for Reid to insist so emphatically on its existence independent of the feeling of grandeur; for everyone agreed that *something* causes the feeling, the only possible disagreement being about what kind of a something it is. What Reid is insisting upon is that the aesthetic value is in the object; the object does not become aesthetically valuable because of any relation to the perceiver: "if we hearken to the dictates of common sense, we must be convinced that there is real excellence in some things, whatever our feelings or our constitution be." [32]

As for objects other than minds — material objects, works of art, natural phenomena — they cannot, strictly speaking, possess the quality of grandeur, according to Reid; it is possessed by mind alone. Grandeur, he writes, "is found, originally and properly, in qualities of mind;... it is discerned, in objects of sense, only by reflection, as the light we perceive in the moon and planets is truly the light of the sun; and ... those who look for grandeur in mere matter, seek the living among the dead." [33] Matter, then, is a sign, or evidence, of grandeur in something else not grand itself. Thus, "When we contemplate the earth, the sea, the planetary system, the universe," we ascribe grandeur to them indirectly by virtue of our conceiving the sublime mind that created them: "They appear truly grand, and merit the highest admiration, when we consider them as the work of God . . . . " And when we perceive grandeur "in" literary works, "we ascribe to a work that grandeur which properly is inherent in the mind of the author."[34] Reid follows here the Platonic tradition that Shaftesbury bequeathed to eighteenth-century British aesthetics. His insistence that grandeur can belong to the mind only, and the obvious association of it with moral qualities, recalls the identification of the aesthetic with the moral on the part of Shaftesbury and the Cambridge Platonists. We shall encounter the same Platonic strain in Reid's theory of beauty and find it still surviving in the aesthetics of Reid's fellow Scot, Archibald Alison.

(8) It remains for us now to examine Reid's account of the beautiful in light of the distinction between "weak" and "strong" objective qualities.

"Our determinations with regard to the beauty of objects," Reid states, "may, I think, be distinguished into two kinds; the first we may call instinctive, the other rational."[35] The distinction is couched in the same terms as that between primary and secondary qualities. In rational judgments of beauty, as in our perception of primary qualities, we have clear and distinct knowledge of the objective quality; such judgments are "grounded on some agreeable quality of the objects which is distinctly conceived, and may be specified."[36] But instinctive judgments are of "occult" qualities, as are our perceptions of secondary qualities: "Some objects strike us at once, and appear beautiful at first sight, without any reflection, without our being able to say why we call them beautiful, or being able to specify any perfection which justifies our judgment."[37]

Now most rational judgments of the beautiful seem to have for their objects the same kind of quality as the grand: a quality of mind, or a quality in nonmental objects which suggests and draws the perceiver to a quality of mind. Reid illustrates this contention with an example reminiscent of Shaftesbury: the beauty displayed by a man of "good breeding."

There is nothing in the exterior of a man more lovely and more attractive than perfect good breeding. But what is this good breeding? It consists of all the external signs of due respect to our superior, condescension to our inferiors, politeness to all with whom we converse or have to do, joined in the fair sex with that delicacy of outward behavior which becomes them. And how comes it to have such charms in the eyes of all mankind; for this reason only, as I apprehend, that it is a natural sign of that temper, and those affections and sentiments with regard to others, and with regard to ourselves, which are in themselves truly amiable and beautiful. [38]

The occult qualities of beauty, the objects of instinctive aesthetic perception, can be compared, as we have remarked, to the secondary qualities. [39] We do not perceive their external nature clearly and distinctly; no reason can be given for the sensation of beauty instinctively felt. But we are not necessarily committed forever to ignorance here: the occult quality of beauty "is a proper subject of philosophical disquisition; and by a careful examination of the objects to which Nature hath given this amiable quality, we may perhaps discover some real excellence in the object, or, at least some valuable purpose that is served by the effect which it produces upon us." [40] The successful outcome of such an examination is the transformation of an instinctive judgment of beauty into a rational one, as in the following example which Reid provides:

The beauties of the field, of the forest, and of the flower-garden, strike a child long before he can reason. He is delighted with what he sees; but he knows not why. This is instinct, but it is not confined to childhood; it continues through all the stages of life. It leads the florist, the botanist, the philosopher, to examine and compare the objects which nature, by this powerful instinct, recommends to his attention. By degrees, he becomes a critic in beauties of this kind, and can give a reason why he prefers one to another. In every species, he sees the greatest beauty in the plants and flowers that are most perfect in their kind.... When he examines the internal structure of these productions of Nature, and traces them from their embryo state in the seed to their maturity, he sees a thousand beautiful contrivances of Nature, which feast his understanding more than their external form delighted his eye.

> Thus, every beauty in the vegetable creation of which he has
> formed any rational judgment, expresses some perfection in the
> object, or some wise contrivance in its Author. [41]

Two points are worth noting here. First, if the transformation of an instinctive judgment of beauty to a rational one means, *in all cases,* coming to perceive a mental quality, there would be no need to juxtapose a "perfection in the object" with "a wise contrivance in its Author," justapose, that is, a material excellence apparently real in the strong sense, with a mental excellence. Thus, although Reid, I think, considered *most* aesthetic qualities to be, ultimately, qualities of mind, there are statements which seem to suggest that at least some nonmental qualities are aesthetically real in the strong sense.

The second point is this. We have claimed that the qualities of beauty and grandeur exist, for Reid, in the strong sense, like the primary (and perhaps the secondary) qualities of bodies. Yet there is an important difference. The aesthetic qualities must be what David Ross has called "consequential" qualities. [42] They are dependent upon other qualities (for the most part, mental qualities) for their existence, although this does not make them any the less real in the strong sense. The Deity is "grand" because he is omnipotent and omniscient and good. Take these qualities away and he ceases to exemplify grandeur. But for all of that his grandeur is not identical with his omnipotence, omniscience, and goodness; it is an "emergent" fourth quality. Interpreting Reid in this way only can we reconcile his apparent insistence upon the existence of aesthetic qualities in the strong sense with his belief that we can in some way "reduce" our instinctive aesthetic judgments about "occult" qualities to rational ones about moral qualities of mind.

(9) It has been stated in recent years that Reid's aesthetics is "the most philosophical and least amateurish of the whole English eighteenth-century speculation." [43] If I believed this, I would have written a study of Reid rather than Hutcheson. But there is no doubt that Reid's aesthetic speculations were philosophical, and were far from amateurish. They deserve more attention than they customarily receive.

I take Reid's major contribution to eighteenth-century British aesthetics to be the accommodation of Hutcheson's sense of beauty to an increased realization of the role of reason in perception in general, and in aesthetic perception in particular. Reid himself had a different view of his primary accomplishment in aesthetics; and perhaps it would be appropriate to close with that.

Reid wrote in a letter to Archibald Alison: "I am proud to think that I first, in clear and explicit terms, and in the cool blood of a philosopher, maintained that all the beauty and sublimity of objects of sense is derived from the expression they exhibit of things intellectual, which alone have original beauty."[44]

What are we to make of this claim? After all, the doctrine which Reid takes credit for originating is hardly a new one; and that the great Neoplatonists lacked, and Thomas Reid possessed, "the cool blood of a philosopher" scarcely requires refutation. Yet there is no evidence that Reid was either an immodest man or an ignorant one. What, then, does he mean to say here that expresses neither an overestimation of his own philosophical talents nor ignorance of the history of philosophy?

What Reid had in mind when he spoke of the cold-blooded philosopher, I imagine, was the philosopher as exemplified by Locke: the plain, no-nonsense, "underlaborer," who eschews metaphysics and speculation in the grand manner. And if this is what he intended, then he was not so far wrong in his claim to be the first philosopher of *that* sort to hold aesthetic qualities to be exclusively "mental," or "intellectual," ones. Where Reid erred, I think, was in selecting this as his aesthetic testament. But we need not make the same mistake. Contemporary aesthetics has far more to learn from Reid's struggles with the sense-reason antinomy than with his ingenious but unfruitful reinterpretation of Neoplatonism.

X

THE RISE OF ASSOCIATION

(1) Reid was the last philosopher or critic of any importance to embrace the aesthetic sense doctrine in anything like its characteristic form; and, in fact, it was a dead issue long before he promulgated his aesthetic theory. In 1759, when Alexander Gerard still spoke the language of internal senses, his meaning was a very different one: the doctrine as Hutcheson had known it was no more. The sense of beauty had been destroyed by its own bosom serpent: the association of ideas.

It would be beyond the purview of this study to trace fully the development of the associationist philosophy in eighteenth-century British aesthetics.[1] But some brief historical remarks are necessary, after which we will examine the use to which Gerard put the association of ideas in reinterpreting Hutcheson's sense of beauty.

(2) The association of ideas, we saw, performed a special function in the aesthetic sense doctrine from the outset; but it was a negative function. For Hutcheson and his followers, association was a useful means of sweeping under the carpet the diversities in taste which seemed to militate against the notion of an implanted universal sense or instinct. But it is a double-edged sword. If the internal sense theorist can make negative use of association to explain how the "inherently" pleasant can lose its attractiveness through habitual association with the unpleasant, or how the neutral or "inherently" unpleasant can gain in attractiveness through habitual association with the plea-

sant, then it must be possible to cut the other way and use his own principle in showing that what may seem "inherently" pleasant or unpleasant has gained its pleasantness or unpleasantness in the same way.

One of the first to make this move was the moralist John Gay (cousin of the poet), who attacked Hutcheson's moral sense doctrine in his dissertations *Concerning the Fundamental Principles of Virtue or Morality* (1731).[2] Gay is in substantial agreement with Hutcheson on two points:

> that [i] the generality of mankind do approve of Virtue, or rather virtuous actions, without being able to give any reason for their approbation; and also, that [ii] some pursue it without knowing that it tends to their own private happiness [i.e., do not act with self-interest as their end in view] ; nay even when it appears to be inconsistent with and destructive of their happiness.[3]

Now the question is: How are we to account for these two phenomena of moral experience? Hutcheson, of course, appeals to inner senses: in this particular case, the moral sense and the sense of benevolence. We cannot give reasons for our moral judgments because they are nonrational; and we act in the interest of others, on Gay's interpretation of Hutcheson, in order to gratify our sense of benevolence, thus revealing that our benevolent actions are altruistic in appearance only.[4]

Gay, then, takes Hutcheson (mistakenly, I think) to be a psychological hedonist, agrees with him that even apparently altruistic actions are self-interested, but refuses to accept the moral sense doctrine as an explanation of the "fact." It is, he maintains, a flight to ignorance and dangerously close to the empiricist's bugbear, innate ideas.

> But this account seems still insufficient, rather cutting the knot, than untying it; and if it is not akin to the doctrine of innate ideas, yet I think it relishes too much of that of occult qualities. This ingenious author [Hutcheson] is certainly in the right in his observations upon the insufficiency of the common methods of accounting for both our election and approbation of moral actions, and rightly infers the necessity of supposing a moral sense (i.e. a power or faculty whereby we may perceive any action to be

an object of approbation, and the agent of love) and public affections, to account for the principal actions of human life. But then
by calling these instincts, I think he stops too soon, imagining
himself at the fountain-head, when he might have traced them
much higher, even to the true principle of all our actions, our own
happiness. [5]

For Gay, then, all benevolent acts are, in the last analysis,
motivated by private interest, even though we may not necessarily have private interest as our end in view. But the question
remains: Why are the majority of moral agents unable to give
their moral reason; namely, self-interest? How is it they *see
immediately* that a benevolent act is right without going
through the elaborate process of reasoning, with self-interest as
its conclusion? Gay's answer is *association:* having long ago connected benevolence with self-interest, we no longer bother
about it. The approbation of self-interest has been psychologic-
ally transferred to benevolence. We feel in performing a benevolent act what long ago we felt only after discovering by reason
that benevolent acts are in our interest. We have gained immediacy through habit, by obliterating the intermediary steps:

[O]ur approbation of morality, and all affections whatever, are
finally resolved into reason pointing out private happiness, and are
conversant only about things apprehended to be means tending to
this end; and . . . whenever this end is not perceived, they are
accounted for from the association of ideas, and may properly
enough be called habits. [6]

A subsequent passage articulates the point still more clearly:

We first perceive or imagine some real good, i.e. fitness to pro-
mote our natural happiness, in those things which we love and
approve of. Hence . . . we annex pleasure to those things. Hence
those things and pleasure are so tied together and associated in
our minds, that one cannot present itself, but the other will also
occur. And the association remains even after that which at first
gave them the connection is quite forgot, or perhaps does not
exist, but the contrary. [7]

Innate moral principles are apparent only, being merely acquired habits of thought and action whose origins and *raison d'être* have been forgotten.

(3) The direct inheritor of Gay's associationism was David Hartley, who systematically developed the doctrine in his influential *Observations on Man* (1749).[8] Hume, too, had made important use of the associationist psychology at about this time in his theory of knowledge. But whereas Hartley applied his theory to aesthetics, Hume did not in any significant way; and thus it is Hartley whom we must consider here.

"I begin with the Pleasures and Pains of Imagination; and shall endeavour to derive each Species of them by Association . . . ," writes Hartley in introducing his brief remarks on aesthetics.[9] Let us examine some instances of his procedure.

Here is Hartley's associationist interpretation of that venerable aesthetic principle, *uniformity amidst variety.*

> Uniformity and Variety in conjunction are also principal Sources of the Pleasures of Beauty, being made so partly by their Association with the Beauties of Nature; partly by that with Works of Art; and with the many Conveniences which we receive from the Uniformity and Variety of the Works of Nature and Art. They must therefore transfer part of the Lustre borrowed from the Works of Art, and from the Head of Convenience, upon the Works of Nature.[10]

To take another example, consonance and dissonance in music are both "original" in their effects, the former of course being naturally pleasing, the latter naturally unpleasant. But as both are used together in musical composition, dissonance gradually becomes pleasing through the connection with consonance. "By degrees the Discords become less and less harsh to the Ear, and at last even pleasant, at least by their Associations with the Concords, that go before, or follow them . . . ."[11]

And when all other associationist explanations fail, we can resort to the "Pleasures of Theopathy": the pleasures we feel in associating any object with thoughts of God, its creator.

> Those Persons who have already formed high Ideas of the Power, Knowledge, and Goodness, of the Author of Nature, with suitable

> Affections, generally feel the exalted Pleasures of Devotion upon
> every View and Contemplation of his Works, either in an explicit
> and distinct Manner [i.e.,consciously], or in a more secret and
> implicit one [i.e., unconsciously].[12]

Hartley himself did not put forth his associationist aesthetics
(such as it is) as an attack upon, or an alternative to, the aesthetic sense doctrine. But it came ready to hand when Gerard set
out to "modernize" the aesthetic senses in the light of continu-
ing criticism.

(4) Gerard, like Shaftesbury, is a transitional figure, although
the breach he spans is of considerably less importance to the
history of aesthetics. It is, nevertheless, crucial to the history of
the sense of beauty. Gerard occupies a position between the
doctrine of inner senses which Hutcheson fashioned out of
Locke, and the later Enlightenment's attempt to interpret the
sense of beauty as an amalgam of acquired habits and responses.
Gerard uses the principle of association, which was to be the
major weapon of his successors, to a greater extent than any
previous aesthetician. Yet he still speaks the language of Hutcheson's inner sense theory — a theory which associationism was
instrumental in rendering obsolete. Thus, although Gerard recognizes a large number of aesthetic "senses," he at the same
time, as a result really, decreases the significance of the term
"sense."

In the *Essay On Taste* (1759), Gerard's major aesthetic work
and the one which will occupy us here, seven "*internal* or *reflex
senses*" are distinguished: the senses (or tastes) of *novelty,
grandeur* and *sublimity, beauty, imitation, harmony, ridicule,*
and *virtue* (a list obviously indebted to Addison and Hutcheson). What significance these "senses" have for Gerard, considering their obvious profusion, is a question I request the
reader to hold in abeyance until the conclusion of this chapter,
at which point, I hope, at least a partially satisfactory answer
will have emerged.

The *Essay* begins with some preliminary remarks on taste and
the internal senses:

A fine taste is neither wholly the gift of *nature*, nor wholly the effect of *art*. It derives its origin from certain powers natural to the mind; but these powers cannot attain their full perfection, unless they be assisted by proper culture. Taste consists chiefly in the improvement of those principles which are commonly called the *powers of imagination*, and are considered by modern philosophers as *internal* or *reflex senses*, supplying us with finer and more delicate perceptions, than any which can be properly referred to our external organs. [13]

That "fine taste is neither wholly the gift of *nature*, nor wholly the effect of *art*" is, of course, a common enough contention. But in the context of Gerard's position, the relation between the acquired and the innate raises a special question because of Gerard's use of the appellation "inner sense." As a recent writer observed, "The seven internal senses are not ultimate principles of human nature: they are compound and derivative faculties."[14] Gerard makes it very clear at a number of points in the *Essay* that he wishes to divorce himself from the traditional concept of the internal senses as innate faculties — "the gift of *nature*." Rather, the internal senses are, for Gerard, "the effect of *art*." He was obviously influenced by the critics of the inner sense doctrine who looked with a jaundiced eye on a theory that in a seemingly arbitrary manner could provide an *ad hoc* "sense" for every occasion. And thus Gerard was anxious to represent the inner aesthetic "senses" as acquired responses, not organs of perception. The association of ideas gave him his principal psychological mechanism.

Such a concept of the inner senses was a step into a new region of aesthetic speculation, necessitated by the sort of criticism Balguy, Berkeley, and Price had been leveling at the moral sense school and, *en passant*, at the sense of beauty. Yet Gerard, as we have remarked, stood midway between the new tradition and the old: his roots were in the old law. Gerard derived his notion of the aesthetic senses, as he himself declared, from Hutcheson. And it was to Hutcheson's later works that his debt was greatest. He seemed to discern (I think correctly) a shift in Hutcheson's position.

> Mr. Hutcheson was the first who considered the powers of the
> imagination as so many senses. In his *Inquiry concerning beauty
> and virtue,* and his *Essays on the passions,* he calls them *internal
> senses.* In his later works he terms them *subsequent* and *reflex*
> senses: *subsequent,* because they always suppose some previous
> perception of the objects about which they are employed; . . . *re-
> flex,* because, in order to their exertion, the mind reflects upon,
> and takes notice of some circumstance or mode of the object that
> was perceived, besides those qualities which offered themselves to
> its attention at first view . . . . In the following essay, the terms
> *internal sense* and *reflex sense* are used promiscuously. [15]

Now what exactly did Hutcheson mean in his later works,
notably the *Short Introduction to Moral Philosophy,* when he
referred to *reflex* or *subsequent* senses? And does Gerard retain
Hutcheson's meaning when he "promiscuously" uses the terms?

In answering the first question, it might be well to return for
a moment to Hutcheson's early position. We determined, after
rather lengthy considerations, that in Hutcheson's first *Inquiry,*
the term "beauty" refers to a pleasurable quality very much like
a *secondary quality.* If this is indeed the case, then the sense of
beauty can be said to perceive external objects. In other words,
it perceives the external world to the same extent that, for
Locke, the external senses do in perceiving secondary qualities.
But there is another kind of perception whereby we perceive
not the external world, even to the extent that the external
senses do for the Lockean; that is the kind of perception that
we sometimes describe as *introspection.* And the sense which
gives rise to such second-order perception is, in the terminology
of Hutcheson's later works, a *reflex* or *subsequent* sense. For
the later Hutcheson, the internal senses, including the sense of
beauty, have become reflexive: "INTERNAL senses," he writes,
"are those powers or determinations of the mind, by which it
perceives or is conscious of all within itself, its actions, passions,
judgments, wills, desires, joys, sorrows, purposes of action." [16]
The sense of beauty has ceased to be a spectator of the external
world and has become a spectator merely of its own prison, the
mind.

Hutcheson appends to his later definition of the internal

senses a rather broad hint as to the source of the doctrine. "This power," he writes, "some celebrated writers call *consciousness* or *reflection*, which has for its objects the qualities, actions or states of the mind itself, as the external senses have things external."[17] What "celebrated writers" does Hutcheson have in mind? Well, the notion of an internal sense monitoring its own habitation can be traced at least as far back as Saint Augustine, who writes of an "interior sense" by which one perceives one's own perceiving.[18] But the example that was closest to Hutcheson both in time and sympathy was, as usual, his spiritual father, Locke, who refers to reflection at times as an *internal sense.*[19] In fact, the aesthetic sense doctrine has now described a perfect circle: from Locke to Locke in two generations.

Now to our second question: Does Gerard retain Hutcheson's concept of the reflexive aesthetic sense? He does, in his fashion: for Gerard, taste is "the perception of the perception" of external objects "in contrast to the direct perception of them by the external sense."[20] But it is a reflexive sense that is acquired, not innate, deriving from Hutcheson's later position, yet moving toward complete rejection of implanted faculties. To appreciate the full extent of Gerard's position, both its indebtedness to Hutcheson and its departure from him, we must examine in some detail the inner workings of the aesthetic "senses." However, there is no need to canvas them all: I have chosen, rather, to concentrate on the sense of beauty.

(5) "Beautiful objects are of different kinds, and produce pleasure by means of different principles of human nature." So begins Gerard's disquisition on "*the sense or taste of Beauty.*"[21] We are not to look, in Gerard, for any single definition of *the* beautiful object, or single faculty for its perception. In these respects Gerard has departed from the inner sense school to which he owed his first allegiance.

But if Gerard's opening remark on the beautiful is a departure, the first definition restores the prodigal: "The first species of beauty is that of figure; and belongs to objects possessed of *uniformity, variety,* and *proportion.* Each of these qualities

pleases in some degree; but all of them united give exquisite
satisfaction."[22] This, of course, is a definition that Hutcheson
would have readily accepted, as far as it goes; but it is not
supposed to be complete, or of universal application.

The question now arises: Why do objects posessing *uniformity, variety,* or *proportion* give rise to pleasure when perceived.
Hutcheson's answer is that there is a *sense* disposed to receive
pleasure from such objects: every Lockean simple idea given in
perception must have an appropriate disposition to receive it.
Gerard, on the other hand, makes no mention here of inner
senses, but (like Price, Edmund Burke, and others) ascribes the
pleasure associated with the perception of such qualities as we
might call "aesthetic" to various perceptual principles. Thus,
the pleasure taken in *uniform* (or *simple*) objects is ascribed by
Gerard, as it was by Price and, in the seventeenth century, by
Descartes and Spinoza, to ease of perception and conception:
"Facility in the conception of an object, if it be moderate, gives
us pleasure . . . . Hence too it is that *uniformity* and *simplicity*
become agreeable. Objects endued with these qualities enter
easily into the mind . . . . "[23] And *variety,* as a foil to *unity,*
pleases, according to Gerard, because it exercises the mind —
the principle of mental exercise being a sacred cow in Enlightenment aesthetics, since its extensive use by L'Abbe DuBos, who
himself inherited it from the seventeenth century.[24] As Gerard
expresses the idea,

> But uniformity, when perfect and unmixed, is apt to pall upon
> the sense . . . . *Variety* is necessary to enliven it . . . . Variety in
> some measure gratifies the sense of novelty, as our ideas vary in
> passing from the contemplation of one part to that of another.
> This transition puts the mind in action, and gives it employment,
> the consciousness of which is agreeable.[25]

Proportion, according to Gerard, is of two kinds: the first is
related to *size,* and the second to *fitness.* There must be a
proportion struck between the whole and its parts: a proportion
relative to the size of the whole and the sizes of its parts "when
none of the parts are so small, in respect of one another, and of
the whole, as to disappear through their smallness, while we

contemplate the whole; and when none of them are so large, that, when we fix our view on them, we cannot distinctly perceive at the same time their relation to the whole, and to the other parts." [26] Proportion thus renders an object and its parts conformable to our perceptual faculties; lack of it has the opposite effect. And whereas proper proportion makes the perceptual process successful, lack of it frustrates that process; and from thence arises the relish for proportion and the distaste for its lack.

> As nothing gives us greater pleasure than what leads us to form a lofty conception of our own faculties, so nothing is more disagreeable than what reminds us of their imperfection. On this account it is, that the want of this kind of proportion disgusts us. It leads us to entertain a low, and consequently ungrateful, opinion of our capacity, by rendering it impossible to form one entire distinct conception of the object. [27]

Disproportion, then, displeases because it gives us a perceptual inferiority complex: an explanation that would have delighted Hobbes, who, we recall, explained laughter as an expression of our superiority.

The second species of proportion, *fitness,* is of course another eighteenth-century shibboleth; it had a firm grip on the Enlightenment mind from Hutcheson to Kant, despite the dissenting voices of a few like Burke. Gerard seems to interpret fitness as a kind of *association;* indeed, the principle of association plays such a prominent role in the perception of the beautiful, even where it is not specifically alluded to, that there is no area in which it cannot be seen to obtrude. For even the "pure" perceptions of unity and variety can, in part, be reduced to the association of ideas. They are "indications of design, wisdom, and contrivance; qualities of mind which we never fail to survey with pleasure."

> When we behold uniformity in a work, we naturally conclude, that it could not be the effect of chance, and that it could scarce be formed without intention. . . . we take pleasure in conceiving the excellence of the cause, and by this the delight is heightened which we find in beholding the effect that suggests that excellence. [28]

Thus, the mind is led by the train of associations from the object to the idea of its (supposed) cause; and in that the contemplation of this associated *idea* is pleasant, the primary object of contemplation, be it pleasurable of itself or not, becomes a sharer in the associated pleasure and basks in a reflected light. A similar process is at work in the perception of fitness: the fitness of an object for its end also betokens a rational agent.

> When therefore we see a work, it leads us by a natural association to conceive its end; prone to comparison, we examine the propriety of the parts in relation to this end; if any of them are prejudicial to it, we are disgusted with the want of skill which this imperfection betrays . . . . But when, on examination, the fitness of all the parts appears, the satisfaction with which we think on the skill and ingenuity thus displayed communicates itself to the effect so closely connected with it by causation . . . . [29]

This is clearly an associationist version of Reid's Neoplatonic view that material objects are beautiful only as signs of mental qualities, although Gerard does not underscore, as Reid does, the "only."

It is obvious that the role of association in aesthetic perception is very different for Gerard than it had been for Hutcheson. The latter looked upon the association of ideas as the chief corrupter of taste, joining what is innately pleasurable with what is not and thus poisoning aesthetic sensibility. The former, on the contrary, "usually treats the functioning of association not as a corrupter of taste but as one of the main occasions for its activity and one of the principal causes of its extension."[30] For Gerard, in fact, association is the mainspring of aesthetic perception in general and the perception of beauty in particular: "There is perhaps no term used in a looser sense than *beauty,* which is applied to almost every thing that pleases us . . . . In all these cases, beauty is, at least in part, resolveable into association."[31]

(6) There are, then, a number of qualities that bear the appellation "beautiful," according to Gerard. Each can be explained in terms of certain operations of the mental faculties

and various associations of ideas. But what do these qualities have in common that they should all be called by the same name? Gerard answers, "by reason of the similitude of their feelings, they are reduced to the same *genus*."[32] The causes of beauty are multifarious and complex, the feeling itself always the same, simple Lockean idea. The sentiment or idea of beauty "is compound in its *principles,* but perfectly simple in its *feeling.*"[33] And this is in part Gerard's justification for calling this complex of associations a "sense" of beauty.

Gerard distinguishes three characteristics of a "sense" which he takes to be definitive:

> [i] It is a power which supplies us with such *simple* perceptions, as cannot be conveyed by any other channel to those who are destitute of that sense. [ii] It is a power which receives its perception *immediately,* as soon as its object is exhibited, previous to any reasoning concerning the qualities of the object, or the causes of the perception. [iii] It is a power which exerts itself *independent of volition;* so that, while we remain in proper circumstances, we cannot, by any act of the will, prevent our receiving certain sensations, nor alter them at pleasure . . . . [34]

As we can see from this passage, *innateness* is no longer considered a *sine qua non* for a "sense." And thus Gerard's *acquired* senses do not fail to qualify as "senses" on this account. Nor is the philosopher any longer convinced by the *immediacy* of aesthetic perception that the "sense" of beauty must be a superadded aesthetic faculty, distinct from the commonly accepted ones, and that it cannot be complex in its function. Burke, for example, had already argued that "this celerity of its operation is no proof that the Taste is a distinct faculty"; for here, as elsewhere in the operation of our complex mental processes, we "are obliged to spell" at first, but eventually we "read with ease and with celerity."[35] Again, the nonvolitional character of sense perception is no bar to calling a complex faculty a "sense." For why, after all, should there not be complex psychological processes as immune to our wills and desires as the seeing of red or the feeling of heat? And since the feeling of beauty is simple, even though its causes are not, the last impediment is removed, and Gerard can conclude that "the powers of taste may, with the greatest propriety, be reckoned senses, though they be derived faculties . . . . " [36] Although Gerard is in perfect agreement with Hutcheson that the idea of beauty is a simple idea, he rejects Hutcheson's assumption that the sense of beauty must, therefore, be a simple faculty.

(7) The aesthetic faculties were, in Hutcheson's later writings, both innate and subsequent. For Gerard, as we have seen, they are no longer innate, but are still subsequent or reflexive. Like the inner senses of Hutcheson's later position, their material is subjective. For the Lockean, an external sense has for its object (though not its direct object) the external world, which it delivers to the mind in the form of ideas of primary and secondary qualities. But the subsequent or reflexive sense has for its object not the external world (even indirectly), but rather ideas that have already been delivered by the external senses and worked over by the mind — in other words, predigested material. Even as the sensation of color is produced by the figure and motion of the external (primary) qualities, so the sensation of beauty is produced by the figure and motion of internal objects: the ideas of primary and secondary qualities.

Now what strikes one about this position is its strange kinship with Locke. But it is a different sort of kinship from that which we observed in Hutcheson's early position. It is not so much an extension of Lockean principles as the first *Inquiry* had been, but rather a return, at least in some important respects, to Locke's own aesthetic theory, in so far as Locke can really be said to have had one at all.

As we saw in our earlier discussions of Hutcheson, beauty for Locke is a complex idea; as such, it is never given directly in perception, as are simple ideas. A complex idea, rather, is constructed out of simple ones by an act of the mind. And it can, "when the mind pleases," be "considered . . . as one entire thing, and signified by one name." [37]

Now for both Locke and Gerard, there is a certain sense in which beauty is a complex idea. For Locke, the idea of beauty is *identical with* a complex idea, and for Gerard the idea of beauty is *caused by* a complex idea. But just as for the Lockean, the word "red" can name either the sensation of red or its cause, so for Gerard, it would seem, the word "beauty" can name either the sensation of beauty or its cause; and in the case of beauty, the cause is a complex idea.

However, for Gerard there is one *simple* idea or feeling that can correctly be called beautiful. Is such also the case for Locke? Here the analogy seems to break down, although not perhaps as drastically as one might think. For Locke does tell us that the complex idea of beauty can, "when the mind pleases," be "considered . . . as one entire thing." It would, I think, be contrary to Locke's intentions to claim that when we do consider the complex idea of beauty in this way, there arises a new simple idea or sentiment of beauty. But it surely is a notion that one might be teased into by reading Locke. In any case, both Locke and Gerard certainly are suggesting that there is a way of experiencing the complex idea of beauty such that its complexity gives way to a wholeness not previously present. But for Locke this wholeness is achieved by a free act of will, whereas for Gerard it is caused by perceptual and psychological processes over which the aesthetic perceiver has no control.

It would certainly be a mistake to exaggerate the kinship between Locke and Gerard. Aesthetic thought, after all, by no means stood still between 1690 and 1759; on the contrary, it was a period of unparalleled activity. Yet one can still feel the influence of Locke, even at a distance. The British critics, as Professor Stolnitz has observed, "were, like everybody else, nurtured on Locke." [38] And this was, apparently, even truer of Gerard at mid-century than it had been of Hutcheson at the outset; all of which gives further evidence, if further evidence were really needed, that, in the words of A. C. Fraser, "Few books in the literature of philosophy have so widely represented the spirit of the age and country in which they appeared, or have so influenced opinion afterwards, as Locke's *Essay Concerning Human Understanding.*" [39]

XI

THE TRIUMPH OF ASSOCIATION

(1) I have presented Gerard as rather an ambiguous figure because he seems to adopt two theories which do not keep very good company together: Hutcheson's doctrine of aesthetic senses, and the doctrine of associationism which, more than anything else, contributed to the downfall of the internal sense aesthetics. I conclude, however, with two thinkers who display no ambivalence in this regard: Archibald Alison and Dugald Stewart. They brought the associationist aesthetics to full flower and, in so doing, laid the ghost of Hutcheson and the sense of beauty to rest.

Gerard, as we have seen, did not put forth the association of ideas specifically as an attack upon, or an alternative to, the aesthetic sense doctrine, but rather as a reinterpretation of it. Others, however, prior to Alison and Stewart, had already seen associationism as rendering appeal to inner aesthetic senses unnecessary. Among these was Joseph Priestley, for example, who wrote in the *Course of Lectures on Oratory and Criticism* (1777):

> Whatever it be, in the sentiment or ideas, that makes a discourse to be read with pleasure, must either be *interesting*, by exciting those gross and more sensible feelings we call passions, or must awaken those more delicate sensations, which are generally called *pleasures of the imagination*. Each of these kinds of feelings are, by some philosophers, referred to so many distinct *reflex*, or *internal senses*, as they call those faculties of the mind by which we perceive them; whereas according to Dr. Hartley's theory,

those sensations consist of nothing more than a congeries or com-
bination of ideas and sensations, separately indistinguishable, but
which were formerly associated either with the idea itself that
excites them, or with some other idea, or circumstance, attending
the introduction of them. It is this latter hypothesis that I
adopt . . . . [1]

We can see Priestley's remark as setting the stage for Alison
and Stewart. For they, too, conceived of associationism not
only as an aesthetic principle acceptable on its own merits, but
also as an answer to the internal sense doctrine in aesthetics: an
alternative to the sense of beauty free from the taint of aprioriism and innate ideas. The last of the eighteenth-century Scottish
aestheticians still felt the presence of the internal sense doctrine
enough to make it the object of their criticism, perhaps because
it had been part of the Scottish philosophy almost from the
start. Hutcheson, the one most often associated with the doctrine, Reid, its latter-day proponent, Gerard, its "modernizer,"
all were Scots. The sense of beauty was the Scots' baby, not
perhaps by birth, but by adoption, which, being an act of free
choice, often makes ties as strong as those of blood.

(2) Before we come to consider the work of Alison and Stewart, it would be useful to review the basic tenets of the aesthetic
sense doctrine. We shall then be able to see directly those they
reject, those they accept, and those they ignore.

The inner sense aesthetics can be summarized in six propositions. I will state them in terms of the beautiful; but, clearly,
they hold for other aesthetic qualities as well.

i. The feeling of beauty is simple and unanalyzable.

ii. The perception of the beautiful is innate; it can be improved, but not implanted, by instruction.

iii. The perception of the beautiful is immediate; it does not
proceed by stages.

iv. The perception of the beautiful is not susceptible of control by the will; under the proper perceptual conditions, an
object is perceived as beautiful despite any contrary wish on the
part of the perceiver.

v. The perception of the beautiful is nonrational and achieved through the agency of an internal sense; this is alleged to follow from i-iv.

vi. The quality in objects which produces the idea of beauty in the perceiver is definable (for example, as *uniformity amidst variety*).

Not every philosopher who espoused the doctrine of aesthetic senses held all six of these propositions; nor, of course, were all of them the sole property of the aesthetic sense school. But Hutcheson, implicitly or explicitly, held them all; and he, after all, was rightly considered by followers and critics alike to be both founding father and leading spokesman of the internal sense school.

(3) At the outset of his *Essays on the Nature and Principles of Taste* (1790), Alison attacked the notion that the feelings of beauty and sublimity are simple feelings (proposition i). This, he believed, was his own special contribution to aesthetics. With regard to the genesis of his theory, Alison stated: "It seemed to me that the SIMPLICITY OF THE EMOTION OF TASTE, was a principle much too hastily adopted; and that the consequences which followed from it [the internal sense doctrine among them] . . . were very little reconcileable with the most common experience of human feeling . . . . " With the aesthetic sense doctrine as his principal whipping boy, Alison rejected the axiom of simplicity and outlined his own projected analysis of the pleasures of the imagination.

> I shall endeavour to show, that this effect is very different from the determination of a SENSE; that it is not in fact a simple, but a complex emotion; that it involves in all cases, 1*st,* the production of some simple emotion, or the exercise of some moral affection; and 2*dly,* the consequent excitement of a peculiar exercise of the imagination; that these concomitant effects are distinguishable, and very often distinguished in our experience; and that the *peculiar* pleasure of the BEAUTIFUL or the SUBLIME is only felt when these two effects are conjoined and the complex emotion produced. [2]

Of course one would like to know precisely what Alison meant by a "complex emotion." If we say, for example, that lemonade has a "complex" taste, being sweet by virtue of the sugar, and tart by virtue of the lemons, we would mean, most likely, that the taste of lemonade is itself a distinct, "simple" taste, but that it is the result of—analyzable into—two components. The taste of sugar or of lemons, that is, sweet or sour, we would say is a simple taste in that it is both experienced as simple and is in fact unanlyzable — irreducible into (taste) components. But now take another example: liver and onions. Like lemonade, it is analyzable into two distinct flavors and is, therefore, a complex taste. However, the ingredients do not blend (chopped liver excepted) as lemon and sugar: the components never give rise to a distinct liver-and-onions flavor as lemon and sugar do to a lemonade flavor; the flavor is always liver *and* onions. Thus, liver and onions, unlike lemonade, is complex both in that it is analyzable into two components and is experienced as two flavors; that is, experienced as complex. The question is, in which sense of "complex" is Alison'a aesthetic emotion complex? Is it experienced as simple or complex: lemonade or liver and onions?

One interesting hint is given us in Alison's none too modest posture as an innovator: "I am conscious," he wrote, "that I have entered upon a new and untrodden path . . . . "[3] If we take this claim at all seriously, we must reject the possibility that Alison thought of the feelings of beauty and sublimity as complex in feeling, for it is hardly a new and untrodden path: it is Locke pure and simple. What is left is the view that the feelings of beauty and sublimity are complex feelings which are experienced as simple. This would distinguish Alison's view from Gerard's, which is that the aesthetic feelings are simple ideas *caused by* complex ones. There is, truth to tell, only a very thin line between Gerard and Alison; and Alison seems to cross it at times. It is often difficult to tell whether his complex emotion of taste is the cause of the ideas of beauty and sublimity or the ideas themselves. What I am suggesting is that the most charitable interpretation we can make, given his innovative stance, is the latter: that, for Alison, the emotions of beauty and sublimity are complex emotions experienced as simple.

But if we accept this interpretation, we cannot accept it *tout court.* For Alison writes, to begin with, "these concomitant effects," that is, the simple emotion and the chain of ideas which make up the complex emotion of taste, "are distinguishable, and very often distinguished in our experience . . . . " This seems to suggest that the emotions of beauty and sublimity are often experienced as complex, but that they are sometimes experienced as simple. In emphasizing that they *are* distinguishable, Alison is clearly intimating that they are more usually not distinguished; that they tend to be taken for simple. Thus, it would seem Alison's real position is that the emotions of taste are a mixed bag: some experienced as simple and some as complex.

Again, the statement that "the *peculiar* pleasure of the BEAUTIFUL or the SUBLIME is only felt when these two effects [the simple emotion and the train of ideas] are conjoined and the complex emotion produced," raises similar ambiguities. And to increase our perplexity we now appear to have two subjective phenomena in the aesthetic experience: a *"peculiar* pleasure" and a "complex emotion" which produces it. One would expect that the "complex emotion" is the emotion of taste, pleasure and all. We shall recur to this *"peculiar* pleasure" after having explored Alison's position more fully. But what we have already seen is that Alison has a difficult time keeping his position distinct from Locke's on the one hand and Gerard's on the other; from the view that the idea of beauty (or sublimity) is a complex idea experienced as such, and the view that the idea of beauty (or sublimity) is a simple idea caused by a com-. plex one.

(4) Alison's complex emotion is composed of two basic elements: (i) a "simple emotion" or "moral affection"; and (ii) "the consequent excitement of a peculiar exercise of the imagination." The simple emotion or moral affection which initiates the complex aesthetic emotion is not itself an emotion of taste, but some "nonaesthetic" emotion, say, fear or love, aroused by the aesthetic object. "Whenever the emotions of sublimity or beauty are felt, I believe it will be found, that some affection is uniformly excited, by the presence of the object,

before the more complex emotion of beauty is felt; and that if no such affection is excited, no emotion of beauty or sublimity is produced."[4]

Now the simple emotion is the triggering mechanism for a chain reaction: that reaction constitutes the succession of ideas which, together with the simple emotion, constitute the complex emotion of taste. What is the nature of this train? It is a string of *connected* ideas. But connected by what? After all, consciousness itself is a string of "connected" ideas; but aesthetic experience is only one part of consciousness. The association of ideas raises such a wide variety of feelings (or ideas) consequent upon the contemplation of one object that it becomes vital for the associationist aesthetics to decide which are valid — relevant to the aesthetic experience — and which are not.

For Alison, the key lies in the leading emotion which excites the train. An aesthetic train of ideas must be characterized by emotive unity: the delight of beauty "is proportioned to the degree in which this uniformity of character prevails."[5] In other words, the degree to which a train of ideas is aesthetic is proportional to the degree to which the original simple emotion is expressed in the ensuing train. And it follows that an object is aesthetic in the degree to which it is capable of exciting some leading emotion; it, too, must possess emotive unity (for which reason, incidentally, Alison favored the tragedy of Corneille to the mixed tragi-comedy of Shakespeare). "If it is true, that those trains of thought which attend the emotions of taste, are uniformly distinguished by some general principle of connexion, it ought to be found that no composition of objects or qualities in fact produces such emotions, in which this unity of character or of emotion is not preserved."[6] Both the aesthetic object and the aesthetic experience, then, possess emotive unity. Alison's language almost has the ring of John Dewey in making the point, although the association of ideas seems hardly the psychological principle capable of achieving the kind of organic integration which, for Dewey, characterizes *an* experience.

How does a train of associations manage to embody or express the leading emotion that has given rise to it? "Express" and "embody" are, perhaps, rather highfalutin words for what, in the end, turns out to be the principle of *resemblance*. Hume had distinguished three relations between ideas "by which the mind . . . is convey'd from one idea to another . . . ": these are "RESEMBLANCE, CONTINGUITY in time or place, and CAUSE and EFFECT." He had also essentially decreed *resemblance* for aesthetics (as had Hobbes) by ascribing it to the "aesthetic" faculty, *imagination*. "'Tis plain," Hume wrote, "that in the course of our thinking, and in the constant revolution of our ideas, our imagination runs easily from one idea to any other that *resembles* it, and that this quality alone is to the fancy a sufficient bond and association."[7] For Alison *resemblance* is "sufficient bond and association" to establish the unity of emotion that characterizes the ideas of beauty and sublimity.

> In those trains . . . which are suggested by objects of sublimity or beauty, however slight the connexion between individual thoughts may be, I believe it will be found, that there is always some general principle of connexion which pervades the whole, and gives them some certain and definite character. They are either gay, or pathetic, or melancholy, or solemn, or awful, or elevating, &c. according to the nature of the emotion which is first excited.[8]

Thus, the complex emotion of taste can be thought of as a train of ideas which resemble each other in that they give rise to emotions of the same kind.

(5) But thus far we have been dealing exclusively with the nature of the complex emotion of taste. We must now turn to the pleasure of taste, the pleasure of beauty or sublimity, which, as we have seen, Alison considers an integral part of the aesthetic experience. There are two relevant questions here: (i) How is this pleasure aroused? (ii) What is its nature?

To answer the first question, we must recall that Alison refers to the aesthetic train of ideas as an "exercise of the imagination." He has, in fact, adopted the then ubiquitous notion of aesthetic pleasure as deriving from mental exercise: the notion which Du Bos inherited from the seventeenth century and passed on to the Enlightenment. Alison adds to this notion an indigenous product of British thought: the principle of aesthetic disinterestedness.[9] Alison maintains that "there is a pleasure annexed, by the constitution of our nature, to the exercise of imagination . . . ."[10] It is this pleasure which the aesthetic train of ideas elicits; the imagination, in following the aesthetic train, is engaged in a kind of exercise: "according to common expression, our imagination is seized, and our fancy busied in the pursuit of all those trains of thought . . . ."[11] But the imagination is not always in a state susceptible to the stimulation of this exercise. It must be free and unimpeded by practical considerations if it is to skip lightly from one idea to another, guided by their resemblance only; in a word, it must be *disinterested.*

> That state of mind, every man must have felt, is most favourable to the emotions of taste, in which the imagination is free and unembarrassed, or in which the attention is so little occupied by any private or particular object of thought, as to leave us open to all the impressions, which the objects that are before us can create. It is upon the vacant and the unemployed, accordingly, that the objects of taste make the strongest impression. It is in such hours alone, that we turn to the composition of music, or of poetry, for amusement. The seasons of care, of grief, of business, have other occupations, and destroy, for the time at least, our sensibility to the beautiful or the sublime, in the same proportion that they produce a state of mind unfavourable to the indulgence of imagination.[12]

The pleasure of taste, then, is in part the pleasure of mental exercise; but it is something more. It is the pleasure which, according to Alison, is given by the simple emotion with which the aesthetic experience begins. And thus aesthetic pleasure — the pleasure of sublimity or beauty — is, according to Alison, a complex pleasure, even as the aesthetic emotion is a complex emotion.

> The pleasure, therefore, which accompanies the emotions of taste, may be considered not as a simple, but as a complex pleasure; and as arising not from any separate and peculiar sense, but from the union of the pleasure of SIMPLE EMOTION, with that which is

annexed, by the constitution of the human mind, to the exercise
of IMAGINATION.[13]

Again the complexity of the aesthetic feeling — in this instance,
the pleasure of taste — is claimed by Alison to cast doubt upon
the inner sense doctrine, a claim increasingly heard in the waning years of the eighteenth century.

This brings us to our second question: What is the nature of
this pleasure of taste? It is complex. But is it experienced as
complex or simple? As in the case of the emotions of sublimity
and beauty, the question seems, in the last analysis, a moot one.
Alison simply does not give us enough of a clue. Perhaps he
didn't see the distinction.

(6) Alison's book is divided into two parts: two *Essays*. We
have, so far, been concerned exclusively with the first: "Of the
Nature of the Emotions of Sublimity and Beauty"; that is, the
nature of aesthetic experience. But in order to understand the
full extent of Alison's departure from the inner sense school of
Hutcheson, we must concern ourselves also with the second:
"Of the Sublimity and Beauty of the Material World"; that is,
the nature of material aesthetic objects.

The second essay deals extensively with five classes of material beauty and sublimity: sound, objects of sight, forms, motion, and the human countenance (added in the second edition).
In each case, Alison applies the same basic principles; and as the
principles, not their specific applications, are our primary interest, we shall concern ourselves for the most part with the preliminary remarks in which these principles are stated.

The experience of taste begins with the arousing of a simple
(nontaste) emotion; and thus the first prerequisite for a material
object being an aesthetic (taste) object is the power to arouse
such an emotion. But, Alison argues, "matter itself is unfitted
to produce any kind of emotion." Matter produces sensations;
and "such sensations might be either pleasing or painful, but
. . . in no case could they be attended with any emotion."[14]

How, then, can a material object (or quality) be an aesthetic
object (or quality), if it lacks the necessary prerequisite; namely, the power to arouse emotion? The answer is *association*.

But although the qualities of matter are in themselves incapable of producing emotion, or the exercise of any affection, yet it is obvious that they may produce this effect, from their association with other qualities; and as being either the signs or expressions of such qualities as are fitted by the constitution of our nature to produce emotion. [15]

The habitual association of a quality that cannot evoke emotion with one that can gradually renders the former emotively potent: "the constant connexion we discover between the sign and the thing signified, between the material quality and the quality productive of emotion, renders at last the one expressive to us of the other, and very often disposes us to attribute to the sign, that effect which is produced only by the quality signified." It seems clear, then, that what Alison means to say when he maintains the seemingly implausible view that matter cannot arouse emotion is simply this. Emotive responses are acquired; and they are acquired by association. The only unlearned responses we make are physical responses to physical stimuli, and these are not emotive responses. Expressed in this way, the view loses some of its implausibility.

Alison enumerates seven kinds of association — not, he points out, an exhaustive list: [16]

i. Qualities of form and color, by which objects of use or pleasure are identified, become, through association with them, capable of arousing the emotions which the objects arouse.

ii. Forms, colors, and sounds associated with "qualities of design, of wisdom, of skill" take on the emotive potency of those qualities.

iii. Such material signs of mental qualities as countenance, gesture, and voice take on, through association, the power of arousing emotion which their significata possess.

iv. Qualities that resemble the natural signs of mental qualities, by a sort of second-order association, gain the power of emotive arousal from the signs which have previously gained it from their significata.

v. There are "resemblances" between certain sensations and certain emotions: "Thus, there is some analogy between the sensation of gradual ascent, and the emotion of ambition — -

between the lively sensation of sunshine, and the cheerful emotion of joy — between the painful sensation of darkness, and the dispiriting emotion of sorrow." It is not clear whether the "resemblance" means that the sensations *feel like* the emotions, or, as some of Alison's examples seem to suggest, that there is a kind of structural isomorphism between them. In any case, the material objects and qualities which *ex hypothesi* give rise, in their pristine state, to sensations, not emotions become through the resemblance of emotions to those sensations capable of arousing the emotions also.

vi. Language contributes to the process of association by serving as a collective memory, a repository of associations acquired by past generations. Each individual is limited by time and situation to a relatively small number of associations; but language gives him the benefit of associations acquired by the whole human race in its collective lifetime.

vii. Finally, each man's own personal associations, consequences of his own special circumstances, contribute to the power material objects have of arousing his emotions.

(7) The first of Alison's *Essays* attacks Hutcheson's aesthetic sense doctrine explicitly by denying the simplicity of the emotions of taste. The second attacks it implicitly by denying the innateness of aesthetic judgment (proposition ii) and the existence of qualities common to all objects of taste in reference to which taste terms may be defined (proposition vi). Both denials follow, as we shall see, from the concept of association. This leaves the immediacy of the judgments of taste (proposition iii), the freedom of such judgments from control by the will (proposition iv), and the nonrationality of judgments of taste (proposition v) as possible survivors of the inner sense school.

As to the immediacy of the judgments of taste, Alison is silent, although the associationists, as we have seen, did not believe immediacy and association to be incompatible doctrines, either in ethics or aesthetics. Quite to the contrary, the association of ideas was an attractive hypothesis just because it could preserve immediacy without recourse to innate senses.

The nonrationality of aesthetic perception is obviously implied by Alison's theory. The aesthetic experience begins with an emotion and consists in the preservation of that emotion through the ensuing train of ideas. This is not to say reason is entirely absent from the realm of the beautiful and sublime; the critic and the philosopher both employ rational methods. But in the judgment of taste proper, emotion is supreme.

The relation between taste and the will is another topic on which Alison is completely silent. But here, too, we can read his opinion in his doctrine. Association is essentially a form of mechanistic psychological determinism. According to the doctrine (which, it should be recalled, had Hobbes as an early proponent), the succession of our ideas follows a predictable course, determined by the laws of association. A recent description of Lord Kames along these lines seems to me admirably suited to Alison as well. "He looked upon the human mind as a machine which determined its nature and therefore its reality in accordance with the laws of association and those corollary laws which an investigation of our ways of knowing had established."[17] There seems little place for volition here.

But to return to the two points at issue between Alison and Hutcheson in the second essay, namely, the innateness of the judgments of taste and the definability of its objects, Alison's denial of both follows directly from his associationist viewpoint. The rejection of innateness clearly follows simply from the fact that associations are *acquired* and are also the *sine qua non* for taste. Alison emphasizes continually, throughout the second essay, that all so-called "beautiful" or "sublime" material objects have acquired these characters. Even the most likely candidates for original beauty, sounds, for example, are reduced by Alison to acquired associations.

> The observations which I have offered on the subject of simple sounds, are perhaps sufficient to show, that the sublimity and beauty of these sounds arise, in all cases, from the qualities with which we have observed them connected, and of which they appear to us as the signs or expressions; and that no sounds in themselves are fitted by the constitution of our nature to produce these emotions.[18]

Even such a hallowed quality as proportion acquires its beauty, Alison maintains, from its association, in this case with fitness, which in turn derives its effect from association with the idea of an intelligent creator. Alison writes, "certain proportions affect us with the emotion of beauty, not from any original capacity in such qualities to excite this emotion, but from their being expressive to us of the fitness of the parts to the end designed." [19] It would seem that Alison is willing to grant nothing to the opposition, not even the "natural" appeal of the most simple, formless, raw perception.

Now it is indeed true that we are not born with our aesthetic responses ready made, and that experience is necessary to form them. It may perhaps be true that this experience consists, at least in part, of the acquisition of associations. But suppose association is necessary for all aesthetic responses to the material world. Is it sufficient, too? Are there not, perhaps, qualities innately suited by their nature and ours to produce aesthetic emotions in the sense of being the only ones suited to the forming of associations? Even if we grant (which is a very large concession indeed) that every quality of material objects which is beautiful or sublime is so by virtue of its associations, must we grant that associations of the kind necessary for aesthetic responses can accrue to all material qualities? In a word, are all qualities of material objects potentially beautiful or sublime?

Alison's answer must be, I think, that all material qualities are potentially aesthetic, although some perhaps may be more prone to the formation of the proper associations because they are the "natural" signs of emotive qualities. But in the final analysis, *any* quality of material objects, no matter how offensive to common sensibility, can become beautiful or sublime because any such quality can, through association, conceivably come to elicit a pleasurable emotion in someone or other. I don't know anyone who is likely to feel a simple sensation of pleasure at the sight of a mangled corpse; but I can see no reason why it might not produce in some individual an association with a quality which would produce such a sensation. And for Alison that is the initial step in a psychological process which might ultimately result in a pleasure of taste. And thus all attempts, including those of Hutcheson and the internal sense theorists, to enumerate those qualities common to all the objects of taste, are misguided, according to Alison. No material quality or object is by nature either "aesthetic" or "nonaesthetic."

(8) One question remains: If material qualities are not capable of eliciting emotive responses except by association with qualities which are, what sort of qualities have the power of emotive arousal? The cat which, as might be expected, is now to be let out of the bag is *mental* qualities. Here Alison aligns himself with the old Platonic tradition of Shaftesbury, and its more recent adherents:

> with a DOCTRINE that appears very early to have distinguished the PLATONIC school; which is to be traced, perhaps, (amid their dark and figurative language), in all the philosophical systems of the East, and which has been maintained in this country, by several writers of eminence — by Lord Shaftesbury, Dr. Hutcheson, Dr. Akenside, and Dr. Spence, but which has no where so firmly and so philosophically been maintained as by Dr. Reid in his invaluable work ON THE INTELLECTUAL POWERS OF MAN. The doctrine to which I allude, is, that matter is not beautiful in itself, but derives its beauty from the expression of MIND. [20]

Of course the doctrines of Alison and his predecessors are, as he himself recognized, parallel but not identical. For the British Platonists of Shaftesbury's and Reid's persuasion, mental qualities are aesthetic and raise aesthetic emotions directly. (Why Hutcheson is included in this list at all is not altogether clear.) But for Alison, no quality, either material or mental, can raise aesthetic emotions directly. What mental qualities, and material qualities by association, can do is arouse simple, nonaesthetic emotions, which, in turn, trigger the complex emotion in which beauty and sublimity consist. Says Alison,

> The conclusion, therefore, in which I wish to rest, is THAT THE BEAUTY AND SUBLIMITY WHICH IS FELT IN THE VARIOUS APPEARANCES OF MATTER, ARE FINALLY TO BE ASCRIBED TO THEIR EXPRESSION OF MIND: OR TO THEIR

BEING, EITHER DIRECTLY OR INDIRECTLY, THE SIGNS OF
THOSE QUALITIES OF MIND WHICH ARE FITTED, BY THE
CONSTITUTION OF OUR NATURE, TO AFFECT US WITH
PLEASING OR INTERESTING EMOTION. [21]

XII

END OF AN ERA

(1) Alison shows every indication of having thought that he had given Hutcheson's doctrine its final and conclusive refutation. But the strength of Hutcheson's reputation was such that in 1810 the doctrine was still alive enough to elicit considerable critical comment in Dugald Stewart's *Philosophical Essays*.

Stewart is a *convenient* figure with whom to close our history of Hutcheson's influence on eighteenth-century aesthetic speculation. I underscore "convenient" for the obvious reason that the *end of an era* is, to some degree, at least, an arbitrary point. But Stewart's *Philosophical Essays* makes as natural a coda to Hutcheson's aesthetic sense doctrine as I have been able to find. Stewart was one of the leading purveyors of the Scottish Common Sense School in the first half of the nineteenth century (and even beyond); and as such he must rank as a most influential molder of nineteenth-century philosophical opinion, particularly in Britain and the United States. But although there is, consequently, some reason to think of Stewart as basically a nineteenth-century figure, his roots are deep in the Enlightenment, and his philosophy was still working out the destiny of concepts that would have been familiar to Hutcheson.

(2) Looking back over eighteenth-century aesthetics from his vantage point, Stewart saw, in the attempt to ascertain the quality or qualities which aesthetic terms such as "beautiful" and "sublime" name, a major failure. Why had the Enlightenment failed here? Not, Stewart thought, for any other reason but that

203

the attempt was misguided, the puzzle insoluble. "It has long been a favorite problem with philosophers," Stewart wrote, "to ascertain the common quality or qualities, which entitles a thing to the denomination of *beautiful;* but the success of their speculations has been so inconsiderable, that little can be inferred from them but the impossibility of the problem to which they have been directed." [1]

The Enlightenment landscape was littered with the ruins of theories, Hutcheson's perhaps the most prominent of all, each attempting to define aesthetic terms by matching them with their objects in a one-to-one relation, or, at least, assigning one term to a relatively small group of qualities which together make a sufficient and necessary condition. But this is a bootless effort, Stewart maintained, because — and here, as we shall see, he is strikingly modern — it was predicated on a false view of language: a view which mistakenly assumed that for a noun or adjective to be meaningful, it must have, in all of its uses, some common referent. As Stewart put it,

> The speculations [of eighteenth-century aestheticians] . . . have evidently originated in a prejudice, which has descended to modern times from the scholastic ages; — that when a word admits of a variety of significations, these different significations must all be *species* of the same *genus;* and must consequently include some essential idea common to every individual to which the generic term can be applied. [2]

Stewart was not the first Enlightenment figure to make this linguistic move. Berkeley, who, as we have seen, had already shaken up the rigid Lockean view of language as solely descriptive, was well ahead of Stewart in denying that general terms must each name some common property or idea. In the introduction to the *Principles of Human Knowledge* he stated that "there is no such thing as one precise and definite signification annexed to any general name, they all signify indifferently a great number of particular ideas." [3] But if Stewart was not the first to enunciate this view of language, he was well in advance of his time in working out its logical details, and certainly the first to apply it to questions of an aesthetic nature.

What linguistic theory does Stewart put in place of the one rejected? His problem is to give some satisfactory account of how a single noun or adjective comes to name many different individuals. The rejected answer was: every general term is a name. Every name must be the name of something; if it refers to different individuals, it must do so by virtue of some characteristic — some second-order "individual" — common to them all. Stewart denies that an adjective used univocally for a number of different individuals must name some property common to them all. To support his contention, he must give a satisfactory account of how such adjectives as "beautiful" can refer to so vast an array of different individuals. He begins by agreeing that common properties of objects are the occasion for their being referred to by the same adjective; but, he argues, no single property (or group of properties) need be held in common by more than two objects for any number of objects to be referred to by the same adjective. All that is necessary is that a continuous chain of connected properties connect any group of individuals referred to by the same adjective. Stewart writes:

> I shall begin with supposing, that the letters A, B, C, D, E, denote a series of objects; that A possesses some one quality common with B; B a quality in common with C; C a quality in common with D; D a quality in common with E; — while, at the same time, no quality can be found which belongs in common to any *three* objects in the series. Is it not conceivable, that the affinity between A and B may produce a transference of the name of the first to the second; and that, in consequence of the other affinities which connect the remaining objects together, the same name may pass in succession from B to C; from C to D; and from D to E? In this manner a common appellation will arise between A and E, although the two objects may, in their nature and properties, be so widely distant from each other, that no stretch of the imagination can conceive how the thoughts were led from the former to the latter. [4]

Stewart has, in fact, come very close to Wittgenstein's concept of "family resemblances" as a substitute for the "common property" theory of language.[5] In his now celebrated examination of language games in the *Philosophical Investigations*, Wittgenstein rejected the notion that for the term "game" to be

meaningful in its various applications, it must have reference to
some characteristic common to all games. There is no common
characteristic, he claimed; only a complicated structure of inter-
locking properties.

> Consider for example the proceedings that we call 'games.' I
> mean board-games, card-games, ball-games, Olympic games, and so
> on. What is common to them all? — Don't say: 'There *must* be
> something common, or they would not be called "games" ' — but
> *look and see* whether there is anything common to all. — For if
> you look at them you will not see something that is common to
> *all*, but similarities, relationships, and a whole series of them at
> that. To repeat: don't think, but look! — Look for example at
> board-games, with their multifarious relationships. Now pass to
> card-games; here you find many correspondences with the first
> group, but many common features drop out, and others appear.
> When we pass next to ball-games, much that is common is re-
> tained, but much is lost. . . . And we can go through the many,
> many other groups of games in the same way; can see how similari-
> ties crop up and disappear.
>
> And the result of this examination is: we see a complicated
> network of similarities overlapping and criss-crossing: sometimes
> overall similarities, sometimes similarities in detail.[6]

(3) Before we leave the subject of Stewart and contemporary
thought, it might be worthwhile to consider a more general
parallel between Stewart's situation at the beginning of the
nineteenth century and the state of value theory during the first
half of the twentieth. I think deeper affinities will be revealed
than just a chance anticipation of Wittgenstein.

I began this discussion by remarking that in 1810 Stewart
looked back over the eighteenth century to see a vast array of
attempts to define aesthetic terms by identifying each with
some quality or discrete group of qualities possessed in common
by objects of the same aesthetic kind. In all cases, Stewart
argued, the attempts had failed. In 1903, G. E. Moore, making a
broader survey of ethical theory, came to the same conclusion.
Moore, like Stewart, asked: Why have they failed? Stewart's
answer was that they have failed because aesthetic terms do not
each refer to some single quality, but to different qualities in

different objects. Moore's answer was that they have failed because "good" does not refer to any *naturalistic* quality or group of qualities: "good is not to be considered a natural object"; it is a single quality, but that quality is nonnatural, "simple and indefinable." "In fact, if it is not the case that 'good' denotes something simple and indefinable, only two alternatives are possible: either it is a complex, a given whole, about the correct analysis of which there may be disagreement; or else it means nothing at all, and there is no such subject as Ethics."[7] Moore envisions no fourth alternative; the second and third are untenable, and so he takes the first.

Moore's argument did not remain within the boundaries of ethical theory. It was quickly adopted by members of the Bloomsbury group, among them Clive Bell, who concurred with Moore in the belief that if a group of objects is to bear the same name, the objects must have some common characteristic: specifically, if the word "art" is to be meaningful, the objects to which *it* refers must have a common characteristic: "For either all works of visual art have some common quality, or when we speak of 'works of art' we gibber . . . . There must be some one quality without which a work of art cannot exist . . . . "[8]

Thus Stewart, in aesthetics, and Moore, in ethics, faced a similar problem. Why, they asked, have we been unable to find some quality common to the objects which the terms of our respective disciplines name? Stewart took one alternative in rejecting the notion that for a term to name different objects, these objects must have some quality or discrete group of qualities in common. Moore took another tack in his insistence that for a term to refer meaningfully to different objects, they must possess a common property. The mistake of previous moralists, rather, was to assume that the common property is natural and analyzable when, in fact, it is neither.

What is of particular interest is that in recent years many value theorists have rejected Moore's alternative and turned toward Stewart's. Wittgenstein himself had already applied the theory of "family resemblances" both to ethics and aesthetics in his lectures at Cambridge. G. E. Moore, who attended many of these lectures, reports:

> He introduced his whole discussion of Aesthetics by dealing
> with one problem about the meaning of words . . . . He illustrated
> this problem by the example of the word 'game,' with regard to
> which he said both (1) that, even if there is something common to
> all games, it doesn't follow that this is what we mean by calling a
> particular game a 'game,' and (2) that the reason why we call so
> many different activities 'games' need not be that there is any-
> thing common to them all, but only that there is 'a gradual transi-
> tion' from one use to another, although there may be nothing in
> common between the two ends of the series. And he seemed to
> hold definitely that there is nothing in common in our different
> uses of the word 'beautiful,' saying that we use it 'in a hundred
> different games' — that, e.g., the beauty of a fact is something
> different from the beauty of a chair or a flower or the binding of
> a book. [9]

And today we have such moralists as Paul Edwards maintaining
that "the features to which moral judgments refer or which
they imply are no more nonnatural than the features to which
judgments about the niceness of foods refer . . . " [10] ; that "
'good' is polyguous as far as its referent is concerned." [11] We
have such aestheticians as Helen Knight arguing that "good," in
its aesthetic applications, "does not name an indefinable quality," [12] although it is indefinable in the sense that it does not
refer to one single quality, or discrete group of qualities, but to
"criterion-characters" which vary with the occasion. And we
have Morris Weitz using Wittgenstein's concept of "family resemblances" in support of "art" as an "open concept," having
reference to "no common properties — only strands of similari-
ties." [13] In many areas of value theory, then, the eighteenth and
twentieth centuries have delivered themselves of similar doctrines; but, in addition, whole segments of development have
been parallel, the direction of evolution being away from an
impacted one-term — one-object concept of language to a looser, more flexible logical model.

(4) Stewart's notion of terms such as "beautiful" and "sublime" *transferring* their applications from object to object has as
its psychological analogue the doctrine of the association of
ideas, to which Stewart also subscribed. He had adopted the

terms "transitive" and "transitivity" from another associationist
aesthetician, Richard Payne Knight.[14] The transference must
begin with some object or class of objects that is originally
sublime or beautiful. This was a point that Stewart felt the need
to emphasize in the face of an associationist aesthetics which
seemed, at times, to fall into an infinite regress from one derived pleasure to another, and was in a way a concession to
Hutcheson and his school. The association of ideas enables

> us to conceive how a thing indifferent in itself, may become a
> source of pleasure, by being connected in the mind with some-
> thing else which is naturally agreeable; but it presupposes, in every
> instance, the existence of those notions and those feelings which
> it is its province to combine: insomuch that, I apprehend, it will
> be found, wherever association produces a change in our judg-
> ments on matters of Taste, it does so, by co-operating with some
> natural principle of the mind, and implies the existence of certain
> original sources of pleasure and uneasiness.[15]

In a word, "If there was nothing originally and intrinsically
pleasing or beautiful, the associating principle would have no
materials on which it could operate."[16] At some point the chain
of associations "must at last arrive at principles of which no
account can be given, but that such is the will of our maker." [17]
That there are "principles of which no account can be given,
but that such is the will of our maker," sounds very like pure,
unalloyed Hutcheson. Where Stewart and his predecessor part
company is in Stewart's reluctance to describe such principles as
internal senses. It is the *external* senses which, for Stewart, are
the source of original aesthetic perceptions. And those more
complex and cerebral pleasures of the imagination, that, for
Hutcheson, demanded the postulating of internal senses, Stewart made the work of the association of ideas.

In the case of beauty, the original objects are objects of sight;
and the first qualities of these objects to be aesthetically enjoyed, to bear the name of "beautiful," are colors. The next are
forms: "When in addition to the pleasures connected with *colours,* external objects present those which arise from certain
modifications of *forms,* the same name will be naturally applied

to both the causes of the mixed emotion." The emotion is *mixed,* be it noted, but experienced as simple:

> The emotion appears, in point of fact, to our consciousness, simple and uncompounded, no person being able to say, while it is felt, how much of the effect is to be ascribed to either cause, in preference to the other; and it is the philosopher alone, who ever thinks of attempting, by a series of observations and experiments, to accomplish such an analysis.[18]

Both color and form please the eye, are pleasures of seeing; yet there are other pleasures which visible objects give that are pleasures not of seeing, but of *understanding.* And if these come to bear the name of "beautiful," it is through association with the eye, which is their avenue to the understanding. Order, fitness, utility, symmetry are by "the *consent* of all mankind," beautiful. And all "are calculated to give pleasure to the *understanding,*" not the organs of sight; "but as this pleasure is conveyed through the medium of the *eye,* they are universally confounded with the pleasing qualities which form the direct objects of its physical perceptions."[19] We have here a classic case of what Stewart calls "transference." Fitness, for example, a pleasure of the understanding, is called "beautiful," a term previously applied to pleasures of sight, because it has in common with pleasures of sight the characteristic of being perceived by the eye.

The only other external sense whose "objects" bear the name "beautiful," Stewart points out, is the sense of hearing. It is another case of transference: "this use of the word appears to me," Stewart remarks, "to be plainly *transitive,* arising, in part, from the general disposition we have to apply to one class of our perceptions, the epithets strictly appropriated to the agreeable qualities perceived by another." However, the qualification "in part" is well taken; for the tendency to transfer the term "beautiful" from the pleasures of the sense for which it was meant to those of another "suggests no reason why the epithet *beautiful* should be applied to agreeable *sounds,* rather than to agreeable *tastes,* or to agreeable *odors.*" This can be explained, Stewart thinks, only by the wider associations which sound can encompass through its *picturesque effect* ("Thus, the clack of a mill . . . conjures up at once to the mind's eye the simple and cheerful scene which it announces; and thus . . . the songs which delighted our childhood, transport us into the well-remembered haunts where we were accustomed to hear them"); and its *expressive power.*[20]

The above examples will, I think, convey something of the way in which Stewart explains the proliferation of aesthetic objects. The procedure is not novel but is characteristic of the associationist aestheticians, although the logical sophistication which Stewart brings to his work is in contrast to that of many of his predecessors. What remains to be pointed out is that Stewart, like Alison, has rejected (by implication) one of the basic tenets of Hutcheson's first *Inquiry:* the definability of aesthetic terms by reference to a common property of aesthetic objects (proposition vi). The use of the association principle also contributes, as in the case of Alison, to the rejection of another doctrine of the inner sense school: the innateness of the aesthetic judgment (proposition ii). We shall see this aspect of Stewart's position explicitly stated in his discussion of *taste,* to which we now turn our attention.

(5) Taste, for Stewart, seems to mean two (not necessarily distinct) things: a disposition to have "aesthetic" feelings in the contemplation of "aesthetic" objects, and the ability to make judgments about what sorts of objects will elicit "aesthetic" feelings. Thus, it is the faculty of the creator, the audience, and the critic, too. But in all cases, Stewart insists, taste is not simple, it is complex; it is not a gift, it is an acquisition:

> . . . Taste is not a simple and original faculty, but a power gradually formed by experience and observation. It implies, indeed, as its groundwork, a certain degree of natural sensibility, but it implies also the exercise of the judgment; and is the slow result of an attentive examination and comparison of the agreeable or disagreeable effects produced on the mind by external objects.[21]

It was the accomplishment of his own immediate predecessors, Stewart acknowledges, to have made the aesthetic sense doctrine a dead issue: "Mr. Burke, Sir J. Reynolds, Dr. Gerard, and Mr. Alison have combatted in our own times, the prevailing doctrines which class Taste among the simple and original faculties which belong to our species." [22]

But what of the celerity with which the judgments of taste are made? Is it consistent with a complex and acquired reaction? For Hutcheson and the early internal sense theorists, as we have seen, the immediacy of aesthetic judgment was reason enough to conclude that it is innate and nonrational. However, for the later critics of the doctrine, this was not the case: surely, they argued, repetition and habit could so ingrain a response that it would indeed be immediate and seem simple and innate when it was, as a matter of fact, no more so than reading or writing. To this latter view Stewart gravitated, comparing taste with "those intellectual processes, which, by often passing through the mind, come at length to be carried on with a rapidity that eludes all our effort to remark it; giving to many of our judgments, which are really the result of thought and reflection, the appearance of instantaneous and intuitive perceptions." [23]

Taste, in its critical and creative employments, is an acquired power of *"discrimination* or *discernment,"* characterized by "the *promptitude* with which its judgments are commonly pronounced." [24] The method of acquiring taste is the "experimental" method: "it is not by reasonings *a priori,* that we can hope to make any progress in ascertaining and separating the respective effects of the various ingredients which may thus be blended in the composition of Beauty," Stewart writes.

> In analyzing these, we must proceed on the same general principles by which we are guided in investigating the physical and chemical properties of material substances; that is, we must have recourse to a series of observations and experiments on beautiful objects of various kinds; attending diligently to the agreeable or the disagreeable effects we experience, in the case of these diversified combinations.

The instrument by which successes and failures are determined in the aesthetic laboratory is our own aesthetic response. "In all these experiments and observations, . . . the result is judged of by attending to our own feelings; as, in our researches concerning *heat,* we appeal to the thermometer." [25]

But there is one crucial difference between the experimental method of the natural sciences and that of aesthetics: a difference which goes further than the vague notion of "habit" toward accounting for the *promptitude* of aesthetic judgments. The natural scientist must manipulate, or at least observe in some special way, the world of nature external to him; and so must the aesthetic "scientist" — but only in the beginning. For the artist and critic, aesthetic objects soon become objects of the imagination which the imagination can call up at will and manipulate in any way required by the "experimental" method. The aesthetic experiment becomes a mental experiment.

> In the infancy of Taste, indeed, the first step is to compare object with object; — one scene with another scene; one picture with another picture; one poem with another poem: — and, at all times, such comparisons are pleasing and instructive. But when the mind has once acquired a certain familiarity with the beauties of Nature and of Art, much may be effected, in the way of experiment, by the power of Imagination alone. Instead of waiting to compare the scene now before me with another scene of the same kind, or of actually trying the effects resulting from the various changes of which its parts are susceptible, I can multiply and vary my ideal trials at will, and can anticipate from my own feelings, in these different cases, the improvement or the injury that would result from carrying them into execution. The fact is still more striking, when the original combination is furnished by Imagination herself, and when she compounds and decompounds it, as fancy or curiosity may happen to dictate. In this last case, the materials of our experiment, the instruments employed in our analysis or synthesis, and the laboratory in which the whole process is carried on, are all alike intellectual. They all exist in the observer's mind; and are all supplied, either immediately by the principles of his nature, or by these principles cultivated and assisted by superinduced habits. [26]

Now the essence of mental activity, particularly imaginative activity, is speed; and therein lies a primary reason for the promptitude of taste. For although the acquisition and operation of taste depend upon an experimental method, with all its stages of trial and error, that method is swift as the "fancy." It is carried on continually; it never wants materials on which to work. The experimental wherewithal is never out of hand — or, rather, out of mind.

> The account which has now been given of the habits of observation and comparison, by which Taste acquires its powers of *discrimination* or *discernment*, explains, at the same time, the *promptitude* with which its judgments are commonly pronounced. As the experiments subservient to its formation are carried on entirely in the mind itself, they present, every moment, a ready field for the gratification of curiosity; and in those individuals whose thoughts are strongly turned to the pursuit, they furnish matter of habitual employment to the intellectual faculties. These experiments are, at the same time, executed with an ease and celerity unknown in our operations on Matter; insomuch that the experiment and its result, seem both to be comprehended in the same instant of time. The process, accordingly, vanishes completely from our recollection; nor do we attempt to retrace it to ourselves in *thought*, far less to express it to others in *words*, any more than we are disposed, in our common estimates of distance, to analyze the acquired perceptions of vision.[27]

(6) To conclude, let us take stock of Stewart's position in relation to Hutcheson's. He denies the simple unanalyzable nature of aesthetic perceptions (proposition i) but maintains, nevertheless, that they are experienced as simple. He rejects the innateness of aesthetic judgments (proposition ii). He affirms, with Hutcheson, that the judgment of taste is immediate (proposition iii). He expresses no opinion as to the volitional or nonvolitional character of aesthetic judgments (proposition iv), but denies their nonrationality (proposition v), maintaining, on the contrary, that rational judgment, in the form of inductive inference, plays a prominent role. Finally, he denies the definability of aesthetic terms such as "beautiful" and "sublime" by reference to common properties of objects (proposition vi). Thus, with regard to the six principal claims of Hutcheson and his school, Stewart rejects three outright, accepts one in modified form, accepts one outright, and stands mute on one. Something of Hutcheson, then, still survived; but the sense of beauty

as he had known it did not exist. The mind's aesthetic eye had closed its rheumy lid forever, enduring as a phrase, but not as a theory.

(7) We have spanned almost one hundred years from our consideration of Hutcheson's first *Inquiry* to the present discussion of Dugald Stewart. The history of aesthetic thought in this period is a complex and tangled web: and even the small part of it we have told is not by any means a direct route from one philosophical terminus to another. Yet there are themes and directions discernible; and now is the time to bring them out. There are, it seems to me, a number of ways of looking at the development of the aesthetic sense doctrine from Hutcheson to Stewart.

Perhaps the most obvious frame in which to put our history is the "nature or nurture" antinomy. For it is easy to see the progression from Hutcheson's innate sense of beauty, to Gerard's acquired "sense," and, finally, to the demise of the sense of beauty in Alison and Stewart, as simply a progression from the notion of aesthetic responses as inborn to the notion of them as learned: from the aesthetic birth of man to the aesthetic education of man.

That this is an oversimplification hardly needs pointing out; for Hutcheson insisted that the aesthetic nature is educable as well as corruptible (to the extent that attention can be developed); and Stewart of course was forced to admit that for *any* aesthetic responses to be acquired, some must be innate. The reply to this is an obvious one: that what we have here is not a difference in kind but one of degree; that Hutcheson *emphasized* nature, and Stewart nurture; that the general direction of thought was from the one emphasis to the other. Such a view has the unmistakable mark of an uninteresting truth, and I let it stand for whatever it is worth.

A second way of looking at the progression from senses to association is to see it as a history of aesthetic and moral psychology, beginning in the dark ages of an a priori psychological Aristotelianism and emerging into the enlightenment of a Newtonian science of the mind (which is the way Hume thought of his associative principles). This is the view, I think, which many eighteenth-century writers took. It is reflected in Burke's wielding of Ockham's razor in Hutcheson's direction, and in Diderot's remark in the *Encyclopédie* that "Hutcheson and his followers try to establish the necessity of an *internal sense of beauty;* but they only succeed in demonstrating that there is something obscure and inscrutable in the pleasure which beauty occasions in us . . . ."[28] For, clearly, if Hutcheson is a psychologist, and his "explanation" of the perception of the beautiful is a sense of the beautiful, then he has conformed to the eighteenth-century stereotype of the scientific nincompoop whose sleeping potion has a dormitive virtue and whose clock runs on clockness. Surely the association of ideas, for all of its weaknesses as a psychological theory, is better psychology than can be found in the inner sense doctrine. And if one reads Hutcheson's first *Inquiry* merely as aesthetic psychology, it can be seen only as a primitive beginning to a century of progress.

If we see the history of the aesthetic sense against the background of the philosophy of perception, a third view emerges. It is, of course, a commonplace notion in the history of philosophy that perception, as Locke construes it, is characterized by "passivity," the mind being a sensitive receiver, recording dumbly the input from the external world, whereas for Kant it is a mind-laden, concept-laden *activity.* And the transformation of aesthetic perception from Hutcheson (who, after all, is a Lockean in his basic assumptions) to Stewart can, with some justice, be described as a progression in which mental processes play an increasingly important role.

Two points, I think, can usefully be made about this general characterization. It is, of course, oversimplified to the extent that both Locke and Hutcheson recognized at least one essential mental activity in perception, as we have seen: that of *attention.* And, second, there is a world of difference between the kind of mental processes that Stewart, for example, injected into aesthetic perception and the kind of deep structure Kant formulated for the general theory of perception. The mind is no more *active* in aesthetic perception for Stewart than it had been for Hutcheson. The association of ideas is, as we have noted, a deterministic system, and the mind is no less passive for being equipped with it.

Taking, rather, the point of view of the literary critic and historian of taste, yet another way emerges of seeing the growth of the sense of beauty, and its demise in the doctrine of association. That way is to see a normative, rather than a psychological or analytic, question at stake. In its most general terms, the difference between Hutcheson and Stewart is that Hutcheson does not allow certain acquired perceptions as beautiful or sublime – in other words, "aesthetic" – which Stewart is willing to allow. Yet the issue here may not be what is or is not aesthetic, but what ought or ought not be counted as such. And this seems to involve, really, deciding either to encourage or discourage certain ways of making or responding to works of art (or other potentially "aesthetic" objects). Thus, a correlation can perhaps be drawn between the history of the aesthetic sense from Hutcheson to Stewart and the history of literary taste, say, from Pope to Blake.

Now for those who tend, for various reasons, to see certain philosophical disputes as disguised disputes about value, such an interpretation of Hutcheson and his followers is naturally congenial. In addition, the proverbial recalcitrance of normative disagreements to rational resolution of course lends support to the interpretation, since the philosophical analysis of the aesthetic is itself such a seemingly irresolvable issue. There is, doubtless, an intermingling of aesthetic philosophy and literary criticism throughout this period, with philosophers engaging in the latter as well as the former, and critics in the former as well as the latter. But although the literary and other tastes of writers have certainly influenced their views, it is by no means obvious that the only issue was a normative one.

Let us say that the question before both Hutcheson (at the beginning of the eighteenth century) and Stewart (at the beginning of the nineteenth) was: What makes a judgment or a perception peculiarly "aesthetic"? (And we shall intend by an "aesthetic" judgment or perception nothing more than a judgment or perception of the "sublime" or the "beautiful.") It might be suggested that this is really a slightly misleading way of asking the question: What kinds of judgments or perceptions ought to be allowed as ones of beauty or sublimity? And, given the normative implications of the terms "beautiful" and "sublime," this begins to look like a matter of *recommending* what responses to art, say, should be cultivated and what responses should be discouraged; what responses should be legitimatized and what responses ruled irrelevant. Perhaps this *is* all that the question amounts to. But that is by no means clear. And we can retain the normative question without throwing out the conceptual one. The question "Is such and such a response to art an *aesthetic* one?" might be construed as "Is such and such a response to art a *proper* one?" But we can also ask "Is an *aesthetic* response to art the only *proper* one?" and "Is the response to art that so and so recommends an *aesthetic* one?" And now we can still ask our conceptual question "What is the *aesthetic*?" independent of the normative one.

What I would say about the matter is this. There is a normative issue present in the argument between Hutcheson and the associationist aestheticians. But that does not preclude there being a conceptual issue as well. And the conceptual issue is the one I have tried to bring out in the preceding analysis of Hutcheson, his followers, and his critics.

APPENDIX A
SOME MINOR FIGURES

(1) To examine every writer on aesthetics in Enlightenment Britain who was influenced by the sense of beauty would be a task of staggering proportions and, at least from the philosophical point of view, one that, I suspect, would not pay sufficient returns on the investment. Nevertheless, some consideration of "disciples" may be called for to limn in more fully our picture of the aesthetic sense doctrine during the mid-1700s. I have chosen, therefore, to discuss three minor writers — William Melmoth, John Gilbert Cooper, and Hugh Blair — as representative of the influence which Hutcheson wielded at this time. My choice of Melmoth and Cooper was dictated mainly by the fact that their names are to be found to some small degree in previous studies of the period.[1] They are hardly first-rate philosophical or critical minds, and their influence on the aesthetic sense doctrine is a trivializing one; but such influences also belong to the history of ideas and cannot be totally ignored. Blair, of course, is of somewhat greater importance, not perhaps as an original philosophical thinker, but certainly as a talented popularizer of various aesthetic and critical ideas.[2]

(2) William Melmoth's reputation seems to have rested, in his own day, on two literary productions: a translation of the *Epistles* of Pliny the Younger, which appeared in 1753, and a series of essays on various topics, published during the 1740s as *Letters of Sir Thomas Fitzosborne*.[3]

219

The thirty-ninth of the *Fitzosborne Letters* is an epitome of Hutcheson's *Inquiry,* with a little bit of this and that from Addison, Sir William Temple, and others. Melmoth conceives of aesthetic sensibility as a God-given gift in the form of a faculty or sense from which the standard of taste is derived and to which it owes its authority. He writes:

> The charms of the fine arts are, indeed, literally derived from the author of all nature, and founded in the original frame and constitution of the human mind. Accordingly, the general principles of *taste* are common to our whole species, and arise from that internal sense of beauty which every man, in some degree at least, evidently possesses.

However, whereas Hutcheson tends to play down the role of "education" in developing aesthetic perception (it being, as we have seen, a perversion rather than a corrective influence, for Hutcheson), Melmoth, in this respect perhaps under the influence of Addison and Temple, acknowledges the innate and the acquired as necessary and equal in the functioning of the aesthetic sense. Thus "taste is nothing more than this sense of beauty, rendered more exquisite by genius, and more correct by cultivation . . . . "[4]

In the tradition of the aesthetic sense theorists, Melmoth presses the analogy between critical judgment and sense perception: the critical process is involuntary, immediate, and therefore nonrational. "There are certain forms which must necessarily fill the soul with agreeable ideas; and she is instantly determined in her approbation of them, previous to all reasonings concerning their use and convenience."[5]

As we have seen, the standard of taste is assured, for Melmoth, by a common aesthetic nature among men in the form of a God-given internal sense. But if such a common ground exists, the fact of manifest differences in taste must be accounted for; it is a problem for Melmoth as it had been for his predecessors and as it must be for anyone whose critical position implies unanimity. Melmoth, like Hutcheson, appeals here to the principle of association, although the term itself is not used and the argument is but brief. Melmoth writes:

> The opposition, however, which sometimes divides the opinions
> of those whose judgments may be supposed equal and perfect, is
> urged as a powerful objection against the reality of a fixed canon
> of criticism: it is a proof, you think, that, after all which can be
> said of fine taste, it must ultimately be resolved into the peculiar
> relish of each individual. But this diversity of sentiments will not,
> of itself, destroy the evidence of the criterion; since the same
> effect may be produced by numberless other causes. A thousand
> accidental circumstances may concur in counteracting the force of
> the rule, even allowing it to be ever so fixed and invariable, when
> left in its free and uninfluenced state. [6]

The "accidental occurrences," I presume, are the chance associations of ideas through which Hutcheson and many others attempted to account for diversity of taste. Melmoth does not explore the position further.

There can be no doubt that Melmoth's critical ideas are purely derivative: there is not one that cannot be traced to his immediate predecessors. Nor has he added any depth to what he has appropriated. In Melmoth the sense of beauty has ceased to have any real epistemological significance; it has behind it neither the profound Platonism of Shaftesbury nor the Lockean empiricism with which Hutcheson imbued the doctrine, although it bears the merest traces of both. The aesthetic nature has become the most obvious sort of mechanism, "programmed" by a Deity of convenience. But perhaps we are too severe; Melmoth, after all, made no real pretensions to philosophy.

(3) In John Gilbert Cooper's *Letters Concerning Taste* (1755) we have a more extensive treatment of the aesthetic sense than is to be found in the *Fitzosborne Letters* and, perhaps, some small contribution of original thought. Cooper identifies taste with an *"internal Sense"* and gives us a description of it in complete conformity with what we have come to expect from such theorists. He writes:

> The Effect of *good* TASTE is that instantaneous Glow of Pleasure
> which thrills thro' our whole Frame, and seizes upon the Applause
> of the Heart, before the intellectual Power, Reason, can descend
> to ratify its Approbation, either when we receive into the Soul

> beautiful Images thro' the Organs of bodily Senses; or the Decor-
> um of an amiable Character thro' the Faculties of moral Percep-
> tion; or when we recall, by the imitative Arts, both of them thro'
> the intermediate Power of the Imagination. [7]

The relationship between the sense of beauty and its objects is
determined by the Deity: "the ALMIGHTY has in this, as well
as in all his other Works, out of his abundant Goodness and
Love to his Creatures, so *attuned* our Minds to Truth, that all
Beauty from without should make a responsive Harmony vi-
brate within."[8] And here aesthetic speculation must end; any
further question would amount to prying "into Matters, which
the Deity, for Reasons known only to himself, has placed above
our limited Capacities . . . " — the age-old Deist dodge.[9]

Cooper's language is reminiscent of Shaftesbury's rhapsodic
tone, and in other respects, too, there are affinities between
them. For Cooper, "TRUTH and BEAUTY are coinci-
dent. . . . "[10] As with Shaftesbury, "truth" is used here in the
sense of "true" proportions — thus, well proportioned, measur-
ing up to some ideal or standard. It is the Neoplatonic tradition,
rather than Hutcheson's empiricism, which Cooper seems to
follow. But what he lacks is Shaftesbury's deep commitment to
rationalism. As W. J. Bate has pointed out, Cooper tends to
luxuriate in feeling[11]; and this separates him from Shaftesbury's
aesthetics of reasoned sensibility as well as Hutcheson's somewhat tame subjectivism in which "perception" is a far more
appropriate word than "feeling" for describing aesthetic judgment.

In apparent response to the charge of aprioriism, which many
critics were leveling against Hutcheson and his school, Cooper
seems to be maintaining that the aesthetic sense need not be
considered an additional psychological principle but, rather, a
distinct operation which the traditionally accepted faculties —
sense organs, intellect, and imagination — perform in concert.
Taste, according to Cooper, "does not wholly depend upon the
natural Strength and acquired Improvements of the *Intellectual
Powers;* nor *wholly* upon a fine Construction of the *Organs* of
the Body; nor wholly upon the intermediate Powers of the
Imagination; but upon an Union of them all happily blended,

without too great a Prevalency in either."[12] That both mental and physical attributes must conspire together in the man of taste is, of course, common knowledge, neither the discovery of Cooper nor his century. But that these faculties, in a certain dynamic relationship, *constitute* what can be termed a "sense of beauty" (a position at least adumbrated here) points to the future: to the later Scottish school and (if we are not reading too much into Cooper) to Kant's "free play of the cognitive faculties," the aesthetic *sensus communis* of the third *Critique*. Here, perhaps, Cooper is breaking new ground or, at least, timidly lifting the spade.

(4) Hugh Blair, the last of our trio, and the most familiar to students of eighteenth-century criticism, published his major critical work, the *Lectures on Rhetoric and Belles Lettres*, in 1783, although according to Blair himself the published *Lectures* essentially reproduced what he had been presenting to his classes at Edinburg since 1759.[13] Blair made no pretensions to originality, but he did claim to have done some hard thinking of his own. He wrote candidly of the *Lectures*,

> The Author gives them to the world, neither as a Work wholly original, nor as a Compilation from the Writings of others. On every subject contained in them, he has thought for himself . . . . At the same time, he availed himself of the ideas and reflections of others, as far as he thought them proper to be adopted.[14]

In his opinion of himself, as in his opinions on more controversial topics, Blair was middle-of-the-road.

Blair defines taste as "The power of receiving pleasure from the beauties of nature and of art." He then asks whether this power "is to be considered as an internal sense, or as an exertion of reason?" opting, on familiar grounds, for the "internal sense":

> It is not merely through a discovery of the understanding, or a deduction of argument, that the mind receives pleasure from a beautiful prospect or a fine poem. Such objects often strike us intuitively, and make a strong impression, when we are unable to assign the reasons of our being pleased . . . . Hence the faculty by

which we relish such beauties, seems more nearly allied to a feeling of sense, than to a process of understanding . . . .[15]

Because the reasons for our critical judgments cannot be determined, Blair seems willing to conclude that there are none and,
therefore, that critical judgments are perceptual. He fails, apparently, to see that *both* our inability to determine reasons *and*
the absence of reasons to determine are compatible with our
judgments' being rational, not to mention the fact that our
inability to determine reasons does not imply absence of reasons. And in spite of his introduction of the notion of intuition,
Blair sees no other alternatives beyond *discursive* reason and
perception.

Blair conceived of taste as a *common* sense: "a faculty common in some degree to all men."[16] And thus he, too, faced the
all too familiar questions which this position raises: If we have a
common aesthetic sense, why do we dispute in matters of taste?
If we do dispute, on what grounds do we seek for resolution?
Blair's answer is, essentially, the answer of old: taste is "in some
degree" innate; but it must be nurtured to its full flowering:
"This inequality of Taste among men is owing, without doubt,
in part, to the different frame of their natures; to nicer organs,
and finer internal powers, with which some are endowed beyond others. But, if it be owing in part to nature, it is owing to
education and culture still more."[17]

It is not surprising to find that the education of feeling, for
the most part, lies with reason. Starting out bravely with a sense
of beauty, Blair now must summon reason in through the back
door. He writes,

But although Taste be ultimately founded on sensibility, it must
not be considered as instinctive sensibility alone. Reason and good
sense . . . have so extensive an influence on all the operations and
decisions of Taste, that a thorough good Taste may well be considered as a power compounded of natural sensibility to beauty,
and of improved understanding.[18]

Are we to conclude, then, that reason forms the standard to
which the sense of beauty conforms, in Shaftesbury's manner?
Is reason the final court of appeal? For Blair there seems to be

no straight answer: like Buridan's ass, he stands transfixed between alternatives — reason on the one side, the sense of beauty on the other. Blair leads us a merry chase from feeling to reason to feeling again; for "the ultimate conclusions to which our reasonings lead, refer at last to sense and perception."[19] Blair is caught up in the same sort of vicious circle attributed falsely to Hume. But whereas Hume understands that the circle must be broken, his fellow Scot seems blissfully unaware that anything at all is amiss.

APPENDIX B

LORD KAMES AND THE
SENSE OF BEAUTY

(1) It may come of something of a surprise to the student of eighteenth-century thought to find Lord Kames, whose name is frequently associated with the doctrine of inner sense, exiled from the body of a work devoted to that doctrine and imprisoned in an appendix. Yet the fact is that although entirely within the moral sense tradition and indeed often cited as an example of its excesses, Kames does not adhere to the internal sense doctrine in aesthetics except in a rather offhand manner. Nevertheless, his fame demands that he at least be put in proper perspective with regard to the doctrine he is often alleged to espouse — my intention here.

Kames's *Elements of Criticism,* perhaps the most widely known work of Scottish aesthetics, is a long book; and if, as is likely, you give up before reaching the bitter end — the appendix, in fact — you will emerge with the impression that Lord Kames had little if anything to do with the school of Hutcheson. Indeed, the term "sense" occurs but rarely in the body of the work; it is in the appendix, which Kames called "Terms Defined or Explained," where his connection with the sense of beauty is revealed. And it is thus with the end of the *Elements* that we must begin.

Kames begins the appendix, significantly enough, with definitions of terms central to the aesthetic sense doctrine: *perception, internal sense, external sense.*

> That act of the mind which makes known to me an external
> object, is termed *perception.* That act of the mind which makes

226

known to me an internal object, is termed *consciousness*. The
power or faculty from which consciousness proceeds, is termed an
internal sense. The power or faculty from which perception proceeds, is termed an *external sense*. This distinction refers to the
objects of our knowledge; for the senses, whether external or
internal, are all of them powers or faculties of mind. [1]

For Kames, the hallmark of perception and consciousness is
passivity. "Senses" are "faculties"; and the verbs "to see," "to
feel," and the like are *active* verbs, and this seems to ascribe
some kind of positive "doing" to the senses. But this is a mistake: the sense does not *do* anything, any more than a piece of
wax *does* something when it is melted by a flame. It is the flame
to which we must ascribe the *doing;* the "power" of the wax is
purely passive: the power *to be* melted. And it is the same with
the senses, whether internal or external:

> A tree in flourish makes an impression on me, and by that means I
> see the tree. But in this operation I do not find that the mind is
> active: seeing a tree is only an effect produced on it by interven-
> tion of the rays of light . . . . Perception accordingly is not an
> action, but an effect produced in the mind. Sensation is another
> effect: it is the pleasure I feel upon perceiving what is agreeable. [2]

Although a distinction is made between internal and external
senses, Kames ascribes all perception, both the internal and the
external varieties, to the mind: "the senses," he says above,
"whether external or internal, are all of them powers or faculties of mind." This point is emphasized in the introduction to
the *Elements*, where Kames makes it clear that the pleasures of
sense, though in certain instances mistakenly placed in the organ of perception, are, in reality, "in the mind." He writes:

> [E]very feeling, pleasant or painful, must be in the mind; and yet
> because in tasting, touching, and smelling, we are sensible of the
> impression made upon the organ, we are led to place there also
> the pleasant or painful feeling caused by that impression; but with
> respect to seeing and hearing, being insensible of the organic im-
> pression, we are not misled to assign a wrong place to the pleasant
> or painful feelings caused by that impression; and therefore we
> naturally place them in the mind, where they really are: upon that
> account, they are conceived to be more refined and spiritual, than

what are derived from tasting, touching, and smelling; for the latter feelings seeming to exist externally to the organ of sense, are conceived to be merely corporeal.[3]

The pleasures of visual perception are considered on a higher level than the pleasures of touch, taste, and smell, not because the latter are corporeal and the former mental; for *both* are mental. Rather, they occupy a higher plane merely because they *seem* to be mental (and are indeed mental), whereas the so-called corporeal pleasures of sense, though they are mental, too, *seem* corporeal. Thus, the distinction between mental and physical pleasures of sense is based merely on a "delusion"; but a delusion which we are unable to dispel at the perceptual level and which we would not even be aware of "Were it not that the delusion is detected by philosophy . . . . "[4]

Kames distinguishes sharply between perception and sensation, the former pertaining to external objects, the latter to feelings. But both are, in large measure, mental processes: "internal acts."

> *Perception* is a general term for hearing, seeing, tasting, touching, smelling; and therefore *perception* signifies every internal act by which we are made acquainted with external objects: thus we are said to perceive a certain animal, a certain colour, sound, taste, smell &c. *Sensation* properly signifies that internal act by which we are made conscious of pleasure or pain felt at the organ of sense: thus we have a sensation of the pleasure arising from warmth, from a fragrant smell, from a sweet taste; and of the pain arising from a wound, from a feted smell, from a disagreeable taste. In perception, my attention is directed to the external object: in sensation, it is directed to the pleasure or pain I feel.[5]

Let us review what we know of Kames's position so far. By *perception* we are made aware of external objects, by *consciousness* of internal objects. The power of perception is an external sense, the power of consciousness an internal sense. Both are *passive:* that is the definitive characteristic of senses. Now the term "perception" includes two distinct processes: the first, perception proper, whereby we are made aware of external objects, and the second, sensation, whereby we are made conscious of the pleasures or pains inherent in perception. And this same distinction between perception and sensation holds both for internal and external senses. We are made conscious of a perceptual pleasure or pain — that is, we *sense* it — by an internal mental act which, in the case of vision, locates the feeling (correctly) in the mind, and in the case of the corporeal senses (taste, smell, touch) locates the feeling (incorrectly) in the sense organ itself.

The question before us is whether, in this perceptual scheme, there is a *sense of beauty* (or anything else of the kind). But before we give an answer, we must examine Kames's concept of the beautiful.

(2) Kames's theory of beauty was fully formed ten years before the publication of the *Elements of Criticism* in his *Essays on the Principles of Morality and Natural Religion* (1751), parts of which found their way, with little or no alteration, into Chapter III of the later work. The term "beautiful," according to Kames, is applied to any visual object the perception of which gives pleasure. "With regard to objects of sight, whatever gives pleasure, is said to be beautiful; whatever gives pain, is said to be ugly." And visual beauty is the "original" beauty; all other objects called beautiful are called so in a "figurative" sense only.

> The terms beauty and ugliness, in their original signification, are confined to objects of sight . . . . But though this be the proper meaning of the terms beauty and ugliness; yet, as it happens with words which convey a more lively idea than ordinary, the terms are applied in a figurative sense to almost every thing which carries a high relish or disgust, where these sensations have not a proper name of their own. [6]

Kames makes the customary eighteenth-century distinction between intrinsic beauty and relative beauty (the fitness of means to ends), the latter being a higher species.

> Objects considered simply as existing, without relation to any end proposed, or any designing agent, are to be placed in the

lowest rank or order with respect to beauty and ugliness. But
when external objects, such as works of art, are considered with
relation to some end proposed, we feel a higher degree of pleasure
or pain. Thus, a building regular in all its parts, pleases the eye
upon the very first view: but considered as a house for dwelling
in, which is the end proposed, it pleases still more, supposing it to
be well fitted to its end.[7]

The higher rank of relative beauty is explained by the fact that
it is, in the fullest degree, an intellectual perception.

Intrinsic beauty is an object of sense merely: to perceive the
beauty of a spreading oak or of a flowing river, no more is required but singly an act of vision. The perception of relative beauty is accompanied with an act of understanding and reflection; for
of a fine instrument or engine, we perceive not the relative beauty, until we be made acquainted with its use and destination.[8]

Of course the statement that intrinsic beauty requires merely
an "act of vision" must be unpacked, in the context of Kames's
perceptual model, if we are to be completely accurate. For, as
we have seen, both the perception of external objects and the
sensation of pleasurable or painful feelings are mental acts.
Thus, it would be more accurate to say that whereas the perception of intrinsic beauty involves but two mental acts, (i) an act
of perception by which the external object is brought to consciousness and (ii) an act of sensation by which the feeling of
intrinsic beauty is experienced; the perception of relative beauty requires three mental acts, (i) an act of perception by which
the object is brought to consciousness, (ii) an act of understanding by which the *relation* of means to ends is discovered,
and (iii) an act of sensation by which the feeling of relative
beauty is experienced. Thus, sensation is common to both. But
the process of perception, in the case of relative beauty, is
augmented by an act of understanding, not present in the
mental act by which the external object is merely brought to
consciousness.

(3) Now I think we are prepared to state whether or not
there is a sense of beauty in Kames's general theory of aesthetic

perception. The conclusion must be, it seems to me, that there is not. The perception of the beautiful for Kames involves both the perception of external objects and the sensing of pleasurable feelings; but no internal sense, so far as I can see, plays a part, explicitly or implicitly, in either process. One might be tempted to call the internal act of sensation the province of an inner sense. However, Kames never does so himself, nor indeed would it be consistent with his general theory of perception. For the internal act of sensation can accompany both external and internal perception; and in both cases it is perception which is the province of the senses, not sensation. For Kames, there is no "sense of beauty" properly so called. He has no need for that hypothesis.

Kames's rejection of the sense of beauty and, with it, the mainstream of the aesthetic sense tradition does not, however, mean that he rejected the entire internal sense doctrine outright. On the contrary, he frequently appealed to inner "senses" of various kinds in a none too critical manner, a fact which has brought him a good deal of adverse criticism. Gordon McKenzie writes that Kames, "like most men, held unalterable intuitive beliefs, and being of an inquiring turn of mind he spent a good deal of his time divising arguments which would prove them." [9] All too often, these arguments ended in an innate faculty and, as Spinoza would have said, "the will of God — in other words, the sanctuary of ignorance." [10]

BIBLIOGRAPHY OF WORKS CITED

Aaron, Richard I. *John Locke.* 2nd ed. Oxford: Oxford University Press, 1965.

Addison, Joseph, and Steele, Richard. *The Spectator.* Edited by A. Chalmers. 6 vols. New York: D. Appleton, 1879.

Alison, Archibald. *Essays on the Nature and Principles of Taste.* Boston: Cummings and Hilliard, 1812.

Anon. review of Hume's "Of the Standard of Taste." *Critical Review,* III (1757).

Aristotle. *Nicomachean Ethics.* Translated by Martin Ostwald. New York: Bobbs-Merrill, Library of Liberal Arts, 1962.

Ayer, A. J. *Language, Truth, and Logic.* 2nd ed. New York: Dover Publications, 1946.

Baeumler, Alfred. *Kants Kritik der Urteilskraft: ihre Geschichte und Systematik.* Halle, 1923.

Balguy, John. *A Collection of Tracts, Moral and Theological.* London, 1734.

Barker, Stephen F. *Philosophy of Mathematics.* Englewood Cliffs, New Jersey: Prentice-Hall, 1964.

Bate, W. J. *From Classic to Romantic: Premises of Taste in Eighteenth-Century England.* New York: Harper Torchbooks, 1961.

Bell, Clive. *Art.* New York: Capricorn Books, 1958.

Berkeley, George. *The Works of George Berkeley.* Edited by A. A. Luce and T. E. Jessop. 9 vols. London: Thomas Nelson, 1948-1957.

Blackstone, William T. *Francis Hutcheson and Contemporary Ethical Theory.* Athens, Georgia: University of Georgia Press, 1965.

Blair, Hugh. *Lectures on Rhetoric and Belles Lettres.* 3rd ed. 3 vols. London, 1787.

Borgerhoff, E. B. O. *The Freedom of French Classicism.* Princeton: Princeton University Press, 1950.

Borinsky, K. *Baltasar Gracián.* Halle, 1894.

—————. *Die Poetik der Rennaissance.* Berlin, 1866.

Bosker, A. *Literary Criticism in the Age of Johnson.* New York, 1935.

Bouhours, Dominique. *La Manière de bien penser dans les ouvrages d'esprit.* Paris, 1771.

Brett, R. L. "The Aesthetic Sense and Taste in the Literary Criticism of the Early Eighteenth Century." *The Review of English Studies,* XX (1944).

—————. *The Third Earl of Shaftesbury.* London: Hutchinson, 1951.

Brown, S. G. "Observations on Hume's Theory of Taste." *English Studies,* XX (1938).

Burke, Edmund. *A Philosophical Enquiry into the Origin of our Ideas of the Sublime and Beautiful.* Edited by J. T. Boulton. London: Routledge & Kegan Paul; New York: Columbia University Press, 1958.

Carritt, E. F. "Moral Positivism and Moral Aestheticism." *Philosophy,* XIII (1938).

Cassirer, Ernst. *The Philosophy of the Enlightenment.* Translated by F. C. A. Koelin and J. P. Pettegrove. Boston: Beacon Press, 1955.

—————. *The Platonic Renaissance in England.* Translated by J. P. Pettegrove. Edinburgh, 1953.

Collingwood, R. G. *Principles of Art.* Oxford: Oxford University Press, 1955.

Cooper, John Gilbert. *Letters Concerning Taste. The Fourth Edition. To which are added, Essays on Similar and Other Subjects. The Second Edition.* London, 1771.

Descartes, René. *Compendium of Music.* Translated by Walter Robert. American Institute of Musicology, 1961.

——————. *Oeuvres de Descartes.* Edited by C. Adam and P. Tannery. 13 vols. Paris, 1897-1913.

——————. *The Philosophical Works of Descartes.* Translated by E. S. Haldane and G. R. T. Ross. 2 vols. New York: Dover Publications, 1955.

Diderot, Denis. *Oeuvres Esthetiques.* Edited by Paul Verniere. Paris: Editions Garnier Frères, 1959.

Dryden, John. *Of Dramatic Poesy and Other Critical Essays.* Edited by G. Watson. 2 vols. London: Everyman's Library, 1962.

DuBos, Jean Baptiste. *Critical Reflections on Poetry, Painting, and Music.* Translated by Thomas Nugent. London, 1748.

Durham, W. H. (ed.). *Critical Essays of the Eighteenth Century.* New Haven: Yale University Press, 1915.

Edwards, Paul. *The Logic of Moral Discourse.* Glencoe, Illinois: The Free Press, 1955.

Elledge, Scott, and Schier, Donald (eds.). *The Continental Model.* Minneapolis: University of Minnesota Press, 1960.

Elton, William (ed.). *Aesthetics and Language.* Oxford: Oxford University Press, 1959.

Flew, Antony. *God and Philosophy.* New York: Delta Books, 1966.

Fontenelle, Bernard Le Bovier de. *A Plurality of Worlds.* Translated by John Glanvill. London, 1702.

Frankena, William K. "Hutcheson's Moral Sense Theory." *Journal of the History of Ideas,* XVI (1955).

Fraser, A. C. *Thomas Reid.* Edinburgh and London, 1898.

Garnett, Richard, and Gosse, Edmund. *English Literature: an Illustrated Record.* 4 vols. London: Heinemann, 1903.

Gerard, Alexander. *An Essay on Taste.* Edited by W. J. Hipple, Jr. Gainesville, Florida: Scholar's Facsimiles and Reprints, 1963.

Gibson, J. *Locke's Theory of Knowledge and its Historical Connections.* Cambridge: Cambridge University Press, 1968.

Gilbert, Katherine, and Kuhn, Helmut. *A History of Esthetics.* 2nd ed. London: Thames and Hudson, 1956.

Gracián, Baltasar. *The Oracle.* Translated by L. B. Watson. London and New York: Everyman's Library, 1962.

Grave, S. A. *The Scottish Philosophy of Common Sense.* Oxford: Oxford University Press, 1960.

Grene, Marjorie. "Gerard's *Essay on Taste.*" *Modern Philology,* XLI (1943).

Güttler, C. *Eduard Lord Herbert von Cherbury.* Munich, 1897.

Halberstadt, William H. "A Problem in Hume's Aesthetics." *Journal of Aesthetics and Art Criticism,* XXX (1971).

Hartley, David. *Observations on Man, his Frame, his Duty, and his Expectations.* 2 vols. London, 1749.

Hartshorne, Charles. *Philosophy and Psychology of Sensation.* Chicago: University of Chicago Press, 1934.

Herbert of Cherbury, Edward, Lord. *On Truth.* Translated by M. H. Carré. Bristol, 1937.

Hipple, W. J. *The Beautiful, the Sublime, and the Picturesque in Eighteenth-Century British Aesthetic Theory.* Carbondale, Illinois: Southern Illinois University Press, 1957.

Hobbes, Thomas. *Leviathan.* Edited by C. B. Macpherson. Baltimore: Penguin Books, 1968.

Hogarth, William. *The Analysis of Beauty.* London, 1753.

Home, Henry, Lord Kames. *Elements of Criticism.* 6th ed. 2 vols. Edinburgh, 1785.

Hooker, E. N. "The Discussion of Taste, from 1750 to 1770, and the New

Trends in Literary Criticism." *Publications of the Modern Language Association*, XLIX (1934).

Howard, Robert. *The Dramatic Works of Sir Robert Howard*. 3rd ed. London, 1722.

Hume, David. *Dialogues Concerning Natural Religion*. 2nd ed. London, 1779.

—————. *The Letters of David Hume*. Edited by J. Y. T. Grieg. 2 vols. Oxford: Oxford University Press, 1932.

—————. *The Philosophical Works of David Hume*. 4 vols. Boston: Little, Brown, 1854.

—————. *A Treatise of Human Nature*. Edited by L. A. Selby-Bigge. Oxford: Oxford University Press, 1955.

Hutcheson, Francis. *An Essay on the Nature and Conduct of the Passions. With Illustrations on the Moral Sense*. 1st ed. London, 1728.

—————. *Illustrations on the Moral Sense*. Edited by Bernard Peach. Cambridge, Massachusetts: Harvard University Press, 1971.

—————. *Inquiry into the Original of our Ideas of Beauty and Virtue*. 1st ed. London, 1725.

—————. *Inquiry into the Original of our Ideas of Beauty and Virtue*. 2nd ed. London, 1726.

—————. *Inquiry into the Original of our Ideas of Beauty and Virtue*. 4th ed. London, 1738.

—————. *Reflections Upon Laughter and Remarks Upon the Fable of the Bees*. Glasgow, 1750.

—————. *A Short Introduction to Moral Philosophy*. 1st ed. Glasgow, 1747.

—————. *Synopsis Metaphysicae, Ontologiam et Pneumatologiam Complectens*. Glasgow (?), 1744.

—————. *A System of Moral Philosophy*. 2 vols. London, 1755.

Jensen, Henning. *Motivation and the Moral Sense in Francis Hutcheson's Ethical Theory*. The Hague: Martinus Nijhoff, 1971.

Kallich, Martin. *The Association of Ideas and Critical Theory in Eighteenth-Century England.* The Hague and Paris: Mouton, 1970.

Kant, Immanuel. *Critique of Aesthetic Judgement.* Translated by J. C. Meredith. Oxford: Oxford University Press, 1911.

––––––. *Critique of Pure Reason.* Translated by Norman Kemp Smith. New York: Humanities Press, 1956.

––––––. *Critique of Teleological Judgement.* Translated by J. C. Meredith. Oxford: Oxford University Press, 1928.

––––––. *Foundations of the Metaphysics of Morals.* Translated by Lewis White Beck. New York: Bobbs-Merrill, Library of Liberal Arts, 1959.

Kenny, Anthony. *Action, Emotion, and Will.* London: Routledge & Kegan Paul, 1963.

Kivy, Peter. "Herbert Spencer and a Musical Dispute." *The Music Review,* XXIII (1962).

––––––. "Hume's Standard of Taste: Breaking the Circle." *British Journal of Aesthetics,* VII (1967).

––––––. "*Lectures on the Fine Arts:* An Unpublished Manuscript of Thomas Reid's." *Journal of the History of Ideas,* XXXI (1970).

––––––. "What Mattheson Said." *The Music Review,* XXXIV (1973).

Knight, Richard Payne. *An Analytical Inquiry into the Principles of Taste.* 2nd ed. London, 1805.

Lang, Berel. "Intuition in Bloomsbury." *Journal of the History of Ideas,* XXV (1964).

Lichtenstein, Aharon. *Henry More: The Rational Theology of a Cambridge Platonist.* Cambridge, Massachusetts: Harvard University Press, 1962.

Locke, John. *Essay Concerning Human Understanding.* Edited by A. C. Fraser. 2 vols. New York: Dover Publications, 1959.

Margolis, Joseph (ed.). *Philosophy Looks At the Arts.* New York: Charles Scribner's Sons, 1962.

Martin, C. B., and Armstrong, D. M. (eds.). *Locke and Berkeley.* Garden City, New York: Doubleday Anchor Books, 1968.

McCosh, James. *The Scottish Philosophy.* New York, 1875.

McKenzie, Gordon. "Lord Kames and the Mechanist Tradition." *University of California Publications in English,* XIV (1942).

McKeon, Richard (ed.). *Selections from Medieval Philosophers.* 2 vols. New York: Charles Scribner's Sons, 1929.

Meldon, A. I. (ed.). *Essays in Moral Philosophy.* Seattle: University of Washington Press, 1958.

Melmoth, William. *Fitzosborne's Letters on Several Subjects.* Boston, 1815.

Méré, Chevalier de. *Oeuvres Complètes.* Edited by Charles-H. Boudhors. Paris, 1930.

Moore, G. E. *Philosophical Papers.* New York: Collier Books, 1962.

––––––. *Philosophical Studies.* Paterson, New Jersey: Littlefield, Adams, 1959.

––––––. *Principia Ethica.* Cambridge: Cambridge University Press, 1960.

More, Henry. *A Collection of Several Philosophical Writings of Dr. Henry More.* 4th ed. London, 1712.

––––––. *An Account of Virtue; or, Dr. Henry More's Abridgement of Morals.* Translated by Edward Southwell. London, 1690.

Noxon, James. "Hume's Opinion of Critics." *Journal of Aesthetics and Art Criticism,* XX (1961).

Plato. *The Dialogues of Plato.* Translated by Benjamin Jowett. 2 vols. New York: Random House, 1937.

Plotinos. *Works of Plotinos.* Translated by K. S. Guthrie. 4 vols. Alpine, New Jersey, 1918.

Price, Richard. *A Review of the Principal Questions in Morals.* Edited by D. D. Raphael. Oxford: Oxford University Press, 1948.

Priestly, Joseph. *A Course of Lectures on Oratory and Criticism.* London, 1777.

Raphael, D. D. *The Moral Sense.* Oxford: Oxford University Press, 1947.

Reid, Thomas. *Lectures on the Fine Arts*. Edited by Peter Kivy. The Hague: Martinus Nijhoff, 1973.

—————. *Philosophical Works of Thomas Reid*. Edited by Sir William Hamilton. 8th ed. 2 vols. Edinburgh: James Thin, 1895.

Robbins, D. O. "The Aesthetics of Thomas Reid." *Journal of Aesthetics and Art Criticism*, No. 5 (1942).

Ross, David. *The Right and the Good*. Oxford: Oxford University Press, 1930.

Saint-Evremond, Charles de. *Oeuvres Mêlées de Saint-Evremond*. Edited by C. Giraud. Paris, 1866.

Schilpp, Paul Arthur. *Kant's Pre-Critical Ethics*. 2nd ed. Evanston, Illinois: Northwestern University Press, 1960.

Schueller, Herbert M. " 'Imitation' and 'Expression' in British Music Criticism in the 18th Century." *The Musical Quarterly*, XXXIV (1948).

Selby-Bigge, L. A. (ed.). *British Moralists*. 2 vols. New York: Bobbs-Merrill, Library of Liberal Arts, 1964.

Sellars, Wilfrid, and Hospers, John (eds.). *Readings in Ethical Theory*. New York: Appleton-Century-Crofts, 1952.

Shaftesbury, Anthony Ashley Cooper, Third Earl of. *Characteristicks of Men, Manners, Opinions, Times*. 5th ed. London, 1773.

—————. *The Life, Unpublished Letters, and Philosophical Regimen of Anthony, Earl of Shaftesbury*. Edited by Benjamin Rand. London: Swan Sonnenschein; New York: Macmillan, 1900.

—————. *Second Characters, or the Language of Forms*. Edited by Benjamin Rand. Cambridge: Cambridge University Press, 1914.

Smith, G. Gregory (ed.). *Elizabethan Critical Essays*. 2 vols. Oxford: Oxford University Press, 1959.

Sorley, W. R. "The Philosophy of Herbert of Cherbury." *Mind*, n.s. III (1894).

Spingarn, J. E. (ed.). *Critical Essays of the Seventeenth Century*. 3 vols. Oxford: Oxford University Press, 1957.

Spinoza, Benedict de. *Chief Works of Benedict de Spinoza.* Translated by R. H. M. Elwes. 2 vols. New York: Dover Publications, 1951.

Stein, K. H. von. *Entstehung der Neuren Aesthetik.* Stuttgart, 1886.

Stephen, Leslie. *History of English Thought in the Eighteenth Century.* New York: Harbinger Books, 1962.

Stevenson, C. L. *Ethics and Language.* New Haven: Yale University Press, 1944.

Stewart, Dugald. *The Works of Dugald Stewart.* 7 vols. Cambridge, Massachusetts: Hilliard and Brown, 1829.

Stolnitz, Jerome. " 'Beauty': Some Stages in the History of an Idea." *Journal of the History of Ideas,* XXII (1961).

—————. "Locke and the Categories of Value in Eighteenth-Century British Aesthetic Theory." *Philosophy,* XXXVIII (1963).

—————. "On the Origins of 'Aesthetic Disinterestedness.' " *Journal of Aesthetics and Art Criticism,* XX (1961).

—————. "On the Significance of Lord Shaftesbury in Modern Aesthetic Theory." *The Philosophical Quarterly,* XI (1961).

Wiley, Basil. *The Seventeenth Century Background.* New York: Doubleday Anchor Books, 1955.

Wiley, M. L. "Gerard and the Scots Societies." *The University of Texas Publications: Studies in English,* No. 4026. (1940).

Wittgenstein, Ludwig. *Philosophical Investigations.* Translated by G. E. M. Anscombe. New York: Macmillan, 1953.

Wittkower, Rudolf. *Architectural Principles in the Age of Humanism.* London: Alec Tiranti, 1962.

Yolton, John W. *John Locke and the Way of Ideas.* Oxford: Oxford University Press, 1956.

—————. "Locke's Unpublished Marginal Replies to John Sergeant." *Journal of the History of Ideas,* XII (1951).

NOTES

CHAPTER I

1. Ernst Cassirer, *The Platonic Renaissance in England*, trans. J. P. Pettegrove (Edinburgh, 1953), p. 160.

2. Basil Wiley, *The Seventeenth Century Background* (New York: Doubleday Anchor Books, 1955), p. 125.

3. See C. Güttler, *Eduard Lord Herbert von Cherbury* (Munich, 1897), pp. 163-182.

4. W. R. Sorley, "The Philosophy of Herbert of Cherbury," *Mind*, n.s. III (1894), p. 501.

5. Edward, Lord Herbert of Cherbury, *On Truth*, trans. M. H. Carré (Bristol, 1937), pp. 116, 122.

6. *Ibid.*, pp. 125, 122.

7. Sorley, *op. cit.*, p. 500.

8. *On Truth*, pp. 140, 139.

9. *Characteristicks of Men, Manners, Opinions, Times*, 5th ed. (London, 1773), vol. I, p. 399.

10. *An Account of Virtue; or, Dr. Henry More's Abridgement of Morals*, trans. Edward Southwell, (London, 1690), p. 28.

11. *Ibid.*, p. 8.

12. Aharon Lichtenstein, *Henry More: The Rational Theology of a Cambridge Platonist* (Cambridge, Massachusetts: Harvard University Press, 1962), p. 67.

13. Quoted in Paul Arthur Schilpp, *Kant's Pre-Critical Ethics*, 2nd ed. (Evanston, Illinois: Northwestern University Press, 1960), p. 31. Kant, of course, rejected the moral sense in his mature ethical writings.

14. For some brief accounts of the history of "taste" as an aesthetic concept, see K. Borinsky, *Baltasar Gracián* (Halle, 1894), pp. 39-72; *Die Poetik der Rennaissance* (Berlin, 1866), ch. VI; K. H. von Stein, *Die Entstehung der Neuren Aesthetik* (Stuttgart, 1886), pp. 83-97. For a thorough account of "taste" in Germany and France during the seventeenth

and eighteenth centuries, see Alfred Baeumler, *Kants Kritik der Urteils-kraft: ihre Geschichte und Systematik* (Halle, 1923), pp. 18-82.

15. *The Oracle,* trans. L. B. Watson (London and New York: Every-man's Library, 1962), p. 97.

16. See, for example, "Sur les Plaisirs," *Oevres Mêlées de Saint-Evremond,* ed. C. Giraud (Paris, 1866), vol. I, p. 34.

17. See, for example, "Discours de la Justesse," in *Oeuvres Complètes,* ed. Charles-H. Boudhors (Paris, 1930), vol. I, pp. 95-112.

18. "The *Je Ne Sais Quoi,*" trans. Donald Schier, in *The Continental Model,* ed. Scott Elledge and Donald Schier (Minneapolis: University of Minnesota Press, 1960), p. 230. For a discussion of the *je ne sais quoi* as a critical concept in Bouhours, see E. B. O. Borgerhoff, *The Freedom of French Classicism* (Princeton: Princeton University Press, 1950), pp. 186-200.

19. "The *Je Ne Sais Quoi,*" p. 236.

20. *Ibid.,* p. 229.

21. *Ibid.,* p. 235.

22. *La Manière de bien penser dans les ouvrages d'esprit* (Paris, 1771), p. 402.

23. *Elizabethan Critical Essays,* ed. G. Gregory Smith (Oxford: Oxford University Press, 1959), vol. I, p. 158.

24. *The Dramatic Works of Sir Robert Howard,* 3rd ed. (London, 1722), p. 307.

25. *Of Dramatic Poesy, and Other Critical Essays,* ed. G. Watson (London: Everyman's Library, 1962), vol. I, p. 120.

26. Ernst Cassirer, *The Philosophy of the Enlightenment,* trans. F. C. A. Koelln and J. P. Pettegrove (Boston: Beacon Press, 1955), p. 304.

27. Katherine Gilbert and Helmut Kuhn, *A History of Esthetics,* 2nd ed. (London: Thames and Hudson, 1956), p. 233. The same point is made, and enlarged upon, in Jerome Stolnitz, "Locke and the Categories of Value in Eighteenth-Century British Aesthetic Theory," *Philosophy,* XXXVIII (1963).

28. *The Life, Unpublished Letters, and Philosophical Regimen of Anthony, Earl of Shaftesbury,* ed. Benjamin Rand (London: Swan Sonnenschein; New York: Macmillan, 1900), p. 403.

29. *Characteristicks,* vol. II, p. 74.

30. *Ibid.,* p. 372.

31. *A Plurality of Worlds,* trans. John Glanvill (London, 1702), p. viii.

32. *Characteristicks,* vol. II, p. 295.

33. *Ibid.,* p. 406.

34. *Ibid.*

35. *Ibid.,* p. 427.

36. *Ibid.,* p. 408.

37. *Works of Plotinos,* trans. K. S. Guthrie (Alpine, New Jersey, 1918), vol. I, p. 51 (*Enneads,* I.vi.7).

38. *Characteristicks*, vol. II, p. 427.

39. Letter to Michael Ainsworth, June 3rd, 1709, *The Life, Unpublished Letters, and Philosophical Regimen of Anthony, Earl of Shaftesbury*, p. 405. John Toland was the "pirate."

40. This gap, however, is by no means barren of intellectual effort: witness the large amount of material written between 1698 and 1712, published for the first time by Benjamin Rand in 1900 under the title *Philosophical Regimen.*

41. *Characteristicks*, vol. II, pp. 28-29.

42. *Ibid.*, p. 52.

43. *The Tragedies of the Last Age*, in *Critical Essays of the Seventeenth Century*, ed. J. E. Spingarn (Oxford: Oxford University Press, 1957), vol. II, p. 183.

44. "On the Significance of Lord Shaftesbury in Modern Aesthetic Theory," *The Philosophical Quarterly*, XI (1961), p. 111.

45. *An Antidote Against Atheism* [1652], in *A Collection of Several Philosophical Writings of Dr. Henry More*, 4th ed. (London, 1712), pp. 52-53.

46. *Characteristicks*, vol. II, pp. 414-415.

47. *Ibid.*, vol. I, p. 234.

48. *Ibid.*, p. 336.

49. *Ibid.*, vol. III, p. 161.

50. R. L. Brett, *The Third Earl of Shaftesbury* (London: Hutchinson, 1951), p. 151; my italics.

51. *Characteristicks*, vol. II, p. 411.

52. For one example of Locke's argument on this regard, see *Essay Concerning Human Understanding*, Book I, Chapter III, Section 2.

53. *The Life, Unpublished Letters, and Philosophical Regimen of Anthony, Earl of Shaftesbury*, p. 403. This argument seems almost a sketch of a later and more famous one with which Kant introduced the first *Critique*: "But though all our knowledge begins with experience, it does not follow that it all arises out of experience" (*Critique of Pure Reason*, trans. Norman Kemp Smith [New York: The Humanities Press, 1956], p. 41).

54. *Critique of Aesthetic Judgement*, trans. J. C. Meredith (Oxford: Oxford University Press, 1911), p. 82.

55. *Characteristicks*, vol. III, pp. 164-165.

56. *Ibid.*, vol. I, p. 353.

57. *Second Characters or the Language of Forms*, ed. Benjamin Rand (Cambridge: Cambridge University Press, 1914), p. 177. Shaftesbury died before the completion of this work. The portion from which I have quoted existed only in the form of manuscript notes until published by Rand.

58. *Characteristicks*, vol. I, p. 332.

59. *Ibid.*, pp. 340-341.

60. Two *immediate* predecessors of Hutcheson, L'Abbé Du Bos and

Leonard Welsted, deserve at least brief mention here; for both spoke explicitly of a critical or aesthetic sense. Thus, Du Bos writes in the *Reflexions Critiques sur la Poesie et sur la Peinture* (1719): "We have a sense, which judges of the merit of works, that consist in the imitation of objects of a moving nature. . ." (Jean Baptiste Du Bos, *Critical Reflections on Poetry, Painting and Music*, trans. Thomas Nugent [London, 1748], vol. II, p. 238). And, similarly, Welsted writes in *The State of Poetry* (1724): ". . . To have what we call *Taste*, is having, one may say, a new Sense or Faculty superadded to the ordinarily ones of the Soul, the prerogative of fine Spirits! and to go about to pedagogue a Man into this sort of knowledge, who has not got the Seeds of it in himself, is the same thing, as if one should endeavor to teach an art of seeing without Eyes. . ." (in *Critical Essays of the Eighteenth Century*, ed. W. H. Durham [New Haven: Yale University Press, 1915], p. 366).

CHAPTER II

1. *Inquiry into Beauty and Virtue,* 1st ed. (London, 1725), p. vii.
2. *Inquiry into Beauty and Virtue,* 2nd ed. (London, 1726), p. xxi. This reference to Shaftesbury was added in the second edition.
3. Jerome Stolnitz, "Locke and the Categories of Value in Eighteenth-Century British Aesthetic Theory," p. 47.
4. *Inquiry into Beauty and Virtue,* 1st ed., p. iv.
5. John Locke, *Essay Concerning Human Understanding,* ed. A. C. Fraser (New York: Dover Publications, 1959), vol. I, p. 160.
6. *Inquiry into Beauty and Virtue,* 1st ed., p. v.
7. *Ibid.*
8. *Ibid.,* pp. v-vi.
9. *Ibid.,* p. vi.
10. *Inquiry into Beauty and Virtue,* 4th ed. (London, 1738), "Additions and Corrections."
11. *Inquiry into Beauty and Virtue,* 1st ed., p. viii.
12. *Ibid.,* p. 75.
13. Locke, *op. cit.,* vol. I, p. 58.
14. See J. Gibson, *Locke's Theory of Knowledge and its Historical Connections* (Cambridge: Cambridge University Press, 1968), p. 38.
15. This is not to say that Descartes and those of his ilk were the only objects of Locke's critique, or that what I have suggested here was his only critical purpose. As John Yolton has, I think, pretty conclusively shown, there were those who actually did hold the doctrine of innate knowledge in just the naive form that Locke sometimes attacked, and not in the more subtle form of Descartes and the Continental rationalists. See John Yolton, *John Locke and the Way of Ideas* (Oxford: Oxford University Press, 1956), especially ch. II.

16. *Inquiry into Beauty and Virtue,* 1st ed., p. ix.

17. Joseph Addison, *On the Pleasures of the Imagination,* Paper I, *The Spectator,* ed. A. Chalmers (New York: D. Appleton, 1879), vol. V, pp. 30-31.

18. *Ibid.,* Paper II, p. 33.

19. *On the Sublime,* XXXV.

20. *On the Pleasures of the Imagination,* Paper II, vol. V, pp. 34-35.

21. *Ibid.,* p. 36.

22. *Ibid.,* Paper III, pp. 39-40.

23. Locke, *op. cit.,* vol. II, p. 32.

24. *Ibid.,* vol. I, p. 468.

25. *On the Pleasures of the Imagination,* Paper VIII, vol. V, pp. 68-69.

26. Francis Hutcheson, *Reflections Upon Laughter and Remarks Upon the Fable of the Bees* (Glasgow, 1750), p. 27.

27. The *"Sensus Ridiculi"* is, indeed, included in the list of internal or reflex senses in Hutcheson's Latin treatise, *Synopsis Metaphysicae, Ontologiam et Pneumatologiam Complectens* (Glasgow[?], 1744), p. 55.

28. *Inquiry into Beauty and Virtue,* 1st ed., p. 78.

29. Francis Hutcheson, *An Essay on the Nature and Conduct of the Passions and Affections. With Illustrations on the Moral Sense,* 1st ed. (London, 1728), pp. 4-6.

30. Francis Hutcheson, *A Short Introduction to Moral Philosophy,* 1st ed. (Glasgow, 1747), p. 13.

31. Francis Hutcheson, *A System of Moral Philosophy* (London, 1755), vol. I, p. 15.

32. *Inquiry into Beauty and Virtue,* 1st ed., p. 11.

33. *Ibid.,* p. 10.

34. I am indebted to George Dickie for bringing this point to my attention.

35. *Inquiry into Beauty and Virtue,* 1st ed., p. 11.

36. See D. D. Raphael, *The Moral Sense* (Oxford: Oxford University Press, 1947), p. 19.

37. *Inquiry into Beauty and Virtue,* 1st ed., p. 42.

CHAPTER III

1. *Inquiry Concerning Beauty,* 1st ed., pp. 6-7.

2. I have in mind particularly here Locke's distinction between primary and secondary qualities. See, for example, Reginald Jackson, "Locke's Distinction between Primary and Secondary Qualities," reprinted in *Locke and Berkeley,* ed. C. B. Martin and D. M. Armstrong (Garden City, New York: Doubleday Anchor Books, 1968).

3. Locke, *Essay,* ed. Fraser, vol. I, p. 28.

4. *Ibid.,* vol. I, p. 122.

5. See Richard I. Aaron, *John Locke*, 2nd ed. (Oxford: Oxford University Press, 1965), pp. 111-112.

6. Locke, *Essay*, vol. II, p. 145.

7. *Ibid.*

8. *Inquiry Concerning Beauty*, 1st ed., p. 2.

9. *Ibid.*, p. 3.

10. Locke, *op. cit.*, vol. I, p. 173.

11. *Ibid.*, p. 302.

12. *Ibid.*, p. 214.

13. *Ibid.*, pp. 215-216.

14. *Ibid.*, pp. 146-147.

15. *Inquiry Concerning Beauty*, 1st ed., p. 2.

16. *Ibid.*, p. 7.

17. *Ibid.*, pp. 13-14.

18. Cf. C. D. Broad, "Some Reflections On Moral-Sense Theories in Ethics," reprinted in *Readings in Ethical Theory*, ed. Wilfrid Sellars and John Hospers (New York: Appleton-Century-Crofts, 1952), pp. 369-370.

19. *Inquiry Concerning Beauty*, 1st ed., p. 10.

20. *Ibid.*, p. 8.

21. *Ibid.*, pp. 7-8.

22. *Inquiry Concerning Beauty*, 4th ed., p. 10.

23. *Inquiry Concerning Beauty*, 1st ed., p. 10.

24. *Ibid.*, p. 89.

25. *The Works of George Berkeley*, ed. A. A. Luce and T. E. Jessop (London: Thomas Nelson, 1948-57), vol. II, p. 176.

26. *Inquiry Concerning Beauty*, 1st ed., pp. 15-16.

27. The notion that *uniformity amidst variety* can exist in an arrangement of secondary qualities is implicit, for example, in Hutcheson's discussion on pp. 5-6 of the first edition of the *Inquiry Concerning Beauty*, and even more obvious in the passage as it was revised for editions two, three, and four.

28. Locke, *op. cit.*, vol. I, p. 172; my italics.

CHAPTER IV

1. A. J. Ayer, *Language, Truth, and Logic*, 2nd ed. (New York: Dover Publications, 1946), p. 113.

2. William Frankena, "Hutcheson's Moral Sense Theory," *Journal of the History of Ideas*, XVI (1955); William T. Blackstone, *Francis Hutcheson and Contemporary Ethical Theory* (Athens, Georgia: University of Georgia Press, 1965); Bernard Peach, ed., Francis Hutcheson: *Illustrations on the Moral Sense* (Cambridge, Massachusetts: Harvard University Press, 1971).

3. *Inquiry Concerning Beauty*, 1st ed., p. 73.

4. *Ibid.*, p. 42.
5. *Euthyphro*, XII, 10; trans. Jowett.
6. Broad, *op. cit.*, p. 365.
7. Locke, *Essay Concerning Human Understanding*, vol. II, pp. 8-9.
8. *Ibid.*, p. 9.
9. *Ibid.*, p. 11.
10. *Ibid.*, p. 98.
11. *Ibid.*, p. 105.
12. Berkeley, *op. cit.*, vol. II, p. 37.
13. C. L. Stevenson, *Ethics and Language* (New Haven: Yale University Press, 1944), pp. 21-22.
14. The correspondence between Hutcheson and Burnet is reprinted in the appendix to Professor Peach's edition of Hutcheson's *Illustrations on the Moral Sense*. I have quoted from this (Peach, *op. cit.*, p. 212).
15. *Inquiry Concerning Beauty*, 1st ed., p. 26.
16. See Jerome Stolnitz, "On the Origins of 'Aesthetic Disinterestedness,' " *Journal of Aesthetics and Art Criticism*, XX (1961).
17. *Inquiry Concerning Beauty*, 1st ed., p. 11.
18. *An Essay on the Nature and Conduct of the Passions and Affections*, 1st ed., p. 102.
19. See, for example, Anthony Kenny, *Action, Emotion and Will* (London: Routledge & Kegan Paul, 1963), ch. III.
20. *Inquiry Concerning Beauty*, 1st ed., p. viii.
21. *Ibid.*, p. 7.
22. *Ibid.*, p. 16.
23. *Ibid.*, pp. 4-6. The words in brackets were added in the second edition.
24. Charles Hartshorne, *Philosophy and Psychology of Sensation* (Chicago: University of Chicago Press, 1934), p. 186. Cf. Vincent Tomas, "The Concept of Expression in Art," reprinted in *Philosophy Looks At the Arts*, ed. Joseph Margolis (New York: Charles Scribner's Sons, 1962).
25. Locke, *op. cit.*, vol. I, p. 184.
26. *Inquiry Concerning Beauty*, 1st ed., p. 81.
27. *Ibid.*, p. 84.
28. Locke, *op. cit.*, vol. I, pp. 531-533.
29. *Inquiry Concerning Beauty*, 1st ed., p. 4.
30. *Ibid.*, p. 76.

CHAPTER V

1. Hutcheson, *Inquiry Concerning Beauty*, 1st ed., p. 78.
2. *The Spectator*, ed. Chalmers, vol. V, p. 34.
3. *Ibid.*, p. 35.
4. *Ibid.*, p. 36.

250   THE SEVENTH SENSE

5. *Ibid.*, pp. 34-35.

6. *A Short Introduction to Moral Philosophy*, p. 13.

7. *Ibid.*

8. Thomas Hobbes, *Leviathan*, ed. C. B. Macpherson (Baltimore: Penguin Books, 1968), p. 125 (Part I, ch. 6).

9. Hutcheson, *Reflections Upon Laughter*, p. 7.

10. *Ibid.*, p. 19.

11. *Ibid.*, p. 33.

12. Francis Hutcheson, *A System of Moral Philosophy*, vol. I, p. 16.

13. Hutcheson, *Inquiry Concerning Beauty*, 1st ed., p. 22.

14. William Hogarth, *The Analysis of Beauty* (London, 1753), p. 14.

15. Edmund Burke, *A Philosophical Enquiry into the Origin of our Ideas of the Sublime and Beautiful*, ed. J. T. Boulton (London: Routledge & Kegan Paul; New York: Columbia University Press, 1958), p. 105.

16. Hutcheson, *Inquiry Concerning Beauty*, 1st ed., p. 34.

17. *Ibid.*, p. 40.

18. *Ibid.*, p. 35.

19. *Ibid.*, pp. 16-17.

20. *Ibid.*, pp. 18-22.

21. R. G. Collingwood, *The Principles of Art* (Oxford: Oxford University Press, 1955), pp. 38-39.

22. Hutcheson, *Inquiry Concerning Beauty*, 1st ed., pp. 27-28. "In right-angled triangles, the square on the side subtending the right angle is equal to the squares on the sides containing the right angle."

23. *Ibid.*, p. 29.

24. Hutcheson, *Inquiry Concerning Beauty*, 2nd ed., pp. 32-33.

25. Hutcheson, *Inquiry Concerning Beauty*, 1st ed., p. 29.

26. Stephen F. Barker, *Philosophy of Mathematics* (Englewood Cliffs, New Jersey: Prentice-Hall, 1964), p. 25.

27. Hutcheson, *Inquiry Concerning Beauty*, 1st ed., pp. 25-26. Hutcheson was obviously a novice in music, and he made alterations of this passage in later editions of the *Inquiry* to correct his terminology. "Chord," for example, becomes "Concord."

28. *Ibid.*, p. 33.

29. *Ibid.*, pp. 33-34.

30. See Rudolf Wittkower, *Architectural Principles in the Age of Humanism* (London: Alec Tiranti, 1962).

31. Hutcheson, *Inquiry Concerning Beauty*, 1st ed., p. 36.

32. *Ibid.*, pp. 36-37.

33. For a useful discussion of such theories, mostly in the period 1750-1800, see Herbert M. Schueller, " 'Imitation' and 'Expression' in British Music Criticism in the 18th Century," *The Musical Quarterly*, XXXIV (1948).

34. "What Mattheson Said," *The Music Review*, XXXIV (1973).

35. Hutcheson, *Inquiry Concerning Beauty*, 1st ed., pp. 77-78.

36. This same kind of observation led to various theories of the origin of music from speech. See Peter Kivy, "Herbert Spencer and a Musical Dispute," *The Music Review*, XXIII (1962).

<h2 style="text-align:center">CHAPTER VI</h2>

1. Francis Hutcheson, *Synopsis Metaphysicae, Ontologiam et Pneumatologiam Complectens*, p. 96.

2. *A System of Moral Philosophy*, vol. I, pp. iv-v. Leechman's biographical sketch of Hutcheson comprises the preface to the posthumously published *System*. Leechman also tells us that in 1717 Hutcheson wrote a letter to Samuel Clarke, pressing some of his theological objections. Leechman adds: "Whether the Doctor [Clarke] returned any answer to this letter does not appear from Dr. Hutcheson's papers."

3. *Inquiry Concerning Beauty*, 1st ed., p. 42.

4. *Inquiry Concerning Beauty*, 2nd ed., p. 48. This definition of undirected or undesigned force was added in the second edition.

5. *Inquiry Concerning Beauty*, 1st ed., p. 43.

6. Immanual Kant, *Critique of Teleological Judgement*, trans. J. C. Meredith (Oxford: The Clarendon Press, 1928), p. 54.

7. *Ibid.*

8. See Antony Flew, *God and Philosophy* (New York: Delta Books, 1966), p. 60.

9. *Inquiry Concerning Beauty*, 1st ed., p. 48.

10. *Ibid.*, p. 53.

11. David Hume, *Dialogues Concerning Natural Religion*, 2nd ed. (London, 1779), pp. 47-48.

12. *Ibid.*, p. 58.

13. *Inquiry Concerning Beauty*, 1st ed., p. 91.

14. *Ibid.*, p. 92.

15. *Ibid.*

16. René Descartes, *Compendium of Music*, trans. Walter Robert (American Institute of Musicology, 1961), p. 13. Cf. Descartes's letter to Mersenne, March 18, 1630, in *Oeuvres de Descartes*, ed. Adam and Tannery (Paris, 1897), vol. I, pp. 132-134.

17. Spinoza, *Ethics*, appendix to Part I, *Chief Works of Benedict de Spinoza*, trans. R. H. M. Elwes (New York: Dover Publications, 1951), vol. II, p. 79.

18. *Inquiry Concerning Beauty*, 1st ed., p. 93.

19. *Ibid.*, p. 95.

20. *Ibid.*, p. 96.

21. R. L. Brett, "The Aesthetic Sense and Taste in the Literary Criticism of the Early Eighteenth Century," *The Review of English Studies*, XX (1944), p. 203.

22. Ernst Cassirer, *The Philosophy of the Enlightenment*, p. 321.

23. "Locke and the Categories of Value in Eighteenth-Century British Aesthetic Theory," p. 40.

24. "On the Significance of Lord Shaftesbury in Modern Aesthetic Theory," p. 99.

CHAPTER VII

1. Sir Leslie Stephen, *History of English Thought in the Eighteenth Century* (New York: Harbinger Books, 1962), vol. II, p. 2.

2. Berkeley wrote a treatise on ethics which was lost while he was traveling in Italy.

3. *Critique of Pure Reason*, p. 66n.

4. John Balguy, *A Collection of Tracts, Moral and Theological* (London, 1734), pp. 60-61.

5. *Ibid.*, p. 61.

6. *Ibid.*, pp. 155-156.

7. *Ibid.*, pp. 226-227.

8. *The Works of George Berkeley*, ed. A. A. Luce and T. E. Jessop (London: Thomas Nelson, 1948-1957), vol. III, *Alciphron, or the Minute Philosopher*, ed. T. E. Jessop, p. 116n.

9. *Ibid.*, p. 117.

10. *The Works of George Berkeley*, ed. Luce and Jessop, vol. I, *Theory of Vision Vindicated*, ed. A. A. Luce, p. 252.

11. *Alciphron*, pp. 123-124.

12. Stephen, *op. cit.*, vol. II, p. 3.

13. D. D. Raphael, *The Moral Sense*, pp. 1, 111.

14. "Some Reflections on Moral-Sense Theories in Ethics," p. 363.

15. *A Review of the Principal Questions in Morals*, ed. D. D. Raphael (Oxford: Oxford University Press, 1948), p. 4.

16. *Ibid.*, p. 57.

17. For some recent discussion of this issue, see W. D. Falk, " 'Ought' and Motivation," reprinted in Sellars and Hospers, *Readings in Ethical Theory*; and William K. Frankena, "Obligation and Motivation in Recent Moral Philosophy," *Essays in Moral Philosophy*, ed. A. I. Melden (Seattle: University of Washington Press, 1958). For a discussion of the issue in Hutcheson, see Henning Jensen, *Motivation and the Moral Sense in Francis Hutcheson's Ethical Theory* (The Hague: Martinus Nijhoff, 1971), ch. III.

18. Price, *op. cit.*, p. 59.

19. *Ibid.*, p. 60.

20. *Ibid.*, p. 66.

21. Price's moral and aesthetic "dualism" has been defended in recent years by E. F. Carritt in "Moral Positivism and Moral Aestheticism," *Philosophy*, XIII (1938).

22. Price, *op. cit.*, pp. 20-21.
23. *Ibid.*, p. 64.
24. *Ibid.*, p. 65.

CHAPTER VIII

1. Sections (1)-(4) of this chapter consist (with minor revisions) of a previously published article, "Hume's Standard of Taste: Breaking the Circle," *The British Journal of Aesthetics*, VII (1967). It is reprinted here with permission of *The British Journal of Aesthetics*.

2. *The Letters of David Hume*, ed. J. Y. T. Greig (Oxford: Oxford University Press, 1932), vol. I, p. 40.

3. *A Treatise of Human Nature*, ed. L. A. Selby-Bigge (Oxford: Oxford University Press, 1955), p. 471.

4. As Kant characterized him in the *Critique of Pure Reason*, p. 597.

5. "Of the Standard of Taste," *The Philosophical Works of David Hume* (Boston: Little, Brown, 1854), vol. III, p. 252.

6. *Works*, vol. IV, p. 233.

7. "Of the Standard of Taste," *Works*, vol. III, p. 257.

8. "The Sceptic," *Works*, vol. III, pp. 179-180.

9. *Ibid.*, p. 180.

10. "Of the Standard of Taste," *Works*, vol. III, pp. 265-266.

11. *Ibid.*, p. 265.

12. See, for example, S. G. Brown, "Observations on Hume's Theory of Taste," *English Studies*, XX (1938); and James Noxon, "Hume's Opinion of Critics," *Journal of Aesthetics and Art Criticism*, XX (1961).

13. "Of the Standard of Taste," *Works*, vol. III, p. 260.

14. *Ibid.*, p. 261.

15. *Ibid.*, p. 258.

16. "Of the Delicacy of Taste and Passion," *Works*, vol. III, p. 3n.

17. "Of the Standard of Taste," *Works*, vol. III, p. 263.

18. *Ibid.*

19. *A Treatise of Human Nature*, p. 472.

20. Cf. Kant, *Critique of Aesthetic Judgement*, trans. J. C. Meredith (Oxford: Oxford University Press, 1911): "by the name *sensus communis* is to be understood the idea of a *public sense, i.e.* a critical faculty which in its reflective act takes account *(a priori)* of the mode of representation of every one else, in order, *as it were*, to weigh its judgement with the collective reason of mankind, and thereby avoid the illusion arising from subjective and personal conditions which could readily be taken for objective, an illusion that would exert prejudicial influence upon its judgement. This is accomplished by weighing the judgement, not so much with actual, as rather with the merely possible, judgements of others, and by putting ourselves in the position of every one else, as the result of a mere abstrac-

tion from the limitations which contingently affect our own estimate" (p. 151).

21. "Of the Standard of Taste," *Works*, vol. III, p. 264.

22. *Ibid.*, p. 268.

23. C. L. Stevenson, *Ethics and Language*, p. 138. Stevenson's remark has reference, of course, to ethical disputes, and I have appropriated it for this analysis of Hume's aesthetic theory.

24. *Critical Review*, III (1757), p. 213.

25. Aristotle, *Nicomachean Ethics*, 1094b, trans. Martin Ostwald.

26. *Works*, vol. IV, p. 355. My attention was drawn to this passage by the article of William H. Halberstadt, "A Problem in Hume's Aesthetics," *Journal of Aesthetics and Art Criticism*, XXX (1971), p. 212.

27. Halberstadt, *op. cit., passim.*

CHAPTER IX

1. *Essays on the Intellectual Powers of Man, The Philosophical Works of Thomas Reid*, 8th ed., ed. William Hamilton (Edinburgh: James Thin, 1895), vol. I, p. 275.

2. C. D. Broad, "Some Reflections on Moral-Sense Theories in Ethics," p. 368.

3. Reid, *Essays on the Intellectual Powers, Works*, vol. I, p. 310.

4. *Ibid.*

5. *Ibid.*, p. 312.

6. "The Nature and Reality of Objects of Perception," *Philosophical Studies* (Paterson, New Jersey: Littlefield, Adams, 1959), p. 50. It should be noted that Reid refers to some sensations as unlearned signs of qualities, but does not apparently, believe that all sensations are *unlearned* signs.

7. Reid, *Works*, vol. I, p. 310n.

8. A. C. Fraser, in *Thomas Reid* (Edinburgh and London, 1898), is also, I believe, guilty of this kind of misinterpretation. See, for instance, pp. 64, 141.

9. Reid, *An Inquiry into the Human Mind on the Principles of Common Sense, Works*, vol. I, p. 107.

10. Reid, *Essays on the Intellectual Powers, Works*, vol. I, p. 309.

11. In James McCosh, *The Scottish Philosophy* (New York, 1875), pp. 223-224.

12. Reid, *Essays on the Intellectual Powers, Works*, vol. I, p. 425.

13. Moore, "The Nature and Reality of Objects of Perception," p. 50.

14. For an account of John Sergeant's relation to Locke, see John W. Yolton, "Locke's Unpublished Marginal Replies to John Sergeant," *Journal of the History of Ideas*, XII (1951).

15. Reid, *Essays on the Intellectual Powers, Works*, vol. I, p. 313.

16. *The Philosophical Works of Descartes*, trans. E. S. Haldane and G. R. T. Ross (New York: Dover Publications, 1955), vol. I, p. 248.

17. Reid, *Essays on the Intellectual Powers, Works*, vol. I, p. 313.

18. *Philosophical Works of Descartes*, vol. I, p. 249.

19. Reid, *Essays on the Intellectual Powers, Works*, vol. I, p. 313n.

20. See Peter Kivy, *"Lectures on the Fine Arts:* An Unpublished Manuscript of Thomas Reid's," *Journal of the History of Ideas*, XXXI (1970); and Thomas Reid, *Lectures on the Fine Arts*, ed. Peter Kivy (The Hague: Martinus Nijhoff, 1973).

21. Reid, *Inquiry, Works*, vol. I, p. 117.

22. Reid, *Essays on the Intellectual Powers, Works*, vol. I, p. 490.

23. *Ibid.*, p. 492.

24. *Ibid.*

25. Reid, *Lectures on the Fine Arts*, p. 37.

26. Reid, *Essays on the Intellectual Powers, Works*, vol. I, p. 490.

27. *Ibid.;* my italics.

28. Reid, *Inquiry, Works*, vol. I, p. 141.

29. Reid, *Essays on the Intellectual Powers, Works*, vol. I, p. 493.

30. *Ibid.*

31. *Ibid.*, p. 495.

32. *Ibid.*

33. *Ibid.*, p. 498.

34. *Ibid.*, p. 496.

35. *Ibid.*, p. 500.

36. *Ibid.*, p. 501.

37. *Ibid.*, p. 500.

38. *Ibid.*, pp. 501-502.

39. Reid states explicitly: "some of the qualities that please a good taste resemble the secondary qualities of body, and therefore may be called occult qualities. . . ." (*Ibid.*, p. 490).

40. *Ibid.*, p. 500.

41. *Ibid.*, p. 505.

42. David Ross, *The Right and the Good* (Oxford: Oxford University Press, 1930), p. 88.

43. D. O. Robbins, "The Aesthetics of Thomas Reid," *Journal of Aesthetics and Art Criticism*, No. 5 (1942), p. 36.

44. *Works*, vol. I, p. 89. The letter is dated 3d Feb. 1790; it was sent in acknowledgment for receipt of a copy of Alison's *Essays on the Nature and Principles of Taste*.

CHAPTER X

1. For an account of the associationist aesthetics in eighteenth-century Britain, see Martin Kallich, *The Association of Ideas and Critical Theory in*

Eighteenth-Century England (The Hague: Mouton, 1970).

2. Prefixed to Edmund Law's translation of King's *Essays on the Origin of Evil.*

3. *British Moralists,* ed. L. A. Selby-Bigge (New York: Bobbs-Merrill, Library of Liberal Arts, 1964), vol. II, p. 269.

4. Gay was not the only eighteenth-century moralist to see Hutcheson as a disguised psychological hedonist. Cf. Kant, *Foundations of the Metaphysics of Morals,* trans. Lewis White Beck (New York: Bobbs-Merrill, Library of Liberal Arts, 1959), pp. 61, 61n.

5. *British Moralists,* vol. II, p. 269-270.

6. *Ibid.,* p. 270.

7. *Ibid.,* p. 283.

8. Hartley wrote in the preface to the *Observations:* "About Eighteen Years ago I was informed, that the Rev. Mr. Gay, then living, asserted the Possibility of deducing all our intellectual Pleasures and Pains from Association. This put me upon considering the Power of Association" (*Observations on Man, his Frame, his Duty, and his Expectations* [London, 1749], vol. I, p. v).

9. *Ibid.,* p. 418.

10. *Ibid.,* p. 419.

11. *Ibid.,* p. 426.

12. *Ibid.,* p. 420.

13. Alexander Gerard, *An Essay on Taste,* ed. W. J. Hipple, Jr. (Gainesville, Florida: Scholar's Facsimiles and Reprints, 1963), pp. 1-2. This is a facsimile of the third edition (1780). For an account of the *Essay*'s inception, see M. L. Wiley, "Gerard and the Scots Societies," *The University of Texas Publications: Studies in English,* No. 4026 (1940); and Hipple's introduction to the *Essay,* pp. v-ix.

14. W. J. Hipple, Jr., *The Beautiful, the Sublime, and the Picturesque in Eighteenth-Century British Aesthetic Theory* (Carbondale, Illinois: The Southern Illinois University Press, 1957), p. 68.

15. Gerard, *op. cit.,* pp. 1-2n.

16. Hutcheson, *A Short Introduction to Moral Philosophy,* p. 6.

17. *Ibid.*

18. *On Free Will (De Libero Arbitrio,* Book II, ch. IV and V), trans. R. McKeon, *Selections from Medieval Philosophers,* ed. R. McKeon (New York: Charles Scribner's Sons, 1929), vol. I, pp. 23-27.

19. Locke, *op. cit.,* vol. I, p. 123.

20. Marjorie Grene, "Gerard's *Essay on Taste,*" *Modern Philology,* XLI (1943), p. 45.

21. Gerard, *op. cit.,* p. 29.

22. *Ibid.*

23. *Ibid.*

24. DuBos, *op. cit.,* vol. I, pp. 5, 20, *et passim.*

25. Gerard, *op. cit.,* p. 31.

26. *Ibid.*, p. 34. Hipple has suggested (*The Beautiful, the Sublime, and the Picturesque*, p. 75) that this is essentially the Aristotelian notion of magnitude. See *Poetics*, vii, and *Nicomachean Ethics*, IV.iii.

27. Gerard, *op. cit.*, p. 35.

28. *Ibid.*, p. 36.

29. *Ibid.*, pp. 40-41.

30. Grene, *op. cit.*, p. 52.

31. Gerard, *op. cit.*, p. 43.

32. *Ibid.*, p. 45.

33. *Ibid.*, p. 147n.

34. *Ibid.*, p. 146n.

35. Burke, *Enquiry into the Sublime and Beautiful*, p. 26.

36. Gerard, *op. cit.*, p. 145n.

37. Locke, *Essay Concerning Human Understanding*, vol. I, p. 214.

38. "Locke and the Categories of Value in Eighteenth-Century British Aesthetic Theory," p. 40.

39. Locke, *op. cit.*, vol. I, p. xi (editor's *Prolegomena*).

CHAPTER XI

1. Joseph Priestly, *A Course of Lectures on Oratory and Criticism* (London, 1777), pp. 72-73.

2. Archibald Alison, *Essays on the Nature and Principles of Taste* (Boston: Cummings and Hilliard, 1812), p. vii.

3. *Ibid.*

4. *Ibid.*, p. 57.

5. *Ibid.*, p. 24.

6. *Ibid.*, p. 77.

7. David Hume, *A Treatise of Human Nature*, ed. L.A. Selby-Bigge, p. 11.

8. Alison, *op. cit.*, p. 55.

9. For an analysis of Alison's use of aesthetic disinterestedness and its significance, see Jerome Stolnitz, "On the Origins of 'Aesthetic Disinterestedness,' " p. 137-139.

10. Alison, *op. cit.*, p. 102.

11. *Ibid.*, p. 18.

12. *Ibid.*, pp. 20-21.

13. *Ibid.*, p. 103.

14. *Ibid.*, p. 106.

15. *Ibid.*, pp. 106-107.

16. *Ibid.*, pp. 107-112.

17. Gordon McKenzie, "Lord Kames and the Mechanist Tradition," *University of California Publications in English*, XIV (1942), pp. 94-95. It should be noted, however, that Kames was not a strict determinist; nor is

258THE SEVENTH SENSE

it likely that Alison was either, for Alison, a divine, would not have been likely to give up freedom of the will.

18. Alison, *op. cit.*, p. 141.
19. *Ibid.*, p. 268.
20. *Ibid.*, pp. 417-418.
21. *Ibid.*, p. 421.

CHAPTER XII

1. *Philosophical Essays, The Works of Dugald Stewart* (Cambridge, Massachusetts: Hilliard and Brown, 1829), vol. IV, p. 184 ("On the Beautiful").

2. *Ibid.*, vol. IV, p. 185.

3. *The Principles of Human Knowledge*, ed. T. E. Jessop, *The Works of George Berkeley*, ed. A. A. Luce and T. E. Jessop (London: Thomas Nelson, 1948-1957), vol. II, p. 36.

4. "On the Beautiful," *The Works of Dugald Stewart*, vol. IV, pp. 187-188.

5. This parallel between Stewart and Wittgenstein is recognized in passing in S. A. Grave, *The Scottish Philosophy of Common Sense* (London: Oxford University Press, 1960), pp. 231-232n, as well as in Jerome Stolnitz, " 'Beauty': Some Stages in the History of an Idea," *Journal of the History of Ideas*, XXII (1961), pp. 202-203.

6. Ludwig Wittgenstein, *Philosophical Investigations*, trans. G. E. M. Anscombe (New York: Macmillan, 1953), pp. 31-32e.

7. G. E. Moore, *Principia Ethica* (Cambridge: Cambridge University Press, 1960), pp. 14-15.

8. Clive Bell, *Art* (New York: Capricorn Books, 1958), p. 17. For some suggestive remarks on Moore's influence, see Berel Lang, "Intuition in Bloomsbury," *Journal of the History of Ideas*, XXV (1964), pp. 295-302.

9. G. E. Moore, "Wittgenstein's Lectures in 1930-33," *Philosophical Papers* (New York: Collier Books, 1962), p. 306.

10. Paul Edwards, *The Logic of Moral Discourse* (Glencoe, Illinois: The Free Press, 1955), pp. 139-140.

11. *Ibid.*, p. 142.

12. Helen Knight, "The Use of 'Good' in Aesthetic Judgments," reprinted in *Aesthetics and Language*, ed. William Elton (Oxford: Oxford University Press, 1959), p. 155.

13. Morris Weitz, "The Role of Theory in Aesthetics," reprinted in Margolis, *Philosophy Looks At the Arts*, p. 53.

14. See Richard Payne Knight, *An Analytical Inquiry into the Principles of Taste*, 2nd ed. (London, 1805), pp. 9-18.

15. *Elements of the Philosophy of the Human Mind* [1792], *The Works of Dugald Stewart*, vol. I, pp. 273-274.

16. *Philosophical Essays, The Works of Dugald Stewart*, vol. IV, p. 233.

17. *Elements of the Philosophy of the Human Mind, The Works of Dugald Stewart,* vol. I, p. 273.

18. *Philosophical Essays, The Works of Dugald Stewart,* vol. IV, pp. 197-198.

19. *Ibid.,* p. 240.

20. *Ibid.,* pp. 240-241.

21. *Elements of the Philosophy of the Human Mind, The Works of Dugald Stewart,* vol. I, pp. 271-272.

22. *Philosophical Essays, The Works of Dugald Stewart,* vol. IV, p. 324 ("On Taste").

23. *Ibid.,* p. 318.

24. *Ibid.,* p. 338.

25. *Ibid.,* pp. 329-330.

26. *Ibid.,* p. 337.

27. *Ibid.,* pp. 338-339.

28. Denis Diderot, *Oeuvres Esthetiques,* ed. Paul Verniere (Paris: Editions Garnier Frères, 1959), p. 401.

APPENDIX A

1. References to Cooper occur, for example, in A. Bosker, *Literary Criticism in the Age of Johnson* (New York, 1935), pp. 164-165; W.J. Bate, *From Classic to Romantic: Premises of Taste in Eighteenth-Century England* (New York: Harper Torchbooks, 1961), pp. 53-54; E.N. Hooker, "The Discussion of Taste, from 1750 to 1770, and the New Trends in Literary Criticism," *Publications of the Modern Language Association,* XLIX (1934), p. 79n. References to Melmoth can be found both in Bate (pp. 52-53) and Hooker (p. 79n).

2. "Though he was neither a comprehensive nor a profoundly original writer, Blair was of immense importance as a popularizer of aesthetic and critical speculation. . ." (Hipple, *The Beautiful, the Sublime, and the Picturesque,* p. 122).

3. The first volume of the *Letters* was published in 1742; a second in 1748; the two volumes were first published together in 1749. The work seems to have maintained its popularity throughout the century, going through a number of editions.

4. William Melmoth, *Fitzosborne's Letters on Several Subjects* (Boston, 1815), p. 112.

5. *Ibid.*

6. *Ibid.,* p. 114. Melmoth emphasizes the uniformity of man's aesthetic nature here; but he is not altogether consistent about this. Cf. p. 109.

7. John Gilbert Cooper, *Letters Concerning Taste. The Fourth Edition. To which are added, Essays on Similar and Other Subjects. The Second Edition* (London, 1771), pp. 2-3.

8. *Ibid.*, p. 7.

9. *Ibid.*

10. *Ibid.*, p. 2.

11. Bate, *op. cit.*, p. 53.

12. Cooper, *op. cit.*, p. 27.

13. Hugh Blair, *Lectures on Rhetoric and Belles Lettres,* 3rd ed. (London, 1787), vol. I, pp. iii, 4n.

14. *Ibid.*, p. iv.

15. *Ibid.*, p. 20.

16. *Ibid.*, p. 21.

17. *Ibid.*, p. 24.

18. *Ibid.*, p. 29.

19. *Ibid.*, p. 40.

APPENDIX B

1. Henry Home, Lord Kames, *Elements of Criticism,* 6th ed. (Edinburgh, 1785), vol. II, p. 505.

2. *Ibid.*, p. 506n.

3. *Ibid.*, vol. I, pp. 1-2.

4. *Ibid.*, p. 2n.

5. *Ibid.*, vol. II, p. 508.

6. *Essays on the Principles of Morality and Natural Religion,* in *British Moralists,* vol. II, p. 302.

7. *Ibid.*, p. 303.

8. Kames, *op. cit.*, vol. I, p. 198.

9. Gordon McKenzie, "Lord Kames and the Mechanist Tradition," p. 98.

10. Spinoza, *Ethics,* Part I, Appendix.

INDEX

261